REVISITING HERSTORIES

The Young Lords Party

REVISED EDITION

ALSO BY IRIS MORALES

BOOKS
Through the Eyes of Rebel Women: The Young Lords, 1969-1976
(2016)

Latinas: Struggles and Protests in 21st Century USA, Anthology
Editor and Author (2018)

Voices from Puerto Rico: Post Hurricane María/
Voces desde Puerto Rico: Pos-Huracán María
Editor (2019)

Vicki: A Summer of Change! / ¡Un verano de cambio!
Children's picture book co-authored with Dr. Raquel M. Ortiz (2020)

Latinas: Gender, Race and Class, Vol. 2. Anthology
Co-editor and Author (2025)

A Flag's Journey
Children's chapter book. *(2025)*

ESSAYS ABOUT THE YOUNG LORDS
"Power to the People!"
Palante: Voices and Photographs of the Young Lords, 1969-1971 (2011)

"¡Palante, Siempre Palante! The Young Lords"
The Puerto Rican Movement: Voices from the Diaspora (1998)

"¡Palante, Siempre Palante!" Interview with Richie Pérez
CENTRO Journal, Volume xxi Number 2. (Fall 2009)

DOCUMENTARY
¡Palante, Siempre Palante! The Young Lords
Producer, writer and codirector (1996)
Distributed by Third World Newsreel. www.twn.org

REVISITING HERSTORIES

The Young Lords Party

REVISED EDITION

BY

IRIS MORALES

INTRODUCTION BY

DR. JACQUELINE LAZÚ

Red Sugarcane Press, Inc.
New York, New York

Dedicated to my mother Almida Roldán and the women of her generation who migrated from Puerto Rico and created opportunities for their daughters to have more liberated lives.

To all the organizers and activists who hold our dreams in their actions.

CONTENTS

ILLUSTRATIONS

ABBREVIATIONS

BPP	Black Panther Party
BWA	Black Women's Alliance
BWLC	Black Women's Liberation Caucus
CESA	Committee to End Sterilization Abuse
CCNY	City College of New York
CUNY	City University of New York
DRUM	Detroit Revolutionary Unity Movement
FBI	Federal Bureau of Investigation
GLC	Gay and Lesbian Caucus
GLF	Gay Liberation Front
HRUM	Health Revolutionary Unity Movement
IWK	I Wor Kuen
LGBTQ	Lesbian, gay, bisexual, transgender, and questioning
MPI	*Movimiento Pro Independencia*
PRNP	Puerto Rican Nationalist Party
PRRWO	Puerto Rican Revolutionary Workers Organization
PSP	*Partido Socialista Puertorriqueño* (Puerto Rican Socialist Party)
PRSU	Puerto Rican Student Union
SNCC	Student Nonviolent Coordinating Committee
STAR	Street Transvestite Action Revolutionaries
TLC	Think Lincoln Committee
TWGR	Third World Gay Revolution
TWWA	Third World Women's Alliance
UPR	University of Puerto Rico
WC	Women's Caucus
WU	Women's Union
YWAF	Youth Against War and Fascism
YLO	Young Lords Organization
YLP	Young Lords Party

PREFACE:
FROM GENERATION TO GENERATION

Momentous events in 2019 inspired the writing of *Revisiting Herstories: The Young Lords Party*. That summer, the people of Puerto Rico took to the streets in historic numbers, demanding the resignation of a corrupt colonial governor—demonstrating that collective action can shake the pillars of power. At the same time, the fiftieth anniversary of the Young Lords' founding in New York sparked renewed interest in the organization's radical legacy and lessons. These parallel calls to action—one unfolding in the present, the other from the past—led me to reflect on how social movements begin, how they evolve, and how their stories are carried forward by new generations.

Months later, as the COVID-19 pandemic forced us into isolation, I turned to history. I immersed myself in the anti-colonial movements of Puerto Rico and in the activism of the Young Lords, focusing on the struggles and contributions of the women who helped shape the organization in New York. *Revisiting Herstories: The Young Lords Party* was published in the aftermath of the pandemic. This revised edition expands this exploration, offering a deeper perspective on the organization's evolution, its challenges, and the issues that remain as urgent and relevant as ever.

The summer of 2019 was extraordinary. In Puerto Rico, over half a million people streamed into the streets and highways, demanding the resignation of Governor Ricardo Rosselló.[1] Marchers carried Puerto Rican flags and massive banners that read, *#RickyRenuncia*. (Ricky Resign). The immediate catalyst was the release of hundreds of pages of private chat messages between the governor and his inner circle. These exchanges laid bare a pervasive abuse of power and deep contempt for the Puerto Rican people expressed in sexist, racist, misogynist, homophobic, and other offensive content. The officials made derogatory and insulting remarks about women and LGBTQ+ individuals and even mocked hurricane disaster victims.

Outraged by their blatant disdain, Puerto Ricans from all walks of life joined the demonstrations. The leaked chats were yet another transgression added to decades of government corruption and severe austerity policies. Protesters chanted, *"¡Somos más, y no tenemos miedo!"* (We are more, and we are not afraid). It was a leaderful movement. At the forefront were feminists,[2] Afro-Boricuas,[3] queer activists, young people, and artists. In New York City, Puerto Ricans rallied at Columbus Circle, echoing protesters' demands that the governor resign—I was among them.

As Governor Rosselló made excuse after excuse, the protests grew. More and more people took to the streets, drawing global attention to the enduring reality of U.S. colonialism in Puerto Rico. Though he insisted he would not step down, twelve days of sustained mobilizations ultimately forced his resignation. The power of the people prevailed, and it was a moment of celebration. Jubilant Puerto Ricans of all ages gathered—singing, playing drums, and dancing—in front of San Juan's capitol building and in town plazas across the country. They expressed both joy and relief at the ousting of this agent of colonialism and corruption. As Puerto Ricans in the archipelago celebrated, so did Puerto Ricans across the diaspora—even knowing that another colonial puppet was already waiting to take his place.

When news of the uprising in Puerto Rico broke, former members of the Young Lords Organization were preparing to commemorate the group's founding in New York. The victory on the archipelago energized the celebration, serving as a powerful reminder of the movement that had ignited fifty years earlier.

On July 26, 1969, the Young Lords Organization established a chapter in New York City, calling for "self-determination for Puerto Ricans on the island and inside the United States."[4] Through people-to-people organizing, bold acts of civil disobedience, and mass protests, the Young Lords sparked a grassroots movement against poverty, racism, government neglect, and corporate exploitation. Thousands joined—high school and college students, young mothers, retail and service workers, former gang members, Vietnam War veterans, artists, and community organizers. Most were first-generation Puerto Ricans, born or raised in the United States. Other Latinx and African American young people also enlisted. The diversity of experiences grounded the organization in the realities, suffering, and resilience of low-income and working-class Puerto Ricans.

I joined the Young Lords Organization in New York in 1969. Later renamed the Young Lords Party, then the Puerto Rican Revolutionary Workers Organization. I remained a member for over five years and have documented these experiences in the award-winning film *¡Palante, Siempre Palante! The Young Lords*, the book *Through the Eyes of Rebel Women: The Young Lords, 1969–1976*, and numerous articles. Building on this work, *Revisiting Herstories: The Young Lords Party* offers an in-depth examination of the organization and the rise and decline of revolutionary feminist ideals and campaigns from 1969 through 1972. I write about these experiences as "part of a larger process, as one voice in a dialogue among people who have been silenced,"[5] contributing to an ongoing effort of reclamation and collective understanding.

During this seminal period for U.S. feminists of color, we—women in the Young Lords—brought a focus to gender justice that profoundly shaped the organization's politics and practices. Our activism paralleled that of Black, Latinx, Asian, and Indigenous feminists with whom we shared struggles for racial, economic, and social justice. Any discussion of feminist activism within the Young Lords necessarily draws from the theories of U.S. African American and Chicana feminists, as well as the ideological frameworks of revolutionary nationalist movements.

Revisiting Herstories: The Young Lords Party is a book about activism—and the battle of ideas. Within the organization, tensions arose between male-supremacist beliefs and feminist aspirations. These struggles shaped both how women were treated and the direction of the organizing. Though most of us did not identify as feminists at the time, we actively resisted traditional gender roles and notions of women's inferiority. As a cautionary tale, these experiences underscore the ongoing challenge of reconciling feminist principles with nationalist frameworks and emphasize the necessity of ensuring that women's rights and equality are integral to any revolutionary movement.

This revised edition features an introduction by Dr. Jacqueline Lazú than expands upon her article, "Sí, pero... Truth and Reckonings: Revisiting Herstories: The Young Lords Party."[6] Her incisive essay brings critical insight to the book's major themes, emphasizing its feminist, anti-colonial, and intersectional lens; Puerto Rican and Latinx feminist herstories; and the dynamics of power and accountability in radical movements. Her multilayered analysis draws compelling connections between the history of the Young Lords and its relevance to contemporary political struggles.

Dr. Lazú's work is grounded in more than two decades of research on the Chicago Young Lords Organization (YLO). She has extensively documented the group's evolution and the lives of its members—including the often-overlooked contributions of women who played essential roles. She is the author of *Stone Revolutionaries: The Origins of the Young Lords Movement* and editor of the anthology *The Young Lords Speak: From the Streets of Chicago to Revolutionary Organization*. Both works trace the lasting impact of the Chicago YLO and its pivotal role in shaping the Puerto Rican radical tradition in the United States.

In addition to her scholarly work, Dr. Lazú has been a driving force in preserving the legacy of the Young Lords Organization. She has led public history initiatives to document and share the group's impact and played a key role in securing the city's first official tribute to the organization. A commemorative plaque, installed by DePaul University, recognizes their origins in Chicago. As a longtime Chicagoan, originally from the East Coast, Dr. Lazú brings a unique perspective that deepens our understanding of the Young Lords' significance to the Puerto Rican diaspora and U.S. social justice movement history.

Revisiting Herstories: The Young Lords Party offers a nuanced account of the organization, centering the contributions of women members. While the overall structure of this edition remains largely unchanged, the addition of Dr. Lazú's introduction provided an opportunity to review the original text with fresh eyes. In the process, I expanded and updated sections for greater clarity, added historical and political context, and corrected errors. I also refined the language to improve precision in political analysis and enhance readability. This revised edition provides a broader perspective and deeper insight into the intersection of gender and revolutionary struggle—into the complex interplay between feminist and nationalist objectives.

The political activism of Puerto Rican women in the United States was not new. From the earliest waves of migration, Puerto Rican women fought for justice in workplaces, neighborhoods, schools, and across society. Among many trailblazers were Luisa Capetillo, a labor organizer and feminist in the early twentieth century; Julia de Burgos, a poet, journalist, and nationalist active from the late 1930s through the 1940s; and Evelina López Antonetty, a fierce advocate for education rights and community empowerment from the mid-1960s to 1980. Their work continues to inspire feminists, organizers, and social justice activists today.

The women in the Young Lords Organization ushered in "another cycle of militancy,"[7] focusing on the fight against poverty, racism, sexism, and other societal ills. We drew critical attention to the lived realities of Puerto Ricans in low-income communities, firmly believing that wherever women experienced oppression, it was a woman's issue. As Black warrior poet Audre Lorde so powerfully wrote, "There is no such thing as a single-issue struggle because we do not live single-issue lives."[8] This intersectional understanding was at the heart of our activism—a recognition that the fight for justice must confront multiple systemic inequalities.

Our political ideas flowed from several historical rivers. We identified as socialists and nationalists, united by a central demand: self-determination. As "revolutionary nationalists," we allied with the Black Panther Party in the fight against poverty and white supremacy. As Puerto Rican nationalists, we drew inspiration from the Nationalist Party of Puerto Rico. We organized to end Puerto Rico's colonial status and to challenge U.S. policies that orchestrated the post–World War II mass migration and displacement of Puerto Ricans to U.S. ghettos. As children of this migration, we saw ourselves as colonial subjects— intimately familiar with U.S. imperialism and aligned with anti-colonial movements around the world.

Despite the vital contributions of feminists in the Young Lords Party, these herstories remain largely overlooked in the literature of both the women's liberation and broader social justice movements. Even many accounts of the Young Lords today ignore revolutionary feminist ideas and organizing in favor of male-centered nationalist narratives that continue to dominate. *Revisiting Herstories: The Young Lords Party* challenges this erasure and opens new avenues of study for activists and scholars alike.

The words of historian and women's studies scholar Edna Acosta-Belén have special resonance. She writes:

> Building a historical memory, however, is always a rugged and convoluted terrain of contesting claims, but more so for those populations that have endured the coloniality of being silenced and are seeking to voice their untold stories, and in this way, contribute to the production of new decolonial knowledge.[9]

"Contesting claims" is not only about correcting the erasure of women's stories—it is also about how women of color are represented, both individually and collectively. Are women acknowledged as agents of social change and revolution? And what ideas, actions, and strategies advanced by women of color are being documented and passed on to future generations? At stake is not only how we remember the past but also how we shape the most effective action for the future.[10]

In recounting this herstory, I drew from *Silencing the Past: Power and the Production of History* by Michel-Rolph Trouillot. The renowned Haitian anthropologist and scholar reminds us: "[T]he past does not exist independently from the present."[11] This understanding of the relationship between past and present guided me to examine familiar narratives alongside the gaps and silences. I combed through assorted sources, probing and closely studying fragments and overlooked threads of history.

Chicanx and women's studies scholar Maylei Blackwell describes this process as "retrofitted memory." She writes:

> [S]ocial actors read the interstices, gaps, and silences of existing historical narratives in order to retrofit, rework, and refashion older narratives to create new historical openings, political possibilities, and genealogies of resistance.[12]

Using this lens, I uncovered forgotten or discarded herstories, breathing new life and vitality into the existing—and often recycled—narratives of the Young Lords Party.

While materials on the activism of Puerto Rican feminists in the diaspora from 1969 to 1972 are scarce, the tremendous development in gender studies since then provided a wealth of resources to deepen my analysis. I am grateful for this expanded body of research and scholarship, which allowed for a wider and more detailed examination of the social justice movements of that time. It gave language to concepts and practices that we, as Young Lords, explored intuitively but lacked the vocabulary to articulate. As a result, this revised account offers a more accurate and nuanced portrayal of the role, struggles, and contributions of socialist feminists within and without the organization.

Revisiting Herstories: The Young Lords Party offers an insider-outsider perspective, blending primary sources and scholarly research with lived experience, collective memory, political critique, and personal testimony. It reflects my analysis and interpretation, including a critical assessment of the organization's strengths, errors, and lessons. In revisiting these histories, I remained acutely aware that social justice movements appear different from a distance than they do amid the urgency and intensity of the day-to-day organizing.

As Michel-Rolph Trouillot reminds us, "Historical actors are also narrators, and vice versa."[13] Recognizing challenges posed by memory, and to ground the narrative as fully as possible, I began by creating a chronology of events, drawing on primary sources such as letters, retreat reports, position papers, essays, speeches, and newspaper articles. Interviews with women members, along with articles written by them, contribute essential firsthand perspectives. Research into the philosophies of feminists of color, histories of Puerto Rico, African American liberation struggles, queer movement texts, and scholarship on the relationship between nationalism and feminism provide critical context for a broader analysis.

Also intertwined are my reflections inspired by Lucille Clifton's poem, "Why Some People Be Mad at Me Sometimes." She writes:

> they ask me to remember
> but they want me to remember
> their memories
> and i keep on remembering
> mine[14]

Throughout the text, I use both "I" and "we." The use of "I" reflects my personal views and experiences, while "we" conveys the collective beliefs and actions of the Young Lords and other social justice activists of the time. I retain political terms and phrases in use during that era to remain true to the original, while also incorporating contemporary terminology where needed to help clarify past events for today's readers. My aim is to offer a perspective that respects historical context while encouraging reflection on its relevance today.

Note that "Young Lords" is used broadly throughout this book to refer both to the organization and members. The Young Lords Organization was founded in Chicago in 1968. "Young Lords Organization," when referring to the New York chapter, indicates the period from July 1969 to May 1970. "Young Lords Party" refers to its subsequent phase as a national organization, active from May 1970 to July 1972. Significant organizational events previously covered in *Through the Eyes of Rebel Women: The Young Lords, 1969–1976* are referenced but not discussed in detail.

Revisiting Herstories is for readers interested in Puerto Rican history, feminist movements, radical social justice organizations in the United States, and the complex intersections of race, gender, colonialism, and resistance. It speaks to activists, students, educators, community leaders, cultural workers, and others engaged in grassroots activism—as well as anyone seeking a deeper understanding of how these forces shape our histories, communities, and movements for change.

The book is organized into five parts. Part I, "Another Cycle of Grassroots Militancy," sets the historical context. Chapter 1 opens with the formation of the Young Lords Organization (YLO) in New York in 1969. The second chapter describes the group's early activities and ideology. Chapter 3 focuses on the emergence of the Women's Caucus in 1970 and its initial struggles for gender equality within the organization.

Part II, "Feminists of Color and Gender Justice," explores ideas and practices that shaped the political development of women in the Young Lords. Chapter 4 examines sterilization policies in Puerto Rico and the United States, including campaigns led by feminists of color to challenge coercive and abusive sterilization practices. Chapter 5 highlights the influence of African American and Chicana feminists on the political vision and organizing strategies of women in the Young Lords. Chapter 6 reviews the ten demands presented by the Women's Caucus to the Central Committee and their transformative impact on the organization.

Chapter 7 explores the Young Lords' evolving relationship with LGBTQ+ activism and politics.

In May 1970, the New York chapter of the Young Lords broke from the Chicago organization and reconstituted itself as the Young Lords Party (YLP). The process of building a national organization opened space for women's leadership and advanced the struggle for gender equity. Part III, "We Do Not Live Single-Issue Lives," highlights key YLP initiatives from that pivotal year, during which women played significant roles. Chapter 8 examines the Young Lords' organizing efforts and the takeover of Lincoln Hospital, highlighting the leadership of Puerto Rican and African American women workers. It emphasizes their intersectional demands for better labor conditions, preventative health care, and women's rights. Chapter 9 examines citywide criminal justice reform efforts amid jail uprisings, community protests, and organizing at the Women's House of Detention. Chapter 10 documents the collaboration between the Puerto Rican Student Union and the Young Lords Party to mobilize support for Puerto Rico's independence movement, culminating in a march of 10,000 people to the United Nations.

Part IV, "Nationalisms and Feminisms," traces the escalating tensions between the YLP's nationalist ideology and the feminist organizing within its ranks. Chapter 11 details the critical debate within the Central Committee that shifted the group's focus to opening branches in Puerto Rico. In the United States, the Young Lords Party's turned to building "people's organizations" like the Women's Union (WU). Chapter 12 explores the WU's formation, highlighting its activities and socialist feminist agenda. The final chapter in this section analyzes the Central Committee's embrace of narrow nationalism and the constraints it imposed on the revolutionary feminist vision. By mid-1972, the Puerto Rico project shut down, and the Young Lords Party redirected its focus to political work in the United States. It reconstituted itself as the Puerto Rican Revolutionary Workers Organization (PRRWO), which remained active until 1976.

Part V, "Reckoning with the Past," reflects on the recurring themes and challenges that shaped the histories of the YLO, YLP, and PRRWO. Chapter 14 details the repressive tactics and destructive role of the FBI and New York City police in the deterioration of the organization. Chapter 15 examines the internal dynamics that derailed the socialist feminist agenda. The final chapter draws connections between these historical struggles and contemporary movements—particularly those confronting global poverty, deepening inequality, and gender-based violence—challenges intensified by the COVID-19 pandemic.

During the 1960s and 1970s, U.S. feminists of color challenged patriarchy, male supremacy, classism, and systemic racism in pursuit of a more just and humane society. Puerto Rican, African American, Indigenous, Asian, and other women activists mobilized for economic, gender, and racial justice—protesting in the streets and organizing in neighborhoods, workplaces, and schools. They connected their local struggles to global movements and forged solidarity with international "Third World" feminists, linking the fight for justice across borders.

The activism of women in the Young Lords Party brought a socialist feminist perspective to organizing within the Puerto Rican diaspora—grounded in lived experience, political imagination, and grassroots struggle. *Revisiting Herstories: The Young Lords Party* delves into this complex history, illuminating concerns, resistance, and aspirations that continue to be relevant to contemporary movements for justice, equality, and collective liberation. By recovering overlooked and erased narratives and herstories, the book deepens our understanding of the past and sharpens our insight into ongoing political struggles.

Iris Morales
New York City
2025

INTRODUCTION
BY DR. JACQUELINE LAZÚ

I met Iris Morales for the first time in 2024, after many years of working on the history of the Young Lords Organization (YLO), when I was invited to review *Revisiting Herstories: The Young Lords Party* for the *CENTRO Journal,* a publication of the Center for Puerto Rican Studies at Hunter College. Although I am an East Coast native who first encountered the Young Lords through the stories and imagery of the New York chapter, I have spent over two decades researching the original YLO in Chicago, founded by José "Cha Cha" Jiménez. Born from neighborhood struggles as a street gang, the Chicago group fought displacement and police violence, reclaimed public spaces, ran free clinics and breakfast programs, and co-founded the Rainbow Coalition with the Black Panthers and Young Patriots. The movement later expanded to New York and other cities, where it took on new dimensions. New York became central in the public imagination, shaping how the Young Lords have been remembered and represented.

From the beginning, I was committed to telling the Chicago story on its own terms, recovering a history that had been buried, misrepresented, or overshadowed. My distance from the New York story was a methodological choice, grounded in the specific political and spatial conditions that shaped the Chicago movement and in my accountability to the community that entrusted me with their narrative. Still, I was deeply influenced by the work of Iris Morales, whose voice made visible the gendered silences and structural exclusions across all chapters of the organization. Her work offered a language and a framework for what had not yet been fully named in the scholarship or in public memory.

In that context, I read widely and closely across everything written by and about the broader Young Lords movement. Morales's work stood out. In addition to *Revisiting Herstories,* she has built an expansive body of work grounded in justice, political education, and historical recovery. Her groundbreaking documentary *¡Palante, Siempre Palante!* was one of the first public-facing projects to capture the complexity of the New York

Young Lords from within, offering a visual archive for a generation that had never seen themselves reflected in revolutionary history. Her books *Through the Eyes of Rebel Women: The Young Lords 1969–1976* (2016), *Voices from Puerto Rico: Post-Hurricane Maria* (2019), *Latinas: Struggles & Protests in 21st Century USA* (2018), and *Latinas: Gender, Race, and Class* (2024) extend this project by centering women's voices, documenting community resilience, and exposing the structural conditions that shape Puerto Rican life both on the archipelago and in the diaspora. As founder of Red Sugarcane Press, Morales has also supported the publication of other critical works by and about Afro-Caribbean, Latinx, and diasporic authors whose stories might otherwise remain untold. She has modeled a feminist, intergenerational, and decolonial approach to publishing, which understands knowledge as a collective and political project. Her role in shaping the archive, the literature, and the memory of the Young Lords cannot be overstated.

That Morales had to produce, publish, and distribute much of her work while simultaneously creating pathways for others demands critical reflection. In a movement so deeply shaped by Puerto Rican diaspora women, it is striking that a work of this scope and significance emerged without institutional support. This is not an isolated case. It reflects a broader pattern in which Puerto Rican women in the diaspora are consistently absent from the spaces where narratives are legitimized, where funding decisions are made, and where history is curated. The systems that shape who is remembered and who is erased are not neutral. While Puerto Rican radical traditions are rooted in a refusal of colonial logics, they have too often excluded the diaspora and failed to fully recognize the knowledges and political labor of women, nonbinary, and Afro-descendant people. Some shifts are beginning to take place, but they remain selective and insufficient. These silences fracture generational continuity and obscure the full shape of our intellectual and political traditions. Morales's work exposes and challenges these omissions. It reminds us that the struggle over history is also a struggle over power, and that naming what has been erased is essential to building something more just, more complete, and more accountable.

Following the publication of the *CENTRO Journal* review, I reached out to Iris to introduce myself and thank her for her work. Her writing had always held weight for me, unflinching, purposeful, and rooted in lived experience. It shaped how I understood integrity on the page and made reaching out feel just nerve-wracking enough to prove I took the work seriously. Cha Cha and other Chicago Young Lords had also spoken of her with admiration and the kind of respect that made clear she was not someone to be dismissed. Still, I wanted her to know what the book meant to me. She replied with warmth and asked to read the review, and I quickly saw that generosity and conviction are as central to her spirit as precision and resolve. A few weeks later, she wrote back to say she was deeply moved and that the review had captured her intentions in ways few others had. That exchange opened a space of mutual recognition and a shared commitment to the hard work of recovering histories that still resist being told. When she invited me to write this introduction, I said yes without hesitation. It felt like a continuation of the conversation her work had started long ago and like an act of solidarity rooted in shared purpose.

Revisiting Herstories is structured with intention, weaving personal narrative with political analysis, archival documents, and the voices of other women in the Party, movement elders, feminist scholars, and radical thinkers who have long grappled with the challenges of liberation work. Grounded in memory but propelled by critique, the book creates a layered, polyvocal history that resists simplification. Moving between testimony and reflection, Morales illuminates the contradictions that shaped the organization from within. She holds space for the women whose labor sustained the YLO and the Young Lords Party (YLP): mothers, students, service workers, and survivors, while demanding we confront the sexism that devalued their contributions. "From the beginning, women were integral to the Young Lords Organization in New York," she writes, naming not only their presence but their conditions. Many were survivors of domestic violence, addiction, and poverty. This personal yet collective framing refuses romanticization and instead centers structural analysis, connecting the feminization of poverty, labor exploitation, and gendered expectations as forces that shaped women's lives inside and outside the movement. Morales's method is political in that it connects the intimate to the structural and insists that history must be told from the vantage point of those most impacted.

Nostalgia is deliberately resisted. Morales places tension and contradiction in full view, particularly when tracing the Young Lords' evolving leadership structure. She addresses internal distortions of power, showing how the organization's commitment to democratic centralism was gradually undermined by a small group within the Central Committee who began to consolidate authority. Participatory decision-making gave way to top-down control, often justified in the name of efficiency or ideological purity. Morales does not gloss over these shifts. She confronts the gap between the organization's stated values and its internal practices, especially around gender. For example, while the Young Lords called for women's equality, they also endorsed "revolutionary machismo," a term that codified the very patriarchal values they claimed to reject. Through this analysis, the book becomes more than a memoir. It is a political document that asks us to reconsider how memory, power, and accountability function in radical spaces. Naming harm, Morales shows, is not divisive. It is necessary. Solidarity requires a commitment to transformation, and this commitment must begin with clarity about the ways power operates within our own movements.

What makes *Revisiting Herstories* so powerful is that Morales does not write to vindicate herself or settle old disputes. She writes with clarity and purpose, recovering suppressed histories and holding space for accountability. She models what it means to remain in principled relationship with a movement even when its practices fall short of its ideals. Her inclusion of internal documents broadens our understanding of what counts as evidence and challenges who has the authority to interpret it. Morales shifts our attention from the spectacle of public action to the quieter, often erased labor of collective struggle. Her approach reveals the inner life of radical organizing, a space shaped by conflict, care, contradiction, and persistence. She reminds us that archiving is never neutral. It either reinforces or disrupts the stories we inherit.

The book's title signals not only a return to the past but a reshaping of the terrain itself. "Herstories" are not footnotes. They are the scaffolding of the movement. Without them, the house of revolution collapses. Morales builds a method deeply informed by Black and Latina feminist traditions, echoing the insights of Cherríe Moraga and Gloria Anzaldúa, who taught that theory emerges from lived experience, from the body and from the margins, and of bell hooks and Audre Lorde, who insisted that the personal and political must be held together in the practice of liberation. Morales also engages, implicitly, the decolonial calls of María Lugones and Sylvia Wynter to center erased epistemologies and resist Western, linear narratives of history. In this sense, *Revisiting Herstories* is a methodological intervention. Morales remaps the past through the lives and voices of those most often silenced, offering memory as a radical practice of reworlding and intellectual liberation.

The stakes of this work extend beyond the Young Lords Organization and the Young Lords Party. Morales challenges the divide between memory and documentation, showing that lived experience is a form of historical evidence. She brings the receipts. Her careful use of internal records centers the often-overlooked labor of women and makes visible the structures that tried to erase them. This is feminist memory work in action, not an additive gesture but a reconfiguration of historical authorship. Morales blends personal storytelling with political analysis to create a more honest and layered account of the movement. Her method reflects the insights of feminist scholars who understand memory as a space where power is shaped and contested. Cherríe Moraga reminds us that memory is not merely retrieval. It is resistance, an act of cultural survival and political clarity. Morales builds from these teachings and models what it means to reclaim narrative as a tool of liberation.

The book unfolds across five carefully curated parts that layer memory with political analysis, revealing the vision, labor, and strategies of the women in the Young Lords. From the opening pages, Morales connects contemporary uprisings in Puerto Rico with the radical legacy of the Young Lords, calling recent protests "a leaderful movement" and situating herself within that lineage. This framing sets the tone for a project that is both historical and insurgent. Each section builds from the last, tracing the rise of the Women's Caucus, the development of gender justice frameworks through coalition work with Black and Chicana feminists, and the challenges of advancing a feminist agenda within a revolutionary nationalist party. Morales does not shy away from contradictions. She centers them, showing how they shaped political clarity and exposed the limits of the organization's rhetoric.

The structure itself models a nonlinear, feminist approach to history that prioritizes depth over chronology, and collective struggle over singular heroes. Intersectionality is not applied in hindsight; it emerges organically, rooted in lived experience and sharpened through organizing. Morales moves between archival documents, personal reflection, and political analysis to expand what counts as historical evidence and who holds interpretive authority. Her attention to the tensions between nationalism and feminism, and between memory and documentation, gives the book its intellectual weight. What results is not just a recovery of women's contributions, but a reframing of the movement's meaning and legacy. In Morales's hands, structure becomes method. It offers a way of telling history that is grounded in feminist praxis and attuned to the unfinished work of liberation.

Revisiting Herstories also models a transnational conversation rooted in the realities of a people split by colonial displacement. Drawing on what Gloria González once described as the "divided nation," Morales resists frameworks that privilege island-based over diaspora organizing. She reminds readers that Puerto Rican resistance cannot be understood through a single geography. Chapter 10 offers a vivid example. Puerto Rican students in New York, through the Puerto Rican Student Union, advanced local demands such as open admissions and ethnic studies alongside broader commitments to Puerto Rico's independence. Their activism addressed racism, classism, and machismo, insisting, "Unless we act now, we may be the last Puerto Ricans on this planet." That declaration reflected a broader anxiety about forced migration, cultural loss, and systemic neglect. Morales brings this history into urgent dialogue with the present, showing that the struggle for Puerto Rican liberation has always unfolded across multiple fronts and demanded strategies that bridge local and global, personal and collective.

In this revised edition, Morales sharpens her analysis with an urgent call to understand the Young Lords through a feminist, anti-colonial, and deeply intersectional lens. She situates her voice within a collective project of reclamation and insists on the distinction between personal and collective memory. "I" reflects lived experience. "We" affirms shared political vision. Her insistence on these terms signals a refusal to separate scholarship from struggle. This edition does not rewrite the original. It deepens it, revealing ideological tensions between male supremacy and socialist feminist aspirations. Morales does not shy away from exposing contradictions within the movement. Instead, she frames them as critical moments of transformation. By documenting the rise of the Women's Caucus, the collaboration with LGBTQ+ movements, and internationalist solidarity through labor and student activism, Morales places the Young Lords within a broader liberation movement committed to confronting all systems of inequality. She reminds us that confronting the past honestly is necessary to build anything enduring in the present, and that feminism, in this context, is not a sidebar to revolutionary struggle. It is the struggle.

As someone who has spent decades researching the Chicago Young Lords and grappling with the silences around women's roles in that context, returning to Morales's work while preparing this introduction felt especially charged. The questions she raises about accountability, memory, and power resonate with the tensions I have encountered in archives and in conversations with Chicago activists. In both New York and Chicago, women did much of the organizing, caretaking, writing, and repairing, yet their contributions were rarely centered. Morales gives language to that gap and challenges us to engage its implications. In Chicago, many women, like the men, entered the Young Lords through its roots as a street organization, adding a crucial class dimension to their political formation. This shaped both their radical potential and the obstacles they faced, including gendered violence and exclusion from leadership. Public history offers one way to navigate these silences by creating spaces beyond official archives and male-centered narratives. In 2023, I co-curated *Encendidas: Women of the Young Lords in Chicago, 1965 to Present* at The Honeycomb Network in Humboldt Park. The exhibition celebrated women's labor and leadership while inviting reflection, dialogue, and future contributions. Morales reminds us that "historical actors are also narrators," and in that spirit, *Encendidas* offered a space for women to be seen and heard on their own terms, contributing to what she calls "an ongoing effort of reclamation and collective understanding."

Reading *Revisiting Herstories* now, I am struck by its insistence on intergenerational dialogue as a political practice. Morales offers no closure. She revisits the past critically, refusing nostalgia while making room for contradiction, discomfort, and growth. Her commitment to memory work as both personal and collective labor invites us to confront the politics of representation that continue to shape how history is told. Morales names this as a struggle for truth and transformation, one that requires "critical thinking, truth telling, and radical hope." That call feels urgent today, as Puerto Rican and diasporic histories remain under constant negotiation. I return to this book not because the story is unfamiliar, but because Morales equips us to teach, curate, and write with greater clarity and accountability. Her work reminds us that how we tell the story matters and that liberation depends as much on the integrity of our methods as on the ideals we claim to uphold.

—JACQUELINE LAZÚ
Spring 2025

Dr. Jacqueline Lazú is a Society of Vincent DePaul Professor at DePaul University, where she teaches in Modern Languages and is affiliated with Latin American and Latino Studies, African and Black Diaspora Studies, Critical Ethnic Studies, and Criminology. A scholar of Latinx and Caribbean social movements, she focuses on cultural production, diaspora, and public memory. She is widely recognized for her scholarship on the Young Lords and the Puerto Rican diaspora in Chicago, including the books *The Young Lords Speak: From the Streets of Chicago to Revolutionary Organization* (Haymarket, 2025) and *Stone Revolutionaries: The Origins of the Young Lords Movement* (Duke, 2026), and has curated exhibitions such as *Encendidas: Women of the Young Lords in Chicago 1965-Present* and *Tengo Lincoln Park en mi Corazón: Young Lords* in Chicago. Her work bridges scholarship, public history, and community-based education with a focus on social transformation.

PART I.
ANOTHER CYCLE OF GRASSROOTS MILITANCY

Revolution is a great act of imagination and creativity where we fight for a future that does not yet exist.[1]

—Zuleica Romay Guerra, Director Afro-American Studies
Casa de las Américas, Havana, 2021.

Fig. 1. The Young Lords Party. New York City. June 1970.
(Courtesy: Michael Abramson)

1.
HUMAN RIGHTS, NOT JUST CIVIL RIGHTS

> No one person starts, let alone sustains, a movement.
> A movement is only made possible when there is a
> collective vision, mission, strategy, working hands,
> walking feet, listening ears, and resources. A movement
> is not spontaneous; it is a cumulative set of human
> circumstances over a period of time when a critical
> mass of people in one accord say, "enough is enough,"
> and we are not going to take disrespect anymore.[1]
>
> —Gwendolyn Patton, From letter on the sixtieth anniversary
> of the Montgomery Bus Boycott, 2015

In the summer of 1969, the Young Lords emerged in East Harlem, New York. The streets were filthy, littered with piles of uncollected garbage because the sanitation department failed to haul it away. Neighborhood residents were fed up with the vermin, the stench, and the respiratory problems it caused. Government officials showed little concern. The Young Lords—a group of Puerto Rican activists—began sweeping the streets every Sunday, bagging the trash, and demanding it be removed. Energized by their actions, local people joined in, pushing accumulated trash into the middle of the street and setting it on fire.

As smoke from the small fires spread, the garbage cleanup turned into a fierce protest. Traffic through the area came to a halt. Sirens blared, screaming through the city streets, as police cars and fire trucks rushed to the scene. Sanitation trucks followed, finally picking up the garbage.[2] Television reporters and camera crews raced uptown to cover the story: young Puerto Rican New Yorkers burning trash and demanding the streets be cleaned. That night, the dramatic footage aired on the evening news. Viewers watched with curiosity, asking, "Who are the Young Lords?"

On July 26, 1969, the protestors had announced the formation of the New York State chapter of the Young Lords Organization (YLO) at a public event in Tompkins Square Park. The group included students from the State University of New York at Old Westbury and youth activists from the Lower East Side and East Harlem who had been meeting since early that year. In June, they read an article in the *Black Panther Party* newspaper about the Chicago Young Lords—a former street gang transformed into a human rights organization fighting for the rights of Puerto Ricans. Inspired by what they read, several of the activists drove to Chicago to meet the Young Lords and returned with authorization to open a New York chapter.

From the beginning, women were integral to the Young Lords Organization in New York. Most of us were Puerto Rican, born or raised in the United States, raised in Spanish-speaking, working-class homes in the city's most impoverished neighborhoods. African American, Cuban, Dominican, Mexican, and Panamanian women, as well as women of Puerto Rican–Filipino and Puerto Rican–South Asian backgrounds, also joined. Our activism was shaped by our experiences with poverty, racism, migration, and gender oppression. We were young—ranging from fourteen to twenty-six years old. Among us were mothers with young children, high school and college students, service and retail workers, homemakers, survivors of domestic violence and of alcohol and drug addiction. English was our primary language, though most of us spoke Spanish and/or Spanglish, a mix of Spanish and English. We were community organizers united by a common cause.

At its height, women comprised one-third to 40 percent of the membership.[3] On our blouses and scarves, we pinned a button that read, *Tengo Puerto Rico en mi corazón,* (I have Puerto Rico in my heart), declaring our love for Puerto Rico and our yearning for home. The only uniform we embraced was the purple beret—a symbol, connecting us with social justice movements and revolutionaries around the world.

Great Puerto Rican Migration after World War II

The story of the Young Lords begins in the Caribbean. The United States' invasion of Puerto Rico on July 25, 1898, marked the start of U.S. colonial rule. In 1917, Congress unilaterally imposed U.S. citizenship on Puerto Ricans, and they were drafted to fight in World War I shortly thereafter. Following World War II, Puerto Rico experienced a mass exodus driven by colonial conditions. Over the next decade, approximately

470,000 Puerto Ricans migrated to the United States.[4] Most came from poor and working-class sectors—uprooted farmers and sugarcane workers, domestics, Afro-Boricuas, and the unemployed—seeking the promise of economic opportunity. The ongoing flow of people between Puerto Rico and the United States kept alive strong connections among separated families, creating what became known as "circular" or "commuter" migration.

In *Puerto Ricans in the United States: A Contemporary Portrait,* scholars Edna Acosta-Belén and Carlos E. Santiago detail the reasons for the migration.[5] The U.S. occupation caused extreme poverty as large absentee American corporations destroyed Puerto Rico's agriculture and sugar industries. They seized ownership of the land, forcing farmers into migrant labor, low-wage jobs, unemployment, and widespread scarcity.[6] Officials attributed Puerto Rico's dire economic situation to "overpopulation," blaming high fertility rates.[7] A mass sterilization program, beginning in the 1930s, targeted Puerto Rican women, resulting in some of the world's highest rates of the procedure.[8]

In 1947, the Puerto Rican government launched "Operation Bootstrap," an industrialization program proposed as a solution to poverty. It granted U.S. companies access to cheap labor and generous tax breaks, while promoting emigration of the archipelago's poorest residents.[9]

Most Puerto Ricans settled in large U.S. cities, such as New York, Chicago, and Philadelphia, but also in smaller towns throughout the Northeast.[10] They encountered xenophobia and limited economic opportunities. Geographer Matthew Gandy describes these conditions in *"Between Borinquen and the Barrio: Environmental Justice and New York City's Puerto Rican Community, 1969-1972."*

> The new arrivals found that they were restricted to menial, poorly paid work—if they worked at all—in combination with overcrowded, dilapidated housing and inadequate access to basic services such as education and health care.[11]

In addition to the economic hardships, Puerto Ricans faced cultural and racial discrimination. They faced language barriers for speaking Spanish and experienced racism and ethnic discrimination as a mixed-race people.[12]

In New York City, Puerto Ricans lived alongside African American migrants from the U.S. South. We shared migration stories and learned about Jim Crow racism. Between 1964 and 1968, uprisings erupted in African American neighborhoods, including Harlem,[13] driven by glaring poverty, entrenched segregation, and rampant police brutality and murders. Many young Puerto Ricans in the United States joined African Americans in the fight against white supremacy and racial injustice.

Malcolm X inspired Puerto Rican activists with his uncompromising vision of Black liberation and humanist aspirations:

> We declare our right on this earth to be a man, to be respected as a human being, to be given the rights of a human being in this society, on this earth, in this day, which we intend to bring into existence by any means necessary.[14]

For many Puerto Rican activists, his words were a powerful call to action.

In 1966, the Student Nonviolent Coordinating Committee (SNCC), a leading civil rights organization in the U.S. South, led the call for "Black Power." Leaders like Ella Baker, Stokely Carmichael, and Jamil Abdullah Al-Amin (H. Rap Brown) championed this new direction. SNCC's call was, in the words of historian and activist Barbara Ransby, "not simply an escalation in militancy but also a shift in vision, philosophy, and structure."[15] It marked a move away from the civil rights era's fight for integration with white America toward a demand advocating for revolutionary societal transformation.[16]

In California, the Black Panther Party for Self-Defense popularized a 10-Point Program, demanding employment, land, housing, justice, and an immediate end to police brutality.[17]

When Martin Luther King Jr. was assassinated in 1968, an outpouring of grief, frustration, and anger ignited uprisings in more than one hundred U.S. cities.[18] By then, many people had lost faith that the United States could be reformed through elections or legislation alone.

Amid deepening poverty and escalating state violence, grassroots organizing gained momentum in communities of color. In 1968, José "Cha-Cha" Jiménez formed the Young Lords Organization,[19] inspired by the Black Panther Party and by Fred Hampton, Chairman of the Chicago chapter. Jiménez and Hampton met in prison and continued their relationship as community organizers. The YLO united with the Black Panther Party and the Young Patriots Organization (a group of poor whites from Appalachia) to form an alliance called "the Rainbow Coalition." Their rallying cry was "Black Power, Brown Power, and White Power."[20]

In a 1970 interview, YLO field marshal Cosmoe Torres, described the group's political evolution:

> It's not that we were a gang one minute and the next we were all Communists. What we had to realize was that it wasn't no good fightin' each other, but that what we were doing as a gang had to be against the capitalist institutions that are oppressing us.[21]

Torres further emphasized the Young Lords' commitment to "human rights, not just civil rights."[22]

Human rights are fundamental, universal, and inherent to all individuals. They include the rights to life and liberty, freedom from slavery and torture, and the right to food, work, and housing. The United Nations' *Universal Declaration of Human Rights*, adopted in 1948, was the first international legal document to outline these rights.[23] Civil rights, by contrast, refer to legal protections granted by individual nations—such as the right to vote or the right to legal counsel—which can vary from country to country.

Nixon's Law and Order Politics

Four months after the Young Lords Organization emerged in Chicago, Richard M. Nixon was sworn in as the thirty-seventh president of the United States on January 20, 1969. Nixon's presidency coincided with the height of the Young Lords' activism. Although Nixon won the popular vote by a slim victory, he won the electoral college by a comfortable margin, largely by appealing to white Americans eager for a return to pre–civil rights norms. His election revealed that these voters rejected appeals for racial, economic, and social justice.

Nixon claimed to speak for the "Silent Majority," for those who were not out in the streets.[24] He vowed to enforce a program of "law and order," a coded promise to preserve the system of white supremacy that kept African Americans and other people of color in subservience. In 1971, he made good on this pledge by launching the so-called "War on

Drugs." This campaign shifted the national conversation away from eliminating the causes of crime to a focus on punishment and criminalization of Black and Brown communities.[25] His administration capitalized on racial fears, portraying African Americans and Latinx populations as the primary threats to U.S. society. These policies laid the groundwork for the mass incarceration of people of color and helped to position the United States as the world's most carceral nation.[26]

At the same time, Nixon's foreign policy intensified global tensions. He expanded the Vietnam War into neighboring Laos and Cambodia, enlarging the U.S. military presence across Southeast Asia. From 1969 to 1970, Nixon ordered a secret bombing offensive that dropped 2.7 million tons of bombs over Cambodia, killing more than half a million people.[27] In Laos, where bombing had begun as early as 1964, per capita tonnage of bombardment was even higher.[28] These escalations sparked global and U.S. protests, as people condemned both the mass civilian deaths and the imperialist objectives of U.S. foreign policy.

Despite these atrocities, Nixon's downfall came not from his domestic repression or foreign aggression, but from the Watergate scandal. In 1974, the House Judiciary Committee recommended Nixon's impeachment—not for the War on Drugs or the genocidal bombing of Cambodia and Laos, but for his role in the burglary and wiretapping of the Democratic Party's national headquarters and his subsequent attempts to destroy tapes that proved his crimes.[29] Facing removal from office, Nixon became the first U.S. president to resign, famously declaring, "I am not a crook."[30]

Nixon's policies—particularly the War on Drugs and his foreign interventions—still echo today in U.S. domestic and international policy.

The Growing Puerto Rican Community In New York City

By the late 1960s, New York City was home to 815,000 Puerto Ricans—the largest Puerto Rican community in the United States at the time.[31] The city's Republican mayor, John V. Lindsay, elected in 1966 and in office until 1973, identified as "a liberal," largely due to his opposition to the Vietnam War.[32] Nonetheless, progressives and social justice activists clashed with his administration amid deepening poverty, labor unrest, racial strife, and increasing "white flight."[33]

Historian Stephen Brier highlights the dramatic demographic transformation of the postwar era:

> Totaling nearly 8 million residents, New York City experienced a major demographic transformation in the postwar era, with nearly one million African Americans and Puerto Ricans replacing an equal number of white New Yorkers who had moved out of the city to nearby suburbs during the 1950s and 1960s.[34]

This shift reshaped the city, as African Americans and Puerto Ricans became the dominant populations in many neighborhoods.

Among New Yorkers, Puerto Ricans experienced the lowest income and education levels, the poorest housing conditions, and the highest percentage of poverty.[35] Puerto Rican women, like my mother and aunts, were a vital labor source in New York's garment industry and factories, enduring harsh working conditions and starvation wages.[36] Jobs were precarious in a volatile labor market, as factories increasingly left the city in pursuit of cheaper labor costs and bigger profits.[37] The disappearance of these jobs displaced Puerto Rican women who had been the backbone of the struggling garment industry since the 1950s.

Sociologist Alice Colón-Warren explains that the loss of factory jobs was at "the structural roots of the declining labor force participation of Puerto Rican women throughout the 1960s."[38] While a small segment of Puerto Rican women—those with English proficiency and some formal education—might be hired as store clerks, administrative assistants, nurses' aides, and other nonprofessional jobs, many others faced chronic unemployment and deepening poverty. Single mothers, in particular, often had no choice but to seek public assistance to support their families.

Even before the term *feminization of poverty* was popular, Puerto Rican communities were already experiencing high rates of female-headed households. Colón-Warren explains the underlying problem was systemic: prevailing labor market discrimination viewed women as secondary, nonessential workers, while gendered social roles placed the burden of childcare squarely on women, often forcing them "to become heads of household."[39] For working mothers, the scarcity of affordable childcare further compounded the challenge. Lacking access to stable employment and reliable childcare, Puerto Rican working women and their children became ensnared in a persistent cycle of poverty.

A new generation of Puerto Ricans coming of age in 1960s was determined to fight the poverty and injustice affecting our parents, communities, and future. Inspired by the era's social justice movements, Puerto Ricans joined these struggles and gained valuable organizing experience. Puerto Ricans protested the Vietnam War, marched for civil rights, and joined picket lines demanding fair hiring practices and better working condition. In a pivotal moment in 1964, Puerto Rican parents, students, and educators joined 450,000 participants in the largest school boycott in U.S. history, aimed at ending de facto segregation in New York City public schools.[40]

In 1967, when police killed an East Harlem youth, Puerto Ricans took to the streets in protest for three consecutive days.[41] Within the city's public university system, Puerto Rican and African American students joined in occupying campus buildings, demanding open admissions, and the establishment of academic programs that reflected the histories and experiences of people of color.[42]

At the same time, Puerto Rican writers, poets, playwrights, artists, and muralists helped forge "Neorican" and "Nuyorican" identities, fusing experiences from both New York and Puerto Rico. The Nuyorican movement emerged as a powerful literary and cultural force, giving voice to the oppressive social, political, and economic realities confronting Puerto Ricans in the United States and Puerto Rico.

In March 1969, a busload of Nuyorican and African American youth from New York traveled across the country to the National Chicano Youth Conference in Denver, Colorado, organized by the Crusade for Justice. Over 1,500 young people attended,[43] including the group from New York, whose bus was sponsored by the Real Great Society, an East Harlem organization founded by former gang leaders and young professionals.[44] At the conference, the New Yorkers met members of the Young Lords Organization, including its Chairman, José "Cha Cha" Jiménez. Among the attendees were Carlito Rovira and myself. Little did we know that later that year, a Young Lords chapter would open in New York, and we would become members.

The Young Lords Emerge In New York

On July 26, 1969, the Young Lords officially established the New York chapter. Like the Black Panther Party and other nationalist groups of the era, the YLO adopted a paramilitary structure with a strict hierarchy, a chain of command, and rigorous rules of discipline. This model was, in part, a response to the widespread belief that the U.S. government had declared war on progressive movements. That year, FBI director J. Edgar Hoover declared the Black Panther Party "the greatest threat to the internal security" of the United States, underscoring the intense climate of surveillance and infiltration that existed.

The Young Lords Organization was structured as a male paramilitary hierarchy. Information flowed from top to bottom through various levels on a "need-to-know" basis, intended to keep sensitive information out of the hands of FBI and police infiltrators likely embedded in our ranks. At the top of the hierarchy was the Central Committee, the governing and final decision-making body. In New York, the initial members included Felipe Luciano as Deputy Chairman, Juan González as Deputy Minister of Education and Health, Pablo "Yoruba" Guzmán as Deputy Minister of Information, David Pérez as Deputy Minister of Defense, and Juan "Fi" Ortiz as Deputy Minister of Finance. Sixteen-year-old Ortiz was the youngest, while González, at twenty-two, was the oldest. The men selected each other as leaders—there were no elections.

The Central Committee members were the public face of the organization—the primary spokesmen, interacting with the press, negotiating with officials, and meeting with political and movement leaders. Each was in charge of a ministry made up of "captains," "lieutenants," cadres, and Young Lords-in-training. These ranks formed the operational backbone of the organization, carrying out the day-to-day activities, running "serve the people" programs, conducting political education classes, taking part in protests, and selling *Palante*, the Young Lords' newspaper. Larger and more sustained efforts were called "offensives."

The organization's governing principle was "democratic centralism." In theory, this concept balanced power between the Central Committee and the rank-and-file. "Democratic" emphasized open discussion and debate at general membership meetings, giving cadres a voice in decision-making. Every member was expected to abide by the majority consensus, regardless of personal views. "Centralism" referred to the Central Committee's role in maintaining "unity in action" by implementing the collectively agreed-upon decisions. Over time, however, the principle of democratic centralism was corrupted, as the Central Committee increasingly bypassed participatory decision-making processes.

In October 1969, however, the Young Lords Organization was still in the early stages of establishing itself in the community when the Central Committee released its most important and unifying document: the *13-Point Program and Platform*. This statement articulated the organization's core philosophy and beliefs. Below, I introduce several of its points, which are examined in greater depth in the chapters that follow.

Point 1 articulates the Young Lords' primary goals and dual commitment to Puerto Ricans: "We want self-determination for Puerto Ricans: liberation on the Island and inside the United States." For the Young Lords, *self-determination* meant the right of a people or nation to freely decide their political status, control their economic, social, and cultural development, and reclaim ownership of their land and resources.

Point 2 expands this vision calling for "self-determination for all Latinos," explicitly naming Chicanos in the Southwest, the people of Santo Domingo, and others in Latin America resisting U.S. imperialism.

The demand for self-determination extended to Indigenous struggles to reclaim land, preserve cultural identity, and assert political autonomy in the face of the ongoing settler violence aimed at erasing Native populations. Although the term *settler colonialism* was not widely used at the time, it is applicable. Scholar Roxanne Dunbar-Ortiz defines it as "the founding of a state based on the ideology of white supremacy, the widespread practice of African slavery, and a policy of genocide and land theft."[45] Settler colonialism relies on violence, forced removal, and cultural erasure to dismantle Indigenous ways of life. From its inception, the United States has functioned as a settler colonial state.

Point 3 calls for the "liberation of all Third World people," declaring that "Black people, Indians, and Asians slaved to build the wealth of this country," and affirming that "Third World people have led the fight for freedom." At the time, the term *Third World* was widely used to express solidarity with oppressed and exploited peoples of Asia, Africa, and Latin

America, as well as their diasporas. It embodied a politics of internationalism and a commitment to a shared anti-imperialist struggle.

In Point 4, the Young Lords identify as "revolutionary nationalists" dedicated to racial justice and community control over essential institutions—such as policing, healthcare, education, housing, and transportation. The Young Lords describe "Latin, Black, Indian, and Asian people inside the u.s. as *internal colonies*, whose "experiences of ghettoization, police brutality, and racialized oppression under U.S. capitalism" mirrored colonial conditions abroad.[46]

The 13-Point Program demands the withdrawal of U.S. military forces from Puerto Rico and all oppressed nations and communities, while also calling for the release of political prisoners and prisoners of war. It affirms solidarity with global liberation movements.

While the 13-Point Program grounded the Young Lords in anti-imperialist and socialist traditions, it also revealed internal tensions. Point 10, for instance, states: "We want equality for women," yet it simultaneously endorses "revolutionary machismo," reflecting an ongoing acceptance of patriarchal values and a reluctance to confront systemic male domination. This contradiction undermined the program's declared commitment to the liberation of all oppressed peoples.

The final points of the platform align with other revolutionary movements of the time. Point 11 proclaims, "We believe armed self-defense and armed struggle are the only means to liberation."

Point 13 expresses the ultimate vision of the Young Lords:

> We want a socialist society. We want a society where the needs of the people come first and where we give solidarity and aid to the people of the world.

In *The Case for Socialism*, author Alan Maass writes:

> At its heart, socialism is about the creation of a new society, built from the bottom up, through the struggles of ordinary working people against exploitation, oppression, and injustice—one that eliminates profit and power as the prime goals of life, and instead organizes our world around the principles of equality, democracy, and freedom.[47]

The 13-Point Program ends with the rallying cry: *Hasta la victoria siempre*—Always until victory—declaring an unwavering commitment to the struggle for human liberation.

Power to the People: The New Left

The Young Lords were part of the "New Left," consisting of activist organizations that emerged in the 1960s and 1970s to fight U.S. government policies and press for deep structural change. In *Rethinking the New Left: An Interpretative History*, historian Van Gosse summarizes the transformative impact of this era:

> From the 1950s through the 1970s, a series of social movements surged across America, changing the relationship between white people and people of color, how the U.S. government conducts foreign policy, and the popular consensus regarding gender and sexuality. Together, these movements redefined the meaning of democracy, and "power to the people" is what linked them together. They constituted a "movement of movements" that was considerably greater than the sum of its parts.[48]

Under the New Left umbrella, a broad range of groups organized diverse populations around numerous issues, using varied strategies and tactics. Within this framework, the *Third World Left* emerged as a powerful movement led by African American, Latinx, Asian, and Native peoples. While the term "Third World" held varied meanings across groups, it broadly referred to their shared political commitments: solidarity with global anti-colonial struggles, opposition to U.S. imperialism, and a belief in movement building "from below"—originating in the most disenfranchised communities and sectors.[49]

At the forefront were African American organizations, especially the Black Panther Party and other groups committed to Black self-determination and social justice. Puerto Rican organizers, likewise, built a left rooted in the dual struggle against colonialism in Puerto Rico and for the rights of Puerto Ricans in the United States. Feminists of color were central to these movements, bringing forward liberatory theories and practices, forming caucuses, and creating autonomous women-led organizations and committees. Socialist feminists, in particular, challenged male dominance within the movement while fighting for the rights of women of color and the liberation of all oppressed people.

The New Left groups did not operate in isolation. Collaborations and coalitions flourished, fostering collective action and advancing shared goals. These alliances facilitated the exchange of ideas and strategies across racial, national, and ideological lines, deepening the impact of each organization. In an era of rapid political and social change, the New Left became a vital force for social transformation during the late 1960s and 1970s.

Fig. 2. "We Want a Socialist Society." East Harlem. 1970.

(Courtesy: Michael Abramson.)

2.
SERVING THE PEOPLE. "WE ARE REVOLUTIONARY NATIONALISTS"[1]

> Great transformations do not begin from above
> nor with monumental and epic deeds, but with
> movements small in size and that appear irrelevant
> to politicians and analysts from above. History is
> not transformed by packed squares or enraged crowds,
> but ... by the organized conscience of groups and
> collectives that know and recognize one another,
> below and to the left, and build another politics.[2]

—*Insurgent Subcommandante Marcos*, Chiapas, México, 2018

In the fall of 1969, the Young Lords Organization opened a storefront office at 1678 Madison Avenue, between 110th and 111th Streets in East Harlem. This space became the main hub of YLO activity in New York until April 1970, when the group opened a second storefront in the Bronx. During this period, the organization attracted self-sacrificing and loyal members from low-income backgrounds who were not afraid, but eager, to knock on doors to spread the word of revolution.

This chapter describes the YLO's early activities and evolving ideology. Through grassroots activism and bold political actions, members challenged systemic injustices while offering programs responding to immediate community needs. The day-to-day activities blended revolution with reform, as the Young Lords organized for long-term change while delivering tangible benefits to people's lives.

At the East Harlem storefront, David Pérez, the Deputy Minister of Defense, welcomed new recruits for orientation. He reviewed the 13-Point Program and the rules of discipline, emphasizing that attendance at general membership meetings and political education classes was mandatory. All members were expected to sell the organization's newspaper, distribute flyers, and engage in local door-to-door organizing. Although the orientation process evolved over time, these core membership requirements remained consistent.

At the storefront, members attended meetings, received assignments, and connected with neighborhood residents. The officer of the day, at the front desk, answered the telephone, welcomed visitors, and distributed daily tasks. Through community organizing and "serve the people" programs, the Young Lords advanced the idea of socialism, emphasizing that though the U.S. government had the resources to meet people's basic needs, it systematically failed to do so.

Fig. 3. Officer of the Day. Connie Morales. East Harlem. 1970.
(Courtesy: Michael Abramson)

Many YLO initiatives focused on the needs of mothers and children, including free breakfast programs, clothing giveaways, and preventative health screenings. Like the Black Panther Party, the breakfast program was a top priority. Each weekday, Young Lords picked up food donations, prepared and served meals to children, then escorted them to school. Other members organized free clothing drives and coordinated health screenings.

Members of the Ministry of Education facilitated weekly political education classes for both the Young Lords and community residents. The Information Ministry played a crucial role in coordinating press conferences with English- and Spanish-language media, ensuring the

YLO's message reached a broad public. Young Lords also assisted individuals who arrived at the office with housing disputes, workplace issues, or police brutality complaints. These encounters frequently led to long-term organizing campaigns. Young Lords responded swiftly to spontaneous incidents in East Harlem—especially those involving police violence—and participated in citywide protests and demonstrations.

Among key community organizers in the East Harlem branch were women. Sonia Ivany participated in the 1969 summer garbage offensive and was the first woman to join the Young Lords Organization in New York. She was Cuban, a New York University student, and a new mother of a baby girl. Mirta González, also a mother with a young daughter, was Puerto Rican, and active in community projects. Alongside her were Iris Benítez, who was Afro–Puerto Rican, and Denise Oliver who was African American. Together, they helped organize "serve the people" programs—a term derived from the *Quotations of Chairman Mao Tse-Tung*, the "Little Red Book" we studied for political guidance. In addition to their community organizing responsibilities, González, Benítez, and Oliver were cadres in the Information Ministry and wrote news pieces for the *Y.L.O.* newspaper in Chicago.

Confronting The Lead Poisoning Crisis

Following the summer garbage offensive, the Young Lords turned attention to another public health crisis: lead-poisoning. Landlords often used cheap lead-based paint on tenement walls that easily peeled and crumbled to the floor. These hazardous paint chips posed a serious threat to small children, who, if they ingested them, could suffer brain injury, seizures, or even death. Although aware of the problem, politicians failed to address it.[3]

In response to the ongoing danger, a group of Young Lords sprang into action along with workers and medical students from East Harlem's Metropolitan Hospital. On the morning of November 24, 1969, approximately thirty activists sat-in at the New York City Department of Health, occupying the deputy commissioner's office.[4] They demanded access to lead-testing kits that the city possessed but was not using. As a result of the sit-in, the city officials surrendered more than two hundred urinary lead detection kits.[5]

The Young Lords wasted no time putting the kits to use. For several Saturdays, Young Lords, hospital workers, and medical students gathered outside the East Harlem storefront. Going door to door in teams, they collected urine samples and educated residents about lead-poisoning. Women played a crucial role in these efforts, persuading mothers to allow their children to be tested.

The results were alarming: 30 percent of the children tested positive for lead exposure.[6] It was an outrage! Puerto Rican and African American children were being poisoned in their own homes due to the negligence and greed of landlords, politicians, and health officials. Jack Newfield, a respected journalist from the *Village Voice* newspaper, helped expose the scandal.

Reforms followed. The city's Department of Health created a bureau to order housing repairs in lead-poisoning cases and initiated a prevention program that included screening preschool children in Head Start programs and day-care centers.[7]

These activities were an example of the Young Lords' commitment to bring life-saving services and reforms to underserved communities.

Puerto Rican Radicals at the People's Church

Among the early YLO programs in East Harlem were the free breakfast programs for children. The first one at the Emmaus House on East 116th Street, served thirty children. Additional sites opened at the Theater Arts Center on East 110th Street and at St. Mark's Church in the Lower East Side. Local merchants donated the food, and Young Lords cooked and served it. Mothers in the community enthusiastically embraced the program. By October 1969, the Young Lords were scrambling to find additional space to meet the growing waiting list.

The First Spanish United Methodist Church, located at 111th Street and Lexington Avenue, was largely unused during weekdays. Several Young Lords went to speak with the pastor, Reverend Humberto Carranza, a Cuban exile, requesting space to run a free breakfast program and establish a free day-care center for mothers in the community. Carranza, who was vehemently opposed to the Young Lords' socialist politics, refused.

On December 7, 1969, Young Lords returned to the church on a testimonial Sunday when any person could address the congregants. As Deputy Chairman, Felipe Luciano rose to speak, several policemen were already waiting inside the church. They jumped him and broke his arm. In the ensuing brawl, police arrested thirteen persons, including four YLO women members: Sonia Ivany, Elena González, Mirta González, and Denise Oliver, along with journalist, Erika Sezonov.[8] They were charged with disrupting church services, felonious assault, and riot.

Iris Benítez, of the Information Ministry, documented the incident in the Chicago *Y.L.O.* newspaper, noting that "the highest bail was set … on Mirta González, Lieutenant of Information, and Daoud Velásquez, Captain of Information."[9] The Young Lords mobilized immediately to raise bail funds, securing the release of all members within twenty-four hours.

Three days after Christmas, the Young Lords returned to the church, drawing attention to the poverty and urgent need for social programs in East Harlem. In a dramatic appeal, the Young Lords barricaded the church doors and hung a sign from a side window that read, "*La Iglesia de la Gente*"—"The People's Church."

By the time police arrived, a spirited press conference was already underway. Iris Benítez, Pablo "Yoruba" Guzmán, and Juan González addressed reporters. "The church is supposed to serve the people, help them, and work with them. This is a public building that does not pay taxes," they explained.[10] Later, Benítez detailed the events leading up to the takeover on the Young Lords' *Palante* radio show.[11] News traveled at lightning speed, bringing thousands of supporters to the church.

The militant speeches of young Puerto Ricans, Afro-Boricua leaders, women of color, and the working-class character of the group, made a strong public impression. The urgency with which the Young Lords spoke was a clarion call, revealing the stark divide between poor working-class Puerto Ricans and powerful church and government elites. As the takeover unfolded, the Young Lords welcomed neighborhood residents, activists, and other supporters into the space.

During the next eleven days, the Young Lords offered "serve the people" programs, including breakfast and clothing distribution, a day-care center, health services, a liberation school, community dinners, poetry readings, theatrical performances, film screenings, and guest speakers. Frequent performers included Nuyorican poets Pedro Pietri and José Angel Figueroa; the guerrilla theater group Third World Revelationists; and folkloric musicians Pepe and Flora. One evening, children put on a play, spotlighting the theme, "no one wants to be poor." Activists, artists, and supporters all contributed to the revolutionary effort, solidarity, and joy at the People's Church.

On New Year's Eve, community residents and activists filled the church to ring in "the decade of the people." The atmosphere was electric as Pablo "Yoruba" Guzmán, Deputy Minister of Information, spoke to the lively and animated crowd. "The People's Church is part of a global struggle," he declared to loud applause.[12] The room erupted with shouts and callouts—"Right on!" "Speak, brother!" "¡Así se habla!"—as people rose to their feet, clapping, cheering, and nodding in agreement. U.S. imperial power is "the common enemy of the peoples of the world, even those who live within its borders,"[13] he continued, emphasizing the need to fight from within the "belly of the beast." The energy was electric, charged with the shared urgency of the movement.

On January 8, 1970, the People's Church occupation came to a dramatic end. New York City police stormed the building and arrested 106 Young Lords and supporters. As they loaded into police vans, fists raised high, they sang *"Qué bonita bandera es la bandera puertorriqueña,"*—"What a beautiful flag is the Puerto Rican flag."

The People's Church takeover marked a new phase of Puerto Rican radicalism and militancy in the diaspora. The activities at the church showed a powerful alternative for community voices to be heard in the public discourse—one rooted in direct, action-driven challenge to the systemic neglect faced by poor people. The Young Lords rejected the passive, top-down, let's-wait-and-see, bureaucratic anti-poverty program approach promoted by mainstream reformers at the time.

Newspapers, magazines, radio programs, and television networks covered the Young Lords' activism, generating far-reaching interest and excitement. Defiant young Puerto Ricans challenging systemic poverty and disdain were like a burst of sunlight, reviving faith in the power of ordinary people to take action and spark social change. The urgency of the fight against poverty and injustice was unifying and energized the community.

Defining Puerto Rican Identity in the U.S. diaspora

Amid the social and political upheaval of the era, young Puerto Ricans in the United States grappled with questions of identity. Two central concerns emerged: What unites Puerto Ricans living in the United States? And what is the relationship of the Puerto Rican diaspora to Puerto Rico? According to historian and women's studies scholar Dr. Edna Acosta-Belén, the Young Lords Organization was among the groups that shaped a new vision of Puerto Rican identity, unity, and political engagement within the diaspora during this transformative period.

Despite the geographic distance, Puerto Ricans maintained a strong sense of collective identity—a belief in being "one people"—reinforced by frequent travel between the United States and the archipelago. Visits to family and friends, the sharing of migration stories, and the preservation of cultural traditions helped sustain these ties. As historian Jorge Duany observes, Puerto Ricans developed "imagined communities" that bridged both locations and participated in the social and political life of each.[14]

For the Young Lords Organization, this "imagined community" was expansive. It included all persons of Puerto Rican descent, regardless of whether born in Puerto Rico, had ever visited the archipelago, or spoke Spanish. The Young Lords embraced a radical *puertorriqueñidad,* affirming a shared culture, history, and legacy of resistance to colonialism as central to a broader struggle for self-determination and political liberation. As Acosta-Belén observes, the Young Lords' vision of national identity also explicitly embraced Afro–Puerto Ricanness—a history and heritage long suppressed by colonial forces.[15]

In the United States, the Young Lords popularized *puertorriqueñidad* through the prominent display of the Puerto Rican flag on T-shirts, berets, pins, posters, and other forms of political art and paraphernalia. Yet Young Lords insisted that cultural expression alone would not achieve liberation. For the YLO, nationalism was not solely cultural—it was inherently political. To that end, the Young Lords drew a sharp distinction between revolutionary nationalism and cultural nationalism, emphasizing that cultural identity had to be linked with the political struggle to achieve transformative change.

At the same time, the Young Lords recognized that identifying as a nationalist or pro-independence supporter in Puerto Rico was an invitation to being *fichado*—marked as a subversive—and subjected to police surveillance and repression.[16] Colonialism was not just a political condition but fundamental to Puerto Rican identity.

Writing in the May 1970 issue of the Young Lords' *Palante* newspaper, Deputy Chairman, Felipe Luciano asserted:

> Puerto Ricans, wherever they are, whether in the united states or *Borinquen* (Puerto Rico), constitute a colony and their oppression is that of a colonial people.[17]

This understanding of Puerto Ricans as a colonized people was foundational to the Young Lords' revolutionary nationalism and call for solidarity across the diaspora. It fused ideas of socialist ideologies, the African American liberation movement, and global anti-colonial struggles. The ideology was not static, evolving over time in response to both internal tensions and external shifts in the political landscape.

Major Political Influences

Black Liberation Movements and the Black Panther Party

Central to the Young Lords' revolutionary nationalism was combating racism. Point 4 of the 13-Point Program stated: "We are revolutionary nationalists and oppose racism." This commitment reflected the lived experiences of Puerto Ricans in the United States, who faced systemic poverty, racism, and discrimination. It was also shaped by the civil rights and Black liberation movements, which provided powerful models of resistance and organizing. Puerto Ricans and African Americans frequently joined forces in struggles against racist institutions, forging unity in the fight for justice. Many Young Lords had been active in these movements and maintained strong relationships with African American political leaders and movements.

In the day-to-day political work, the Young Lords tackled multiple forms of racial oppression. We organized against institutionalized injustices in the lives of Puerto Rican and African American low-income communities—unemployment, substandard housing, police brutality, inferior education, and a horrendous public health system. These bonds of struggle were reflected in the membership: approximately 20 percent of Young Lords were African American.

The Black Panther Party (BPP) had a profound influence on the ideology and practices of the Young Lords Organization. Both the Panthers and Young Lords combined community-based organizing with a critique of capitalism as the root cause of poverty and oppression. Each identified as revolutionary nationalist and socialist, grounding their activism in anti-imperialist and class-conscious politics. As BPP cofounder Huey P. Newton stated in a 1968 interview, "[T]o be a revolutionary nationalist you would by necessity have to be a socialist."[18]

The Panthers and the Young Lords believed that liberation could not be achieved within the existing capitalist economic and political system. Newton further explains:

> We realize that this country became very rich upon slavery and that slavery is capitalism in the extreme. We have two evils to fight, capitalism and racism. We must destroy both racism and capitalism.[19]

He underscores the connection between the accumulation of wealth through the enslavement of Black people and the foundations of capitalism, concluding that the struggle against racism and capitalism was inseparable—and that white supremacy was central to both.

Scholar-activist Loretta Ross expands on this analysis by emphasizing the intersectional nature of white supremacy: how it operates in concert with other systems of oppression, including class, gender, and religion. "Racism is a fundamental feature of white supremacy," she writes, "but not its totality."[20] Activist Elizabeth "Betita" Martínez adds that white supremacy is "a system of exploitation and oppression of continents, nations, and peoples of color ... for the purpose of maintaining and defending a system of wealth, power, and privilege."[21] Both Ross and Martínez highlight white supremacy as a global interconnected system comprising numerous oppressive ideologies and practices.

To the broader discourse on anti-Black racism, the Young Lords brought forward the distinct experiences of Puerto Ricans—especially

Afro-Boricuas. After World War II, hundreds of thousands of Puerto Ricans migrated to the United States, primarily from the most economically marginalized sectors, including Black communities. Pablo "Yoruba" Guzmán, the Young Lords' Minister of Information and a second-generation Afro-Boricua-Cubano, powerfully articulates the reality of anti-Blackness faced by Afro-Puerto Ricans. He writes, "[B]efore people called me a 'spic,' they called me a 'nigger'"[22]— underscoring that he experienced anti-Black racism before being racialized as Puerto Rican.

Guzmán situates the experiences of Black Puerto Ricans within the broader history of Black people throughout the Americas. In a 1970 report to the cadre, he writes:

> It is important for us to study the history of Blacks in the Americas, because it is part of Puerto Rican history, in terms of Black slaves in Puerto Rico and how they came into the culture, and in terms of our better understanding the development of Blacks in the United States, who are the major force in the Amerikkkan revolution. ... To study Black history is to complete the study of Puerto Rican history and vice versa.[23]

Guzmán thus connects the histories of African Americans and Afro-Puerto Ricans to a larger Afro-diasporic transnational community.[24]

In addition to confronting institutional racism, Young Lords challenged the racism embedded within Puerto Rican and Latinx culture, language, and history, rejecting the pervasive myth of racial equality often espoused within Latinx communities. The Young Lords tackled issues of racism "between Puerto Ricans and Blacks, and between light-skinned and dark-skinned Puerto Ricans," explaining these divisions as internal contradictions among the people—distinct from structural antagonisms with the ruling class. Still, the Young Lords insisted that addressing internalized forms of racism was essential to the transformation of society.

A *Palante* article titled "Puerto Rican Racism," published in 1970, emphasized that "Puerto Ricans don't like to talk about racism or admit that it exists among Puerto Ricans."[25] Puerto Rico's racial hierarchy, rooted in Spanish colonial rule, defined whiteness along a continuum of gradations that asked: *how much white ancestry do you have?* This system promoted the idea of *mejorar la raza*—bettering the race—by urging individuals to marry lighter-skinned partners "to whiten" the population. Enslaved Africans, their children, and their descendants were relegated to the lowest tier of this racial hierarchy.

Following the U.S. invasion in 1898, this system was compounded by the U.S. racial hierarchy of "one-drop rule"—the notion that any trace of Black ancestry classified a person as Black.[26] The U.S. system further elevated whiteness as a socially desirable ideal and tool of racial domination, intensifying anti-Black racism in Puerto Rico.

As "aids in resisting the silence around Blackness,"[27] the Young Lords Party popularized the terms *Afro-Boricua* and *Afro-Puertorriqueño*, lifting up and celebrating African heritage and culture. A likely forerunner to these terms was *Afro-Borincano*, appearing in the 1930s writings of Arturo Alfonso Schomburg, the Afro-Boricua who built a vast collection of documents related to Black history and the African diaspora.[28] His collection later became the foundation of the Schomburg Center for Research in Black Culture located in New York City.

The Ideology of the Young Lords Party, a pamphlet published in 1971, emphasized Afro-Boricua identity.[29] Articles in *Palante* highlighted the African roots of Puerto Rican culture, the legacy of slavery in Puerto Rico, and the histories of African-descended communities such as "Loiza Aldea."[30] At a time when information on Black Puerto Rican history was scarce, the Young Lords brought these narratives—and the issue of anti-Black racism within Puerto Rican communities—to the forefront.

The Young Lords also challenged racialized discrimination that pushed Puerto Ricans and other communities of color into unemployment, poverty wages, substandard housing, inferior schools, and inadequate health care. As a mixed-race people, Puerto Ricans did not fit neatly into the Black-white binary of U.S. society.[31] Instead, Puerto Ricans were often categorized as "colored" or "other." As a group—particularly the poor and working class, whether light- or dark-skinned—Puerto Ricans faced systemic discrimination based on class, nationality, ethnicity, and language. The Young Lords recognized this as another form of racism and sought to dismantle racialized systems of oppression.

In doing so, the Young Lords broadened understanding of the struggles Puerto Ricans faced and advocated against all forms of racism.

The Puerto Rican Nationalist Party

El Partido Nacionalista Puertorriqueño—the Puerto Rican Nationalist Party (PRNP)—was another major influence on the Young Lords. Unlike the Black Panther Party and the Young Lords Organization, the PRNP was not socialist,[32] but it was firmly anti-colonial. Under the leadership of Pedro Albizu Campos, the PRNP waged a fervent struggle against U.S. colonial rule from the 1930s through the 1960s, seeking to establish Puerto Rico as a free and sovereign nation. The legacy of the nationalist resistance deeply shaped the Young Lords, who referred to themselves as "children of the Nationalist Party."

To understand the influence of the Puerto Rican Nationalist Party, it is essential to examine its pivotal role in the struggle against U.S. colonial rule. Following the invasion in 1898, U.S. colonial control extended into nearly every facet of Puerto Rican society. By the 1930s, it was clear that the U.S. government had no intention of granting Puerto Rico its independence.

In 1935, after police killed four Nationalists accused of plotting a bombing,[33] two young activists—Hiram Rosado and Elías Beauchamp—retaliated by assassinating Colonel Francis Riggs, the U.S.-appointed police commander.[34] They were immediately arrested and executed inside police headquarters.[35] Soon after, Pedro Albizu Campos and other Nationalists were charged with seditious conspiracy and sentenced to prison. Albizu Campos was sentenced to six to ten years.[36]

The political repression continued. On March 21, 1937, peaceful demonstrators gathered in the city of Ponce to demand the release of the Nationalists political prisoners and to commemorate the abolition of slavery in Puerto Rico. Acting on orders from the U.S.-appointed Governor Blanton Winship, police opened fire on the unarmed crowd, killing twenty-one people and wounding more than two hundred.[37] *La Masacre de Ponce* (the Ponce Massacre) became a defining symbol of the relentless violence of U.S. colonial rule in Puerto Rico.

The global political climate also shaped the political discourse around Puerto Rico's status. In 1945, the founding of the United Nations (UN) ushered in a call for decolonization, emphasizing the principle of self-determination. The UN compiled a list of "non-self-governing territories" and called on colonial powers to take steps toward granting them independence. Puerto Rico's inclusion on this list drew renewed international attention to its colonial status and increased pressure on the U.S. government to address the archipelago's political future in accordance with international law and the UN Charter.

In response, the United States moved to obscure its colonial domination. In 1947, the U.S. government permitted Puerto Ricans to elect their governor for the first time. Luis Muñoz Marin, leader of the Popular Democratic Party, won the 1948 election. While this move appeared to grant limited local autonomy, it primarily served as a U.S. strategy to maintain control while projecting an image of democratic self-rule in Puerto Rico.

Soon after taking office, Muñoz Marin signed *La Ley de la Mordaza* (the Gag Law), aimed at suppressing political dissent. It criminalized activities advocating for Puerto Rico's independence, singing patriotic songs, or displaying the Puerto Rican flag. Its harsh repression of freedom of expression led to the imprisonment of thousands and further consolidated U.S. control.

Amid growing demands for independence and mounting pressure from the United Nations, Congress passed Public Law 600 on July 3, 1950. Signed by President Harry Truman, the law allowed Puerto Rico to draft a constitution for internal self-governance, while retaining the archipelago firmly under U.S. congressional authority.[38] Recently released from prison, Albizu Campos denounced the measure as a facade that preserved colonial rule under the guise of democratic reform. He argued that the electoral process would not end U.S. domination.[39] In response to this new political framework, the Nationalist Party began to secretly organize a series of armed uprisings.[40]

On October 30, 1950, Nationalist leader Blanca Canales Torresola led an armed revolt in the town of Jayuya.[41] The U.S. government declared martial law, deploying National Guard troops and conducting aerial bombing on the town using P-47 Thunderbolt fighter planes.[42] In the aftermath, more than 400 people were arrested.[43]

On November 1, 1950, in an effort to draw international attention to continuing U.S. repression in Puerto Rico, Nationalists Oscar Collazo and Griselio Torresola attempted an attack on the Blair House in Washington, D.C., where President Truman was staying. Torresola was killed, and Collazo was arrested and sentenced to twenty-nine years in prison.[44] In the roundup of activists that followed, Albizu Campos was arrested again and sentenced to eighty years.[45]

Although Public Law 600 rebranded Puerto Rico as a "Commonwealth" (*Estado Libre Asociado*), it did not alter its colonial status. Nonetheless, this political maneuver enabled the U.S. government to remove Puerto Rico from the United Nations' list of "non-self-governing territories" in 1953, projecting a false image of self-governance.

On March 1, 1954, Nationalist Party members Lolita Lebrón Soto, Rafael Cancel Miranda, Irvin Flores Rodríguez, and Andrés Figueroa Cordero entered the U.S. Capitol and fired shots from the visitors' gallery of the House of Representatives, wounding five congressmen. Lebrón unfurled the Puerto Rican flag and shouted, "¡*Viva Puerto Rico Libre!*" All four were convicted and sentenced to prison terms ranging from seventy to eighty-five years.[46]

By 1964, Albizu Campos, still imprisoned and gravely ill, accused the U.S. government of subjecting him to radiation poisoning—an accusation the U.S. government vehemently denied. He was released on April 21, 1965 and died soon after in Puerto Rico from radiation-induced cancer.[47] Nearly three decades later, in 1994, the U.S. Department of Energy confirmed that radiation experiments had, in fact, been conducted on prisoners without their consent—including on Albizu Campos.[48]

Historian Manuel Maldonado-Denis describes the Nationalists' battle as "the highest expression of rebelliousness" against imperialism,"[49] emphasizing that the PRNP became "a profound symbol of resistance among the people and in the revolutionary national consciousness."[50]

In solidarity with this legacy, the Young Lords organized for self-determination, believing that Puerto Ricans—whether in Puerto Rico or the diaspora—were affected by the economic, psychological, cultural, and racial exploitation of U.S. colonialism.[51]

The Young Lords Organization, Black Panther Party, and Puerto Rican Nationalist Party shared similar views on armed revolution. They believed that when political avenues fail to achieve justice or social change, and when people's rights and lives no longer progress under the rule of those in power, then armed revolution is not only justified but necessary.

In sum, the Black Panthers, the Young Lords, and the Puerto Rican Nationalists shared a commitment to challenging U.S. imperialism and fighting for the liberation of colonized peoples.

Revolutionary Nationalism and Gender Justice

Puerto Rican women joined the Young Lords Organization drawn by its revolutionary ideals, direct-action strategies, and the visible presence of women activists. Other Latinas and African American women also joined, inspired by the 13-Point Program and its commitment to "the liberation of all oppressed people." As women of color, we saw the organization as a vehicle for political engagement and radical change.

From the outset, however, the liberatory aspirations of women clashed with the Young Lords' nationalist ideology and its traditional gender framework. While the 13-Point Program denounced capitalism, racism, colonialism, and imperialism, it made no mention of patriarchy—an omission, signaling women's oppression was not an organizational priority.

This contradiction was not unique to the Young Lords. Across the revolutionary nationalist movements of the 1960s and 1970s, women's rights were routinely subordinated to nationalist objectives. Leadership remained overwhelmingly male, and demands for gender equality were met with opposition. As feminist historian Anne McClintock notes, nationalism tends to reinforce gendered hierarchies that consolidate male power and restrict women's participation.[52]

Committed to revolutionary goals, women in the Young Lords refused to accept marginalization and challenged the patriarchal structures and traditional gender roles. While we did not call ourselves feminists at the time, we collectively questioned double standards and male chauvinist practices. We insisted that gender justice be fully integrated into the Young Lords' nationalist agenda. Through these struggles, a feminist consciousness emerged—shaped by our lived experiences, political practice, and study.

Our perspective aligned with that of African American, Chicana, Asian, and Indigenous women, who, like us, were fighting on multiple fronts for economic, racial, gender, and social justice. Across the movement, we engaged with issues affecting poor and working-class women of color: reproductive rights, gender-based violence, equal pay, affordable childcare, and state-sanctioned violence. Feminists within the Young Lords popularized the phrase "the revolution within the revolution" as a rallying cry, underscoring that the fight for gender justice must continue as long as inequality persists.

Women's activism was central to transforming the Young Lords Organization, introducing feminist ideas into both its politics and community work. Socialist feminist members advanced a political analysis that emphasized the interconnectedness of gender, race, and class oppression. For us, women's liberation was not a secondary concern—it was essential to both national and class liberation. We asserted that no nation could be truly free while its women remained oppressed.

The chapters that follow examine these tensions in greater detail, tracing the complex and often contested relationship between feminism and revolutionary nationalism within the Young Lords.

3.
RISE OF THE WOMEN'S CAUCUS

The sky is a conga drum stretched tight
for a bembe of the gods.[1]

—Ana Lydia Vega, "Cloud Cover Caribbean"

The People's Church takeover was a galvanizing moment for the Puerto Rican diaspora. News of the December 7, 1969 police attack and arrests of Young Lords at the First Spanish United Methodist Church spread quickly. Thousands of supporters arrived to express solidarity with the families and children of El Barrio. The public took particular note of the activism of women, especially the arrests of Young Lords Sonia Ivany, Elena González, Mirta González, and Denise Oliver.[2]

Outside the church, women delivered fiery speeches through bullhorns. Inside, Iris Benítez, a young Afro-Boricua, spoke to reporters, explaining the reasons behind the takeover. Other women organized "serve the people" programs, offering food, health services, and more. Their active involvement inspired a wave of new recruits. Puerto Rican, Latinx, and African American women saw in the Young Lords direct action strategies a pathway to liberation. While personal histories and motivations varied, many women of color saw their emancipation as inseparable from the struggle for social justice, leading to an exponential increase in women members.

This chapter traces the early activities of women in the Young Lords Organization—highlighting the formation of the Women's Caucus and the rise of feminist consciousness within the group. Given the visible leadership roles women held at the People's Church, new female recruits joined with the expectation of participating in substantive political work. However, women were generally relegated to behind-the-scenes tasks—assisting male leaders, doing clerical work, logistical coordination, and housekeeping. Even as women's numbers increased, the Central Committee remained largely unresponsive to feminist concerns.

It was particularly shocking to hear YLO leaders openly mock the white women's liberation movement. In one instance, Pablo "Yoruba"

Guzmán, Deputy Minister of Information, attributed their activism to sexual frustration. He wrote: "These chicks are all frustrated—that's their main problem. What they really need is a good—you know."[3] Such remarks revealed entrenched male supremacy, entitlement, and underlying hostility toward women.

Although most of us—myself included—had never been involved in the white women's movement, we rejected the contempt men directed at them. We recognized that the disdain shown toward white feminists extended to the liberatory aspirations of women of color.

"How can YLO leaders claim to be for the liberation of all oppressed people when they demean half of humanity? we asked. "Do they want liberation only for men?"

Becoming a Force: The Women's Caucus

The rampant machismo within the Young Lords Organization led several "old-timers"—women who had joined before the church occupation—to call a meeting one Sunday. We saw the need for a collective women's voice in a paramilitary male-led organization and knew we would be stronger together than as individuals. Attendees all expressed similar reactions to the macho and male chauvinist culture. "We joined to fight for the rights of Puerto Ricans not to perpetuate machismo, parading under the guise of a Puerto Rican revolution."

As the feminist historian Anne McClintock notes, "[F]eminism is a political response to gender conflict, not its cause."[4] We aimed to raise awareness about the systemic oppression of women of color and to demand equality. To remain YLO members, we had to confront the organization's macho culture and the Central Committee's backward ideas.

The first caucus participants included Iris Benítez, Denise Oliver, Lulu Carreras, Connie Morales, Martha Duarte (Arguello), Nydia Mercado, Olguie Robles, Doleza Miah, Cookie, Emma, Olgita, myself, and other women whose names I no longer recall. We were young, ranging in age from fourteen to twenty-six years old. Several mothers with young children, though unable to attend the Sunday meetings, stayed informed and provided feedback that enriched our collective development.

Fig. 4. Mirta González, Connie Morales, and Iris Benítez. 1970.
(Courtesy: Michael Abramson.)

For most participants, the caucus sessions were our first encounters with women-led discussions focused on gender oppression and women's liberation. Without a blueprint to follow, we learned from each other. Any woman could introduce a topic or share a reading. In our free-flowing conversations, we discussed the many forms of oppression, racism, and exploitation that affected our lives. We shared experiences related to jobs, reproductive rights, and caregiving responsibilities. Members expressed a strong desire to organize in the community to confront institutionalized gender discrimination and to advocate for reproductive justice, accessible childcare, and an end to sexual violence. Some members emphasized the second-class status of women in the home—expected to cook, clean and take care of children, husbands, and extended family. Others described the ways male domination was replicated within the Young Lords Organization itself.

During our initial meetings, we shared the reasons for joining the organization. Some women had been active in the civil rights and Black Liberation movements, student and workplace struggles, or organizations such as ASPIRA and the United Bronx Parents. We spoke about the women who inspired us—our mothers, *tías, abuelas, primas,* and other family members—as well as iconic revolutionary figures such as Sojourner Truth and Lolita Lebrón.

Each caucus member was encouraged to share her views, and decisions were made by consensus. Every voice was heard. After everyone had shared, someone might say, "It looks like we're all in agreement." When a hot topic sparked mixed opinions, we voted by a show of hands. Our decision-making process was more inclusive and democratic than what often occurred in other YLO meetings.

The Women's Caucus focused primarily on the conditions facing Puerto Rican women, but also on other Latinas and African Americans. We identified as women of color, recognizing both shared and distinct struggles, and the unique ways that systems of exploitation, violence, and separation shaped our lives.[5]

In the words of the Santa Cruz Feminist of Color Collective:

> "[W]omen of color" enables a way of seeing the world through a lens that refracts light in many ways to reveal a world full of possibilities, a world that is constantly shifting and in motion.[6]

"Women of color" was a coalitional term,[7] embracing the possibility of a larger "we" and the interconnectedness of our herstories.[8]

Our experiences with migration and displacement gave us a transnational and anti-imperialist outlook. By connecting the experiences of "women marginalized in the United States and outside of it,"[9] we expressed solidarity with "Third World women"—a term referring to women in Africa, Asia, and Latin America and to their descendants in the United States and around the world.

At the time, we used the words "sex," "women," and "gender" interchangeably, lacking the nuanced understandings of gender fluidity, gender nonconformity, cisgender and non-binary identities, and more that are recognized today. Nevertheless, the Women's Caucus was committed to ending gender-based oppression.

The Women's Caucus was a safe space where we could break the silence surrounding women's oppression. Like the *testimonio* tradition in Latin America and throughout the Third World, we sought "to bring to light a wrong, a point of view, or an urgent call for action."[10] Women described the sacrifices they made to take part in political activism. Working mothers juggled jobs and childcare, often bringing their children to the Young Lords' storefront office when they had no babysitter or could not afford one.

Women with full-time jobs dedicated their evenings and weekends to the political work of the organization. Several members were their family's primary breadwinners, enabling their partners to act as "full-time revolutionaries." Although women held jobs, paid the bills, cared for the children and the home, and contributed to political organizing, their immense labor—both at home and as activists—was frequently unrecognized and undervalued. Partners and others often criticized them for not participating in enough "real political work."

During caucus sessions, we examined beliefs inherited from society, families, schools, and media that fostered feelings of powerlessness, self-hatred, and inferiority regarding our abilities, physical appearance, and skin color. We explored the meaning of concepts like "colonized mentality," "internalized oppression," and "nonconscious" ideology. We gained insights from reading Frantz Fanon's *The Wretched of the Earth* and *Black Skin, White Masks,* which illuminated how colonizers impose their culture and ideas, embedding them in the consciousness of the people they oppress.

Violence against women of color was so pervasive that each member had a story to tell—recounting incidents of verbal assault, beatings, rapes, and other forms of violence, even at the hands of fathers and brothers. Several women reported that their partners warned them, "What happens between a man and a woman is private and not to be discussed with anyone." It was a threat. Refusal to obey could result in a punch in the face—or worse. By labeling such violence "private," men sought to silence women and conceal the emotional and physical abuse they inflicted. Caucus members also shared strategies to fend off sexual advances, including from men in the social justice movement.

As comrades and friends, we were determined to transform the dominant social order. Women and gender studies scholar Kristie Soares describes what that Women's Caucus provided: "a model for decolonial feminist praxis that creates alternate forms of kinship, prioritizes care of self and community, and claims public space for nontraditional performances of femininity and masculinity."[11]

Through the sharing of confidences and knowledge, members of the Women's Caucus developed a feminist consciousness,[12] a collective identity as Puerto Rican, Latina, and African American women—united by similar hopes, dreams, and politics.

Fig. 5. Women's Caucus Meeting. Early 1970.
(Courtesy of Michael Abramson.)

We were eager to bring feminist ideas into the organization and the broader Puerto Rican community. Members were ready to challenge institutionalized gender discrimination and advocate for reproductive justice, accessible childcare, and an end to sexual violence. Though we didn't use the term "feminist" at the time, we resonated deeply with the idea that Isabel Allende later expresses in *The Soul of a Woman*:

> Feminism, like the ocean, is fluid, powerful, deep, and encompasses the infinite complexity of life; it moves in waves, currents, tides, and sometimes in storms. Like the ocean, feminism never stays quiet.[13]

The members of the Women's Caucus envisioned new ways of being and aspired to equality and freedom.

Unmasking Machismo and Male Chauvinism from Within

As the membership of the Young Lords Organization grew, the Women's Caucus welcomed new recruits to our Sunday meetings. During these gatherings, we studied the 13-Point Program and Platform. Point 10 addressed the status of women, declaring: "We want "equality for women. Machismo must be revolutionary…not oppressive."[14]

Initially, we did not question the idea of "revolutionary machismo." We took pride in the program's statement of "equality for women" and were told that no other nationalist group made such a public commitment. But as we examined the concept more closely, we recognized its fundamental contradictions. Rather than rejecting machismo outright, Point 10 implied it could somehow be transformed into a positive force.

In its explanation, the Central Committee attempted to link machismo and capitalism, stating:

> Under capitalism, our people have been oppressed by both the society and our own men. The doctrine of machismo has been used by our men to take out their frustrations against *their* wives, sisters, mothers, and children.[15]

In our experience, machismo was more than male "frustrations." It extended beyond men acting out or venting their disappointments onto the women in their lives. Machismo was a deeply entrenched system of beliefs and behaviors, passed down through generations—one that upheld male dominance and normalized verbal and physical violence. The oppression of women was systemic—not simply the result of bad attitudes. Our demand was the abolition of machismo, not its rebranding. The Central Committee's explanation revealed reluctance to relinquish the structural privileges and control that men held under capitalism and patriarchy.

The members of the Women's Caucus demanded that the notion of "revolutionary machismo" be removed from the 13-Point Program in order to build a more progressive and visionary organization—one committed to both societal and personal transformation. Many activists across the movement likewise rejected the concept as both contradictory and absurd. After all, how do you make machismo revolutionary? Would anyone seriously argue that "racism must be revolutionary and not oppressive"?

Yet despite the widespread criticism, the term "revolutionary machismo," remained in the 13-Point Program for more than a year, until December 1970. The revised version stated: "We want Equality for Women. Down with Machismo and Male Chauvinism!" The accompanying description was updated as follows: "Men must fight along with sisters in the struggle for economic and social equality." However, the revision still failed to address the systemic exploitation of women, the role of patriarchy, or the personal and collective transformation necessary to achieve gender justice.

Point 10 also claimed, "Our women are equals in every way within the revolutionary ranks." In practice, however, men held the leadership and decision-making roles, while women were assigned administrative tasks, logistical support, and domestic chores. This gendered division of labor[16] mirrored the very capitalist and patriarchal structures we sought to dismantle.

To be clear, while we opposed the male supremacist ideology within our ranks, we did not view Puerto Rican or other oppressed Third World men as "the enemy." We understood that male chauvinism and machismo were systemic political problems—rooted in structures of power, not biological or character defects.

Caucus members fiercely challenged male supremacist ideas with a zeal beyond what most men wanted to hear. We scrutinized every manifestation of male supremacy and privilege, large and small. We called out the inferior treatment of women in the home, the workplace, in political organizations, and in society at large. Many men tired of our enthusiasm.

The Central Committee—composed of Felipe Luciano, Juan González, Pablo "Yoruba" Guzmán, David Pérez, and Juan "Fi" Ortiz—accused us of taking time away from "real political work" and ordered the Women's Caucus to stop meeting. After discussing it, we agreed: "They can't dictate how we spend our free time," and we continued to meet.

When the Central Committee members learned that we met, they were livid. How dare we defy their authority? They charged the Women's Caucus with violating a direct command—a serious offense under the organization's rules, which required obedience to Central Committee directives.

In those days, all Young Lords participated in martial arts self-defense classes run by the all-male Defense Ministry. At the end of the next session, the sensei summoned the caucus members to the center of the room and ordered us to line up in rows. The men fanned out to the edges of the large room to watch. Then a loud voice barked: "You have violated a direct Central Committee order for which you are now being disciplined. Give me one hundred pushups."

He caught us by surprise. We exchanged glances but complied. Then he shouted a second command. "Give me one hundred sit-ups." Again, we darted looks to each other, hesitating, asking with our eyes, should we comply? Should we refuse? Ultimately, we compiled. We felt humiliated but got through the grueling workout—winded, bodies aching, but proud. Our anger fueled us. It was the kind of energy Audre Lorde described as vital for transformation: anger that leads to growth and "corrective surgery."[17]

Some men, standing along the walls, hung their heads in embarrassment, avoiding eye contact, uncomfortable with the Central Committee's raw display of male ego and domination. In contrast, we held our heads high, feeling we had taken a collective step toward women's independence. Justice, we knew, was undeniably on our side.

After that episode, the Women's Caucus emerged more united than ever. The confrontation opened the floodgates. We voiced our grievances with renewed boldness. We examined every form of male chauvinism, from disrespectful language to physical assault and abuses of power.

Sexual objectification and harassment were urgent problems. Men commented on women's bodies and acted as if we should thank them for their so-called "compliments." But we expected revolutionary men to treat us as comrades—not as walking body parts or mindless bodies.

Members of the Women's Caucus condemned the hypocrisy of men who claimed to be "for the people" while using their Young Lords membership to pursue sex with young women. Some men spoke as though lying to women about their intentions was a harmless display of manhood, wearing those lies like badges of honor. "You dishonor the purple beret," some of us said. Many women in the community echoed our outrage, remarking, "Some men join the Young Lords just to get into women's pants." This macho behavior turned away potential recruits. "These men aren't serious about revolution," many concluded.

Some men in the movement assumed we welcomed their sexual advances. A woman who rejected them might be labeled a "butch," a "lesbian," or a "cold fish"—all intended as insults. While not all male Young Lords engaged in this conduct, many onlookers, both male and female, excused it as "just part of the Latin culture." That justification enraged us. "If the culture degrades women, then the culture must change," we insisted. "If you claim to be a revolutionary, you have to 'walk the talk.'" We repeatedly asked, "What type of society are we trying to create?"

Our concerns mirrored those raised by women today. How do we end gender-based abuse and violence? "Without consequences, our principles mean nothing," we argued. Long before the #MeToo movement, the Women's Caucus demanded male accountability. Men who harmed women should face consequences. Some of us threatened to resign if the Central Committee failed to act. "Why should a woman risk her life in an organization that does not respect women?" we asked. Men unwilling to support the liberation of half of humanity were not revolutionaries—they were impostors, fakers, and opportunists.

Intersectional Awakening in the Women's Caucus

Within the revolutionary nationalist movements across the United States, feminists of color organized to advance liberatory ideas and practices. The Women's Caucus in the Young Lords Organization raised critical questions about the relationship of the struggle for gender justice to both the revolutionary nationalist and Puerto Rican independence movements. A central debate emerged: Should the fight to end gender oppression be addressed as part of the social justice agenda, or should it wait until after the revolutionary struggle had been won?

In March 1970, several members of the Women's Caucus tackled this question on a Young Lords' *Palante* radio show in an episode titled *Women in the Colonies*.[18] The participants included Iris Benítez, Myrna Martínez, Denise Oliver, and me. During the discussion, Benítez stated, "We are first revolutionaries, second, Puerto Ricans, and thirdly, women." I added: "It's not to say that one comes before the other. Both national and gender oppressions work together."

Our exchange reflected the ongoing and evolving discussions within the Women's Caucus, which had not yet reached consensus. The radio program offered an early glimpse into the emerging dialogue on the intersection of feminism and nationalism—a topic that would be fiercely debated in the months ahead.

At the time, however, our focus was confronting male chauvinism and discriminatory practices within the Young Lords Organization. We were determined to defeat the deeply rooted belief that women of color were inferior—and to dismantle the behaviors and practices flowing from this belief.

Male Chauvinism–Female Passivity: A False Equivalence

A couple of months later, in May, the Central Committee—Felipe Luciano, Juan González, Pablo "Yoruba" Guzmán, David Pérez, and Juan "Fi" Ortiz—held a leadership retreat. The agenda was full of weighty topics, such as the Young Lords' political philosophy, the main organizing priorities, and the relationship with the Chicago Young Lords Organization. According to Guzmán, the retreat also included extensive discussions about male chauvinism. He summarized their conclusion on this topic:

> The attitudes of superiority that brothers had toward sisters would have to change, as would the passivity of sisters toward brothers (allowing brothers to come out of a macho or chauvinist, superior bag).[19]

While members of the Central Committee acknowledged that men needed to change their attitudes of superiority toward women, they simultaneously presented the idea of female 'passivity' as an equally signifi-cant issue—revealing an unwillingness to accept full responsibility. This framing—of "male-chauvinism-female passivity"—shifted blame onto women for supposedly allowing men to behave in macho or chauvinist ways. It downplayed men's accountability and portrayed women as complicit in their own oppression. In effect, it echoed a classic form of victim blaming: "Look what you made me do!" Yet when women did as-sert themselves, they were often criticized as too aggressive or opinion-ated.

The "male-chauvinism-female passivity" framework created a false equivalency between the power held by men and women. Much like the earlier notion of "revolutionary machismo," it reflected a continued re-luctance to recognize the systemic oppression of women.

Members of the Women's Caucus understood "female passivity" differently. For us, it was not about blaming women. What the Central Committee labeled as passivity, we recognized as "internalized oppres-sion," an outcome of historical legacies, systemic exploitation, and per-vasive ideologies that instilled inferiority complexes in women. It re-flected an internal struggle against deeply ingrained beliefs and system-atic social conditioning that taught women to see themselves as less ca-pable, less worthy, and subordinate to men.

Our aim was to break free from these patterns—what we came to understand through the writings of Franz Fanon as a "colonized mental-ity" or the internalization of inferiority, and "non-conscious ideology," the subconscious adoption of the oppressors' worldview. In their place, we sought to nurture liberatory ways of thinking and being that could uplift everyone. We viewed the fight against passivity not as self-blame but as an opportunity—a path for personal growth and transformation—a step toward becoming more empowered revolutionaries.

Chains on Our Mind: The Power of Words

The Women's Caucus explored many strategies to transform the political, cultural, and power dynamics of the organization. Among them was a conscious effort to change language. We came to understand that the dismantling of capitalist ways of thinking and behavior required an intentional struggle toward "a new way of being"[20]—for both men and women. New ways of thinking demanded new words—ones that did not rely on the sexist, racist, misogynist, and exploitative language inherited from a society built on exploitation and the subjugation of women.

Committed to personal and collective transformation, we worked to eliminate from our communications those words and phrases that perpetuated inequality or demeaned women. For example, we rejected being called "girls," a term that infantilized adult women, and we opposed patriarchal identifiers such as "so-and-so's wife," which reduced women to men's property and ignored a women's autonomy and desire for independence. Instead, we advocated for gender-inclusive and gender-neutral language. Phrases like *people power* replaced *manpower*, and *humanity* supplanted *mankind*. We adopted inclusive terms such as "brothers and sisters," *hermanos y hermanas*, and *compañeros y compañeras*. We also introduced new conceptual tools—such as *triple oppression*, *sexism*, *sexual fascism*, and *the revolution within the revolution*, to name just a few.

In our quest for new language and practice, the Women's Caucus found support among male allies. Richie Pérez, then a captain in the Information Ministry and a highly respected leader, wrote an essay in 1971 criticizing the words "chicks" and "broads" as dehumanizing.[21] "Words do show an attitude," Pérez argued. "And, if you want to change that attitude, you have to begin by changing the words that you're using."

Huey Newton, Black Panther Party Chairman, addressed similar concerns in his "Letter to the Revolutionary Brothers and Sisters about the Women's Liberation and Gay Liberation Movements."[22] Acknowledging the widespread use of derogatory language against gay people, Newton urged activists to eliminate slurs like "faggot" and "punk" from their vocabulary. He called these words obstacles to building solidarity.[23]

The Women's Caucus also worked to raise awareness and replace racist terms and concepts commonly used in Spanish. For example, Denise Oliver, then Minister of Finance, addressed the racism inherent in labeling kinky hair as *pelo malo* (bad hair) in her essay "Colonized Mentality and Non-Conscious Ideology," and she criticized other derogatory expressions. "We call Black Puerto Ricans names like *prieto*, *molleto*, and *cocolo*," she wrote. "We 'non-consciously' reject the Blackness we are all a part of." Oliver concluded, "We should not be afraid to criticize ourselves about racism. ... We will never have socialism until we are free of these chains on our mind."[24]

The push for nonracist and nonsexist language gained momentum as a tool for advance revolutionary thinking and practice. The new words we sought to develop were not merely descriptive—they were transformative.

Political Education Inspires New Ways of Being

In addition to our informal study in the Women's Caucus, all members took part in mandatory weekly political education classes. Juan González headed the YLO Education Ministry until September 1970, when he became Minister of Defense of the Young Lords Party. Iris Benítez was the first woman officer in the Education Ministry until March 1970. I was among the initial cadre of the ministry in the East Harlem branch, later joined by Olguie Robles and Gloria Colón. The ministry was responsible for preparing curricula, compiling reading lists, and facilitating weekly classes for members and for the public.

Political education, which we called "P.E.," was empowering and highly valued. Our goal was to nurture a love of learning and political analysis. We encouraged Young Lords to read newspapers, articles, and books. The Young Lords' rules of discipline underscored this commitment: "Political Education classes are mandatory. All members must read at least one political book a month, and at least two hours a day on contemporary matters."

Most Young Lords came through a public school system that undermined the intelligence of Puerto Rican children, making our self-education all the more vital. We embraced political education as a tool for understanding and analyzing policies and ideologies affecting our lives. We viewed theory as a guide to action. Study was so highly valued that every Young Lord, regardless of formal education, carried a book or article to ensure they always had something to read. Through study, we enhanced our critical thinking skills and developed a common language.

Ignorance of women's activities in the Young Lords Organization has led some to mistakenly conclude that the early political education program did not include women-related studies. This is false. From the beginning, class outlines show that all themes in the 13-Point Program were covered in sequential order over thirteen-week cycles. Point 10, "We want equality for women," was studied in the tenth week of each cycle.

Although books about the activism of women of color were scarce, the first political education rotation focused on the inspirational herstories of Puerto Rican anti-colonialists and abolitionists. We read about figures like Lola Rodríguez de Tió and Mariana Bracetti, both key fighters against Spain's colonial rule. Rodríguez de Tió wrote the patriotic lyrics to "La Borinqueña," Puerto Rico's national anthem. Bracetti helped organize the 1868 insurrection known as *El Grito de Lares* (the Cry of Lares) and created the original Lares flag.

We also learned about the twentieth-century labor organizer and women's rights advocate Luisa Capetillo, who organized workers and unions and wrote Puerto Rico's first feminist manifesto in 1911.[25] Juana Colón, a descendant of slaves and a labor organizer, cofounded the first Socialist Party in Puerto Rico and was active in the tobacco workers' movement.[26] Ana Roqué de Duprey emerged as a suffragist leader who published *La Mujer*, Puerto Rico's first women's newspaper.[27]

We studied the activities of Nationalist Party militants like Lolita Lebrón and Blanca Canales, both imprisoned for armed actions against U.S. colonialism. We read the poetry of Julia de Burgos and learned of her involvement with the Nationalist movement. Our studies also included the contributions of African American activists and feminists such as Harriet Tubman, who led hundreds of enslaved people to freedom, and Sojourner Truth, whose "Ain't I a Woman?" speech remains foundational to feminist thought.[28] We claimed these feminist foremothers and identified with their fight for women's rights and self-determination as part of our legacy.

As the political education program evolved, the second and third P.E. cycles in 1970 expanded to include readings about activist women and feminist ideas. These included selections from *The Black Woman*, edited by Toni Cade Bambara, who asserted that the artist's role was to make the revolution irresistible. We read the pamphlet *Enter Fighting: Today's Woman, A Marxist-Leninist View* by Clara Colón, as well as

Frances Beal's essay, "Double Jeopardy: To Be Black and Female." Additionally, we studied articles exploring early societies where women held equal status with men and how, over thousands of years, the rise of private property led to women's subordination. By the summer of 1970, the Education Ministry assigned readings from "The Woman Question" and Friedrich Engels's *The Origin of the Family, Private Property, and the State,* in which Engels argued that the emergence of class society deepened inequality between men and women.

The "YLP Position Paper on Women," published in September 1970, synthesized ideas from these readings. The final P.E. cycle that year added *The Black Woman's Manifesto,* published by the Third World Women's Alliance. From 1969 through the end of 1970, P.E. classes played a crucial role in educating members about women's oppression and their vital contributions to feminist struggles, framing the fight for women's liberation as inseparable from the struggle for socialism.

Our classes also covered the histories of African Americans, Indigenous peoples, and other communities of color in the United States. *The Autobiography of Malcolm X* sparked discussions about self-determination. In January 1970, *Puerto Rico: A Profile* by Kal Wagenheim was published, and we quickly assigned it as required reading. At that time there were few books in English about Puerto Rican history. The Center for Puerto Rican Studies (*El Centro de Estudios Puertorriqueños*) would not be established until 1973. *History of the Indians of Puerto Rico* by cultural anthropologist and archaeologist Ricardo E. Alegría was a favorite reading about Taínos and Taínas. We had the most difficulty finding books about Black people in Puerto Rico. *Historia de la esclavitud negra en Puerto Rico* by Luis M. Díaz Soler was one source, but it was not widely read because not all members could read Spanish. Our studies of Afro-Boricua history came primarily from pamphlets, conversations with individuals knowledgeable about African history in Puerto Rico, and articles in the *Palante* newspaper.

We also studied works on capitalism and imperialism, engaging with the philosophy of dialectical materialism through the writings of Marx, Lenin, and Engels, as well as *The Little Red Book* and other texts by Mao Zedong. Required readings included *Introduction to Socialism* by Leo Huberman and Paul Sweezy, and *Labor's Untold Story* by Richard

O. Boyer. Our studies also covered international revolutionary movements and the writings of anti-colonial leaders and thinkers such as Amílcar Cabral, Kwame Nkrumah, Patrice Lumumba, Ho Chi Minh, and Che Guevara. The works of Frantz Fanon offered insight into the traumas of oppression and sparked discussions about how we internalize the oppressor's ideas.

Political education opened our minds and hearts to new ways of understanding ourselves and the world. It shaped our political outlook and informed our organizing. We studied every article we could find about the activism of women of color, evaluating models and strategies that might apply to our own context. Our organizing efforts and programs in East Harlem grounded us in the everyday realities facing Puerto Rican women. These experiences empowered us to imagine more liberated roles for ourselves, our families, and our community.

The Women's Caucus flourished.

PART II.
FEMINISTS OF COLOR AND GENDER JUSTICE STRUGGLES

… they are the unsung, unrecognized workhorses who provide cohesion to organization while the men parade their "leadership" at meetings and important functions. The women are tired of playing this role. They want the opportunity to assume organizational, political leadership and responsibility in the movement.[1]

—"Women Who Disagree," *Regeneración*, 1970

4.
STERILIZATION POLITICS
AND REPRODUCTIVE JUSTICE

> Women can never obtain real independence unless her
> functions of procreation are under her own control.[1]

—Antoinette Konikow, *Voluntary Motherhood*, 1923 pamphlet

> Forced sterilization of poor women of color is an
> American tradition.[2]

—Natasha Lennard, *The Intercept*, 2020

At a Women's Caucus meeting in 1970, we read a report from Puerto Rico's Department of Health detailing a 1965 study revealing that 34 percent of women in Puerto Rico between twenty and forty-nine years old had been sterilized. "Sterilization is irreversible and as such the u.s can control the Puerto Rican population," declared the article "Sterilized Puerto Ricans," published in the May 1970 issue of *Palante*.[3] We called it genocide!

Caucus members firmly believed in a woman's right to control her body—to decide whether to have children, and how many—without coercion or interference. Our vision of reproductive freedom included access to birth control, the right to safe abortions, and the end to involuntary sterilization and experimentation on women's bodies. Historian Jennifer Nelson observes that the Women's Caucus advanced "an inclusive reproductive rights agenda that influenced (socialist) feminist politics later in the decade."[4]

Historically, individual men, the family, the state, and other institutions have exerted control over women's reproduction. During slavery and colonization in the Americas, white men wielded total power over the bodies of Black and Indigenous women. Enslavers forced enslaved women to bear children, using their bodies as "factories" to reproduce free labor. They conducted medical experiments on women, or allowed others to do so, not as an exception but as the norm.[5] Sexual violence and the forced separation of families were tools of domination used to compel obedience.[6] Rape was everyday terrorism.[7]

White women rarely opposed the violence performed by their husbands. Many actively participated in the system as brutally as men—a reality documented by historian Stephanie E. Jones-Rogers in *They Were Her Property: White Women as Slave Owners in the American South.*[8]

In the early twentieth century, the eugenics movement surged in popularity in the United States. Eugenicists argued that humanity could be "improved" by encouraging reproduction among those with so-called desirable traits while preventing it among those they labeled "unfit"—typically nonwhite people and the poor. Historian Isabel Wilkerson notes that the architects of the German Third Reich, in debating "how to institutionalize racism, ... began by asking how the Americans did it."[9] In fact, the United States had firmly established eugenic practices well before the rise of Nazi Germany.

Sterilization Politics in Puerto Rico

In Puerto Rico, eugenics and population control policies emerged in the discourse among government officials, philanthropists, physicians, journalists, and writers who debated the roots of poverty in the archipelago. Historian Laura Briggs, in *Reproducing Empire: Race, Sex, Science, and U.S. Imperialism in Puerto Rico,* explains that population control theorists and eugenics proponents identified "overpopulation" as the primary cause. They argued that "the working class was reproducing too much" and blamed the population's so-called "excessive sexuality and fertility."[10]

James R. Beverley, the U.S.-appointed governor in Puerto Rico from 1929 to 1933, asserted:

> I have always believed that some method of restricting the birth rate among the lower and more ignorant element of the population is the only salvation for the Island.[11]

Beverley proposed population control policies based on his belief that the poor and working class—particularly dark-skinned and Black people—were "unfit," the least desirable, and the most ignorant.

The politics of sterilization highlight key distinctions between "birth control as reproductive freedom, contraception as technique, and population control as policy."[12] While colonial authorities pushed for population control, women activists in Puerto Rico fought for reproductive freedom, demanding access to contraceptive information and the decriminalization of restrictive laws.[13]

The Puerto Rican Socialist Party,[14] whose members included sugarcane workers and people engaged in needlework,[15] actively organized to provide such information.[16] In 1925, Dr. José Lanauze Rolón, an Afro-Boricua physician and socialist trained at Howard University, founded the Birth Control League of Puerto Rico to educate and offer information to poor families.[17] Between 1925 and 1932, Puerto Rican health officials opened clinics in San Juan, Lares, and Mayagüez.[18] All eventually shut down due to lack of funding and opposition from the Catholic Church.

Amid these challenges, Puerto Rican women "championed birth control as an unmitigated good thing in the face of ongoing attempts by both colonialists and nationalist men to manipulate women."[19] Bishops in Puerto Rico condemned efforts to expand reproductive freedom, denouncing such initiatives as "the gateway to immorality."[20] Meanwhile, the Puerto Rican Nationalist Party rejected birth control as an imperialist import and "genocidal plot" aimed at exterminating the Puerto Rican population.[21] Nationalists urged Puerto Rican women to bear children as a means of preserving the nation, a position that directly conflicted with the demands of Puerto Rican women seeking reproductive rights and birth control alternatives.[22]

As poverty deepened during the Great Depression, U.S. President Franklin Delano Roosevelt established the Puerto Rico Emergency Relief Administration (PRERA). It launched a pilot program in 1934 that provided contraceptive information and supplies to low-income families. Within two years, sixty-seven maternal clinics[23] had been established, serving over 10,000 women.[24]

However, the program encountered fierce opposition. Catholic Action, a conservative group based in Ponce, condemned the family planning initiative and threatened to campaign against Roosevelt if he did not shut it down.[25] Fearing the loss of Catholic support in his reelection bid, Roosevelt ordered the clinics closed.[26] Though short-lived, the success of the PRERA clinics showed that poor and working-class Puerto Rican women were eager for birth control options and reproductive choices.

Following the closure of the PRERA clinics, eugenics proponents exploited Puerto Rican women's desire for reproductive options. Clarence Gamble, a Harvard–educated-eugenicist and heir to the Procter and Gamble fortune, spearheaded a decades-long campaign that turned Puerto Rico into a laboratory for human experimentation. Gamble had previously funded birth control clinics and contraceptive research in impoverished communities across the United States, including Appalachia and the rural South. He viewed Puerto Rico as an ideal testing ground for his agenda.[27] Arguing that impoverished Puerto Ricans should make way for more "fit" members of society,[28] Gamble launched twenty-three birth control clinics across the archipelago.[29]

The first clinic opened in 1937, the same year Public Law 116 legalized sterilization in Puerto Rico.[30] Gamble's clinics tested unapproved contraceptives on more than 1,500 women,[31] dispensing unreliable methods such as foams and jellies while withholding the more effective diaphragm. He claimed the diaphragm was "too expensive and difficult for Puerto Rican women to use"[32] and promoted sterilization as the most dependable birth control.[33] By the late 1930s, he was flying Puerto Rican doctors to New York City to learn the latest sterilization techniques.[34]

Sterilization was aggressively marketed. Historian Laura Briggs concludes, "the draconian figuring of the Puerto Rican woman by Gamble … as a source of danger to the United States laid the foundations for postwar population control policies."[35] Health workers went door to door promoting U.S. government–subsidized sterilization procedures.[36] The U.S. Agency for International Development funded factories to establish on-site family planning clinics that provided free sterilization.[37]

By 1949, postpartum sterilizations accounted for 17.8 percent of all hospital birth deliveries.[38] The procedure had become routine by the 1950s. Mothers with two or more children were frequently sterilized immediately after giving birth. A 1968 study revealed that over one-third of the women were unaware that tubal ligation was permanent.[39] The failure of medical practitioners to disclose this critical information undermines claims that Puerto Rican women "consented" to the procedure.

The documentary *La operación* by filmmaker Ana María García chronicles the extensive sterilization program carried out in Puerto Rico during the 1950s and 1960s.[40] In the film, Dr. Helen Rodríguez Trías, a

Puerto Rican pediatrician and women's rights advocate, emphasizes the necessity of reproductive choice:

> Birth control exists as an individual right, something that should be built into health programming; it should be part and parcel of choices people have. And when birth control is really carried out, people are given information, and there is facility to use different kinds of modalities of birth control.[41]

In Puerto Rico, women were not provided access to "different kinds of modalities of birth control."

Neither the United States nor Puerto Rican governments invested in safe, reversible contraceptive methods beyond sterilization. Instead, they enabled eugenicists to operate freely, establishing unregulated birth control centers that dispensed ineffective contraceptives while coercing poor and working-class women into irreversible sterilization procedures.

Sterilization Politics in the United States

The Women's Caucus played a crucial role in pressing the Young Lords to mobilize against the mass sterilization of women in Puerto Rico. Caucus members took the lead—writing articles, conducting radio interviews, organizing educational forums, and protesting government and hospital policies. Through these efforts, we learned the extent of coerced sterilization programs across the United States.

In the early twentieth century, over 60,000 individuals were sterilized in thirty-two states under U.S. eugenics laws,[42] with California accounting for one-third of these procedures—approximately 20,000.[43] Alarmingly, Latinas were sterilized at rates 59 percent higher than non-Latinas.[44]

During the 1960s and 1970s, African American, other women of color, and poor women were primary targets of coerced sterilization. In Mississippi in 1964, SNCC leader Fannie Lou Hamer led a campaign against a sterilization bill.[45] The SNCC pamphlet *Genocide in Mississippi* reported that "six out of ten women sterilized by tubal ligation in the state were African American."[46] Hamer herself was a victim of this practice. In 1961, she entered a Mississippi hospital for a cyst removal. While under anesthesia, doctors sterilized her without her consent.[47]

In the 1970s, the Indian Health Service targeted Native American women, claiming they had excessively high birth rates.[48] U.S. doctors sterilized approximately 25 to 42 percent of Native American women of childbearing age, some as young as fifteen.[49] In New York City, hospitals sterilized Puerto Rican women at seven times the rate of white women.[50]

In response to these abuses, Dr. Rodríguez Trías cofounded the Committee to End Sterilization Abuse (CESA) in 1974, along with Maritza Arrastía of the Puerto Rican Socialist Party and other women's health activists.[51] CESA won several lawsuits through the late 1970s, helping establish municipal and federal guidelines to prevent sterilization abuse.[52]

Similarly, Chicanas in California won legal victories against forced sterilization. The film *No más bebés* (No More Babies) highlights a landmark case from the late 1960s and early 1970s, in which Mexican immigrant women sued doctors, the state of California, and the U.S. government.[53] In 2021, California belatedly acknowledged these injustices and compensated thousands sterilized under the state's eugenics laws.[54]

Puerto Rican Women as Guinea Pigs

Mass sterilization was just one of many violations of Puerto Rican women's reproductive rights. During the 1940s and 1950s, all major U.S. pharmaceutical companies conducted research in Puerto Rico,[55] with a particular focus in the 1950s on developing the birth control pill. Margaret Sanger, the founder of Planned Parenthood, played a key role[56]— raising funds and recruiting Gregory G. Pincus, a former Harvard scientist— to conduct human trials in Puerto Rico.[57]

Pincus had a background in fertility research and population control,[58] including controversial experiments on psychotic patients at a Massachusetts state hospital. He was joined by John C. Rock, a Harvard professor and obstetrician. Sanger introduced them to Clarence Gamble, who provided access to his clinics.[59] Together, they targeted women seeking alternatives to both pregnancy and sterilization.[60]

In 1956, Pincus and Rock launched human trials in San Juan, Puerto Rico. At the time, little was known about the effects of the birth control pill. Despite this, they tested the pill on approximately 1,500 women, telling them it was medication to prevent pregnancy while not disclosing the fact that it was experimental and carried potential side effects.[61] Many participants experienced severe symptoms from high hormone dosages, including dizziness, nausea, severe cramping, headaches, stomach pain, and vomiting.[62]

The researchers made no effort to identify the cause of these symptoms. Instead, Pincus dismissed the women's reports as psychosomatic, attributing them to "emotional super activity."[63] Some participants also reported blood clotting, which was suspected in three deaths. Yet the researchers failed to investigate further[64] or conduct autopsies. In fact, Pincus and his team concluded the study without reporting any issues to the Food and Drug Association. The pill was subsequently approved as a contraceptive method on May 9, 1960.[65]

In a 2017 article titled "The Bitter Pill: Harvard and the Dark History of Birth Control," Drew C. Pendergrass and Michelle Y. Raji revisit this shameful and violent history. They conclude:

> For the most part, the popular narrative of the pill is one of celebration. When a 2009 Harvard Gazette story discussed Harvard's role in creating the birth control pill, they did so without referencing the Puerto Rican trials or the asylum testing. Pincus and Rock are largely remembered for their contributions to women's reproductive empowerment, without reference to their troubling methods.[66]

The *Harvard Gazette* attempted to erase the sacrifices, side effects, and deaths suffered by poor and working-class Puerto Rican women. Its narrative buried the unethical and horrific tactics used in the trials, including the fact that U.S. researchers failed to secure informed consent and deliberately withheld critical information about the risks and purposes of the research.

To this day, no one has been held accountable—not the researchers, pharmaceutical companies, nor the U.S. or Puerto Rican governments. No reparations have been granted to the victims or their families. Sanger, widely lauded and acclaimed for introducing birth control to women in the United States, did so at the devastating cost and suffering of Puerto Rican women.

5.
SOLIDARITIES WITH AFRICAN AMERICAN AND CHICANA FEMINISTS

I rarely talk about feminism in the singular.
I talk about feminisms. And, even when
I myself refused to identify with feminism,
I realized that it was a certain kind of feminism
... It was a feminism of those women who
weren't really concerned with equality for all women ...[1]

—Angela Davis, August 5, 2019,
Oral History Interview, National Museum of African American History and Culture

The joy and empowerment we experienced as activists and community organizers stood in stark contrast to the gender discrimination we faced within the Young Lords Organization. We expected revolutionary men to reject the sexism embedded in mainstream society, but instead, they carried those same ideas into their political work. Like other U.S. revolutionary nationalist organizations of the time, the YLO replicated patriarchal structures that reinforced male superiority and relegated women to subordinate roles.[2]

In response to these dynamics, women of color organized. The formation of the Black Women's Alliance in 1968 marked an early and critical intervention, directly challenging the marginalization of women's concerns and affirming that gender equality was essential to the broader struggle for social justice. Throughout the movement, Black, Latinx, Native and Asian feminists found it necessary to establish caucuses within nationalist groups or to form independent women's organizations. They brought visibility to the specific political issues affecting women of color and pressed nationalist movements to expand their revolutionary agendas to include women's rights.

Women in the Young Lords took part in cross-organizational dialogues, drawing insight and strength from this wider feminist resistance. Through these exchanges, we learned new herstories, engaged with feminist theory, developed strategies to confront sexism, and created spaces to advance gender justice. In this process, feminists of color contributed to practical strategies for political change and developed theoretical frameworks that linked the struggle for women's rights with the fights against racism, class exploitation, and colonialism.

As noted earlier, the Women's Caucus did not identify with the term *feminist* at that time. We associated it with the predominately white, middle-class women's movement, which failed to address the oppressions faced by women of color and poor women. We rejected the assumption that white feminists spoke for—or represented—all women. However, the struggle against systems that subjugate and oppress women resonated deeply with us, and we developed our own frameworks for liberation shaped by ongoing dialogue with other feminists of color.

Today, the concept of *feminisms*—in the plural—recognizes a multiplicity of perspectives shaped by distinct experiences, class interests, and analyses of oppression, as well as by diverse strategies for achieving gender justice.

This chapter focuses on the herstories, ideals, and organizing strategies of African American and Chicana feminisms. Tracing solidarities with feminists of color highlights the shared visions and commitments that fueled our collective efforts to dismantle systems of racial, gender, and class oppression.

The African American Feminist Tradition

The Women's Caucus studied the herstories of women of color in the Americas back to slavery and colonization. The Black feminist tradition emerged from the fierce resistance of enslaved women, who fought against the absolute power and control that white people wielded over Black and Indigenous women's bodies.[3] White men raped with impunity, yet Black and Native women were not passive victims. As Angela Davis affirms in *Women, Race, and Class,* "Women resisted and advocated challenges to slavery at every turn."[4] Enslaved women destroyed slaveholders' property, poisoned them, and actively participated in uprisings and rebellions.[5] Some, driven by despair, committed suicide and infanticide rather than endure, or allow their children to suffer, the sadism and brutality inflicted upon them.[6]

From the earliest days of slavery, Black women developed "a distinct political tradition based upon a systematic analysis of the intertwining oppressions of race, gender, and class." Historian Sharon Smith traces this evolution in *Women and Socialism: Class, Race, and Capital.*[7] Sojourner Truth's iconic 1851 speech "Ain't I a Woman?" delivered at the Women's Rights Convention in Akron, Ohio, was an early expression of an intersectional identity. Truth asserted her right to equality as a woman, emphasizing how race and gender exposed her to distinct and more severe oppression compared to white women.

By 1949, Claudia Jones—a Trinidad-born journalist, poet, and Communist Party member—explicitly articulated the idea that Black women's oppression was threefold: rooted in race, gender, and class. In her groundbreaking essay, "An End to the Neglect of the Problems of the Negro Woman!" Jones examines the historical role of Black women, highlighting their "super exploitation" as workers.[8] She wrote, "Negro women—as workers, as Negroes, and as women—are the most oppressed stratum of the whole population." Jones concludes that the liberation of Black women would lead to the liberation of all oppressed people.[9] Historian Erik S. McDuffie describes Jones as a pioneer of "a pathbreaking brand of feminist politics that centers working-class women."[10]

Jones also exposed the long legacy of state-condoned sexual assault against Black women and the criminalization of those who defended themselves. She calls for organized resistance to the systemic rape and sexual violence inflicted on Black women by white men and demands accountability for perpetrators.[11]

In her essay, Jones recounts the harrowing case of Rosa Lee Ingram, a Georgia sharecropper who was assaulted by a white landowner in 1948. When she defended herself from the armed attack, she was swiftly sentenced to death by an all-white jury. Her two teenage sons, who intervened to protect her, were also sentenced to death. After sustained legal campaigns and appeals, their sentences were reduced to life imprisonment. The Ingram family remained incarcerated for over a decade.

Ideas about the multiple and intertwining oppressions that Black women face would later evolve into the concept of *intersectionality*, a term coined by legal scholar Kimberlé Crenshaw in 1989. In a 2017 interview with the African American Policy Forum, Crenshaw explained:

> Intersectionality is a lens through which you can see where power comes and collides, where it interlocks and intersects. It's not simply that there's a race problem here, a gender problem here, and a class or LBGTQ problem there. Many times, that framework erases what happens to people who are subject to all of these things.[12]

Philosopher and scholar Ashley Bohrer's offers a concise working definition in her article "Intersectionality and Marxism: A Critical Historiography":

> In its most basic form, then, intersectionality is the theory that both structurally and experientially, social systems of domination are linked to one another and that, in order both to understand and to change these systems, they must be considered together.[13]

A defining characteristic of Black feminism is its commitment to action—the insistence that the interconnected system of oppression must be addressed simultaneously.[14]

In *Living for the Revolution*, historian Kimberly Springer summarizes how Black feminists transformed the women's liberation movement by challenging Eurocentric and classist interpretations of women's issues.[15] Tracing Black women's resistance in the United States back to slavery and colonization, they rejected the idea of a "singular" feminism. Black and other feminists of color also critiqued the dominance of the white women's liberation movement and its "waves" framework,[16] which divides feminist struggles into distinct historical periods: the "first wave" (1848-1920) focused on women's suffrage; the second (1963-1980s) centered on legal and social equality; and the third (1990s and beyond) on expanding feminist discourse and inclusivity.

However, as Kathleen Laughlin and her colleagues argue in "Is It Time to Jump Ship? Historians Rethink the Waves Metaphor," this framework centers the history of the white women's movement while marginalizing the histories of women of color.[17] In reality, Black, Indigenous, Latinx women had long resisted colonization, slavery, and systemic violence well before the nineteenth-century suffrage movement began.

The Black Women's Alliance

In 1968, women in the Student Nonviolent Coordinating Committee (SNCC) formed the Black Women's Liberation Caucus (BWLC). Cofounders Frances Beal, Fay Bellamy, Mae Jackson, Eleanor Holmes Norton, and Gwendolyn Patton demanded gender equality and challenged the prevailing masculinist discourse of the Black Power movement.[18] Arguing that Black women's issues were urgent and inseparable from demands for social justice, the BWLC warned that the treatment of women during the revolutionary struggle would determine their roles afterward. If women were relegated to roles as mothers, caretakers, homemakers, and assistants to men, they would remain so in a postrevolutionary society.[19]

When the BWLC raised these concerns, some men in SNCC accused the women of being divisive and undermining the unity needed to fight racism, even labeling them "saboteurs" of the Black struggle.[20] In 1970, the BWLC broke from SNCC and became the Black Women's Alliance (BWA), a Black feminist socialist organization.

The BWLC's ideas resonated with members of the Women's Caucus. We were well aware of SNCC's work, particularly of women organizers who ran freedom schools and voter registration drives in the Deep South. We admired Ella Baker, SNCC cofounder and strategist, who believed that a leader's role was "to strengthen the group, forge consensus, and negotiate a way forward"[21] through open, democratic, and collaborative structures. Baker recognized women as "the backbone of the movement" and openly criticized the sexist practices that pervaded it.[22]

Several YLO members met Gwendolyn Patton, BWLC cofounder, during a time when she lived in New York City. A committed SNCC staff member, experienced community organizer, and student activist in Tuskegee, Alabama, Patton also cofounded the National Black Antiwar Antidraft Union and coauthored SNCC's position paper opposing the Vietnam War.[23] She shared insights from her organizing work in the Jim Crow South and spoke candidly about the gendered dynamics in nationalist movements.[24] Patton described SNCC's gendered division of labor as "symbolic of the 'you walk behind us' mentality prevalent in the movement,"[25] while emphasizing the indispensable role of women of color in revolutionary activism and the struggle for social change.

Frances Beal's 1969 essay, "Double Jeopardy: To Be Black and Female"[26] became a foundational text for feminist analysis within the Women's Caucus. Beal critiques the inhumanity of capitalism and its exploitation of both Black women and men. She rejects feminisms that identify gender as the sole source of women's subordination, as well as Black nationalist ideologies that view racism as the only form of oppression facing Black people. Instead, she articulates how race and gender intersect to super exploit Black women workers, reducing them to "a state of enslavement."[27]

Beal's essay also challenges the Black liberation movement, urging men "to be revolutionaries in all aspects,"[28] including the treatment of women. As for the women's liberation movement, Beal declares, "Any white group that does not have an anti-imperialist and anti-racist ideology has absolutely nothing in common with the Black women's struggle."[29] She highlights the critical differences between the experiences of Black women and those of white women—particularly the middle-class women who dominated mainstream feminism.

The Black Panther Party

Founded in 1966 in Oakland, California, the Black Panther Party (BPP) championed Black nationalism, socialism, and armed self-defense. Women joined the Party for the same reasons as men—to fight for Black liberation. Its 10-Point Program declared, "We want freedom. We want power to determine the destiny of our Black Community."[30] Kathleen Cleaver, the Party's communications secretary and member of the central committee, explained that her primary motivation as a Black activist was to help end "the legal, social, psychological, economic, and political restrictions imposed on the human rights of Black people."[31] Cleaver maintained that gender oppression could not be addressed as a standalone issue—it had to be confronted within the Black Panther Party.

Women in the Black Panther Party played a key role in shaping what Ericka Huggins would later describe as "the internal dialogue about gender."[32] Although they generally did not identify as feminists—due to the term's association with the predominantly white women's liberation movement—they embodied feminist principles in practice. As Ericka Huggins reflected:

> I would say that the women who were drawn to the Black
> Panther Party were all feminists. ... [W]e generally be-
> lieved in the political, social, economic, and sexual equality
> of women and girls.[33]

Her comment underscores how women in the BPP advanced gender justice through organizing, redefining feminism on their own terms.

In a 2010 interview with historian Mary Phillips, Ericka Huggins
explicitly identified as a feminist, stating, "I'm a strong believer of Black
feminists or women of color feminists, who believe that we have to uplift
our entire community."[34] Her feminism was grounded in lived experience and political practice. She was the first woman to open a BPP chapter—in New Haven, Connecticut—and in 1969, she was arrested and
charged with conspiracy to commit murder. Separated from her infant
daughter, she spent nearly two years in prison before the charges were
dropped.[35]

By the early 1970s, women made up nearly two-thirds of the Black
Panther Party.[36] As FBI and police repression escalated, many male numbers were incarcerated or killed. Women assumed greater leadership to
sustain the organization. In New York, for example, Janet Cyril managed
the BPP's "serve the people" programs in Harlem while twenty-one Black
Panthers were jailed in 1969.[37] Cyril oversaw the free breakfast programs.
Often, at the end of long days, she visited the Young Lords' East Harlem
office, where several of us would gather with her to discuss politics,
movement challenges, and gender struggles—including the latest incidents of sexism and male chauvinism in our organizations.

Cyril recounted being expelled from the Black Panther four times
for refusing to comply with sexist demands and, as she proudly noted,
for her anti-authoritarian stance.[38] Despite these conflicts, she loved the
Party and always returned to the organization. Like the women of the
BPP, we in the Women's Caucus believed we were on the correct path:
fighting for revolution alongside men while also challenging the systems
that oppressed us.[39]

Third World Women's Alliance

By the summer of 1970, the Black Women's Alliance was evolving
into a new organization under the leadership of Frances Beal. When
Puerto Rican *independentistas* in New York City approached the BWA

wanting to join,[40] their request sparked an internal debate about expanding the organization's mission beyond the Black-white paradigm of racial oppression.[41] Although some BWA members opposed altering the mission or composition, the group ultimately chose to transform into the Third World Women's Alliance (TWWA), a multiracial, women-led and women-centered, socialist organization committed to fighting racism, imperialism, and sexism.[42]

Patricia Romney, a former member, chronicles the TWWA's formation, organizing, and contributions in her book *We Were There: The Third World Women's Alliance and The Second Wave*.[43] Originally, composed primarily of African American and Puerto Rican activists in New York, the TWWA later opened a West Coast branch, expanding its membership to include Asian and Pacific Islander women as well as Chicanas. The organization defined "Third World" to include people of African, Puerto Rican, Native American, Chicana, and Asian descent.[44] It built transnational alliances with women's groups, drawing attention to how U.S. foreign and military policies affected women's lives and linking domestic struggles to global anti-imperialist movements.

Members of the Women's Caucus in the Young Lords Party attended some of the TWWA's early formation meetings. As Puerto Rican and African American socialist feminists, we shared ideological commitments and organizing strategies. However, that summer in 1970, women in the YLP were deeply engaged in major protests and campaigns, as discussed in Part III. We ultimately chose to remain within the Young Lords Party, believing we could most effectively advance the struggles of Puerto Rican women through our work with the organization.

Influence of Chicana Feminists

In California and the U.S. Southwest, Chicanx activists were active in revolutionary nationalist organizations. A pivotal convening took place in March 1969 at the National Chicano Youth Conference in Denver, Colorado. The conference sought to unite various civil rights and social justice movements, including the land-grant struggles in New Mexico and Arizona, the farm workers' movement, student protests, and urban youth uprisings.[45] Over five days, participants produced the *Plan Espiritual de Aztlán*, a political manifesto that emphasized "the cultural values of life, family, and home" as "a powerful weapon"[46] for mass mobilization, with nationalism as the unifying force.

During the conference, a heated debate erupted in a women's workshop attended by fifty to seventy Chicanas regarding the role of women in the nationalist movement.[47] Many participants, frustrated by being assigned to cooking, cleaning, and administrative tasks by male organizers, argued that "women should walk next to, not behind Chicanos."[48] Others maintained that Chicanas "should always stand behind their men." When the workshop facilitator reported back to the full conference, she controversially stated, "It was the consensus of the group that the Chicana woman does not want to be liberated."[49] The comment caused an uproar. Activist Elizabeth "Betita" Martínez, who attended the workshop, later clarified that the statement was meant to reject the white women's liberation movement—not the concept of liberation for Chicanas.[50]

Like many revolutionary nationalists movements in the United States, the Chicanx movement "maintained patriarchal structures of domination"[51] and adhered to a largely masculinist ideology.[52] The idealized Chicanx family upheld a dominant male figure and a submissive female beside him. Chicanx studies scholar Alma García explains that the movement exalted traditional gender roles and celebrated the stereotype of the suffering Chicana as the cultural and familial backbone.[53] According to García, some male leaders defended machismo as a source of masculine pride and a defense mechanism against systemic racism. However, Chicana feminists rejected these rationales and called for a transformation of deeply unequal gender dynamics.[54]

Chicana feminism emerged in direct response to the pervasive sexism within the nationalist movement. Chicanas challenged male leaders and activists "who preached 'power to la raza' while relegating Chicanas to answering phones, making coffee, cooking, and even providing sexual favors."[55] In addition to resisting gender oppression, they articulated an intersectional nature of their struggle—recognizing that women of color experience multiple and overlapping forms of oppression shaped by race, class, and culture.[56] They resisted educational exclusion, the patriarchal influence of the Catholic Church, and other ideologies designed to subordinate women.[57]

Throughout this era of protest and community mobilization, Chicanas remained active,[58] urging Chicano leaders to address women's concerns—such as equal pay for equal work, bicultural and bilingual childcare, abortion rights, and an end to forced sterilization. Despite their tireless advocacy, the male-dominated Chicano leadership largely dismissed their recommendations.

Chicana feminists also built organizations that connected the fight for gender equality to broader movements for racial, economic, and social justice. They affirmed the belief that women's liberation and community struggles are inseparable.

The Brown Berets

The Brown Berets, founded in 1967 in East Los Angeles, quickly expanded across the southwestern United States.[59] Like the Young Lords, most members were in their early twenties and came from working-class backgrounds. The Los Angeles chapter oversaw more than sixty branches, primarily in California.[60] While the Brown Berets promoted nationalism as a unifying force, they vacillated between two currents: cultural nationalism, which emphasized preserving traditions, and revolutionary nationalism, which sought liberation for an oppressed people.[61]

In the fall of 1969, several Young Lords from New York, including myself, traveled to California to meet the Brown Berets and explore potential collaborations. I spoke with several Chicana members who ran the organization's health, social services, and children's breakfast programs. We stayed up late into the night exchanging stories about neighborhood projects and strategies for community organizing. Inevitably, the conversation turned to the role and treatment of women within the movement. My experiences with male chauvinism in the Young Lords Organization were met with knowing nods. The Chicanas shared their stories of being treated as "invisible labor"—assigned roles as cooks, secretaries, and janitors during "conferences, symposiums, [and] meetings," and while producing the group's newspapers and magazines. [62] As women's studies and Chicanx historian Maylei Blackwell observes, "Although this labor was essential to the functioning of the political movement, it was seen as women's work and therefore devalued."[63]

Despite our shared experiences of rampant male chauvinism, the Chicanas in the Brown Berets and I remained committed to challenging the backward thinking of male leaders in order to advance the community and social justice.

About six months later, Chicanas in the Brown Berets took action against the persistent machismo and gender injustice in the organization. Gloria Arellanes—the only woman on the Central Committee of the East Los Angeles chapter and minister of correspondence and finance—had repeatedly raised the grievances of Chicana members, to no effect. Disheartened by the men's refusal to change, Arellanes submitted her resignation on February 25, 1970. According to Chicana studies scholar Dionne Espinoza, Arellanes's resignation letter announced the collective departure of "ALL Brown Beret women." Tired of being treated as "nothings, not as 'revolutionary sisters,'"[64] the women made a powerful and public exit.

After the stormy resignation, they formed *Las Adelitas de Aztlán.* As Espinoza notes, their "gender consciousness and woman-identified solidarity empowered them to break with the Brown Berets and forge a new political identity."[65] They marched in the historic Chicano Moratorium against the Vietnam War, wearing black to signify mourning. Though short lived, Las Adelitas de Aztlán underscored the vital role of Chicanas as independent, committed political actors fighting U.S. imperialism and demanding social justice.

Chicana Feminist Organizations

Historian Maylei Blackwell writes, "Women throughout the Chicano movement were no longer willing to tolerate internal organizational practices and masculinist political culture, which were exclusionary, undemocratic, and unfair."[66] Chicana feminists rejected continued inferior treatment. In 1970, *Regeneración,* the first Chicana feminist journal, published a blistering critique titled "Women Who Disagree," condemning the gendered division of political work as a form of male privilege that disregarded Chicanas as revolutionary activists.[67]

Chicanx nationalists, both male and female, often equated feminism with antinationalism, accusing Chicana feminists of divisiveness and retaliating against them. Blackwell documents a range of "silencing mechanisms" used to undermine feminist voices.[68] Nationalists accused feminists of being traitors, labeling them as *vendidas* (sell-outs) and *malinche* (traitors or collaborators). Other insults, such as *agringadas* (white-identified) and *las Chicanas con pantalones* (pants-wearing Chicanas), accused them of "cultural betrayal and assimilation into non-Chicano values and life-style."[69]

Lesbianism, in particular, was cast as an extreme form of feminism. Chicana historian Alma García explains, "Clearly, a cultural nationalist ideology that perpetuated stereotypical images of Chicanas as good wives and mothers found it difficult to accept a Chicana feminist lesbian movement."[70] The backlash against lesbians was severe, ranging from verbal assaults to systemic marginalization. In response, Chicana lesbians pursued various strategies: some formed separate organizations; others built lesbian coalitions; and many remained within the Chicano movement to challenge homophobia from within.[71]

Chicana feminists developed distinct political agendas, and launched campaigns grounded in feminist principles. These efforts included the formation of Comisión Femenil Mexicana, in 1970—the first national organization dedicated to developing Chicana leadership within the movement and the community. In 1971, Chicana students founded *Hijas de Cuauhtémo*, a feminist newspaper. That same year, the first national conference of *la Raza* women was held in Houston, Texas, drawing more than six hundred Chicanas from across the country.[72] Chicanas also turned to literature as a tool for activism—writing became a political act.[73]

Feminists of color advanced the social justice movement by centering the intersections of race, class, gender, and sexuality—issues marginalized by both nationalist movements and mainstream white feminism. African American and Chicana feminists, in particular, pushed beyond the constraints of male-dominated nationalist agendas and the narrow focus of the middle- and upper-class white women's movement. As members of the Women's Caucus, we learned from these collective experiences, recognizing deep parallels and points of connection between our struggles.

6.
DEMANDS OF THE WOMEN'S CAUCUS

Sometimes we are blessed with being able to choose
the time, and the arena, and the manner of our
revolution, but more usually we must do battle
where we are standing.[1]

—Audre Lorde, *A Burst of Light*

By March 1970, women in the New York chapter of the Young
Lords were actively engaged with the organization's work and
programs. Yet despite ongoing discussions and debates, we continued to experience machismo and male chauvinism. Our ideas and
contributions were consistently undervalued, routinely dismissed, or
treated as secondary to the revolutionary agenda.

So, why did we stay? Like many African American and Chicana activists, we grappled with a difficult and deeply personal question: Where
could we most effectively direct our efforts to collectively fight the oppression facing our communities?

As young Puerto Rican activists from working-class backgrounds,
raised in the United States, we committed to advancing the rights of
Puerto Ricans. Organizational options were limited—and male chauvinism was present in all of them. Many of us joined the Young Lords because of its 13-Point Program and bold, direct-action strategies. At the
time, Puerto Rico's leading *independentista* organization in New York,
the Movimiento Pro Independencia, was focused on building support for
Puerto Rico's anti-colonial struggle but was not organizing directly for
the rights of Puerto Ricans living in the United States.

Despite the YLO's patriarchal structure, the Women's Caucus believed it was possible to challenge—and ultimately change—the Central
Committee's backward ideas and policies. After all, the 13-Point Program stated: "We want equality for women."

Caucus members were determined to push for change from within,
viewing our efforts as a necessary deepening of the organization's commitment to liberation. Remaining in a male-dominated structure was a

calculated act—grounded in the belief that transformation was possible. Still, we confided in one another: if the leadership failed to respond, many of us were prepared to exit, just as our African American and Chicana sisters had done in similar circumstances.

The Women's Caucus Presents Ten Demands

The unity of the Women's Caucus gave us confidence to challenge male chauvinist ideas and male-centered practices. A major issue was the low number of women in leadership positions, including on the Central Committee. Between July 1969 to May 1970, few women held officer roles, with the notable exceptions of Mirta González and Iris Benítez. González served as information lieutenant as early as December 1969, and Benítez held the same role from January to March 1970 before taking on the role of education lieutenant from March to May 1970. The Women's Caucus sought to increase the number of women in leadership, believing women would best represent our collective interests.

Denise Oliver and I summarized the discussions from the Women's Caucus and drafted the following ten demands to present to the Central Committee:

1. Appoint women to leadership positions, including the Central Committee.
2. Provide childcare for members.
3. Hold men accountable for acts of male chauvinism.
4. Organize campaigns to address issues affecting Puerto Rican and other women of color in the community.
5. Expand political education regarding the history and oppression of women.
6. Increase coverage of women's concerns in the *Palante* newspaper and include more women writers.
7. End the "no women" policy of the Defense Ministry.
8. Assign women as public representatives and spokespersons.
9. Remove "revolutionary machismo" from the 13-Point Program and Platform.
10. Recognize the right of women to caucus.

We believed these demands were essential to advancing the organization's revolutionary politics and transforming its practices.

When the Central Committee members—Felipe Luciano, Juan González, Pablo "Yoruba" Guzmán, David Pérez, and Juan "Fi" Ortiz—reviewed our demands, several responded with hostility. "We're a revolutionary organization. Our struggle is for the liberation of all Puerto Ricans, not just women," one declared dismissively, revealing a narrow and masculinist perspective. "But liberation is not just for men either," we countered, challenging the assumption that gender justice could be deferred. "Now is not the time to deal with these issues," a few insisted, signaling that they did not view the struggle against gender oppression as an urgent political concern. As feminist scholar Anne McClintock observes: "To insist on silence about gender conflict when it already exists, is to cover over, and thereby ratify, women's disempowerment."[2]

The Central Committee accused us of "divisiveness and disunity," a charge all too familiar from the experiences of Black and Chicana feminists who were similarly dismissed within their movements. Some men even mocked our demands as a "white woman's thing," criticizing us for pushing ideas they claimed were foreign to Puerto Rican culture, as if women's liberation was only for white women.

In an attempt to pacify us, a few Central Committee members conceded that women's issues were important but insisted, "They will be addressed after the revolution." It was a clear brushoff—kicking the can down the road. We rejected it. For us, women's rights could not be postponed. They were integral to the revolutionary struggle. The exchange between the Women's Caucus and the Central Committee underscored the ideological fault lines within the organization and the persistent marginalization of feminist critique in leftist movements of the era.

As we pressed our demands, the most open-minded Young Lords began to advocate with us. Slowly, the Central Committee responded, and the Women's Caucus helped initiate changes.

"No Women" Policy Defeated

In their self-proclaimed roles as "warriors" and "protectors," the all-male Central Committee and Defense Ministry had imposed a "no women" policy, claiming women were physically and mentally unfit for defense and security work. They ignored the long history of Puerto Rican women—in liberation movements and in the YLO—who had taken bold, often life-threatening actions in pursuit of justice. The men's outdated ideas did not withstand scrutiny, and the "no-women" policy was quickly defeated.

As a result, the Central Committee appointed Connie Morales, a young mother from the Bronx who had joined during the People's Church takeover, as the first woman to serve in the Defense Ministry. She was soon joined by Marta Duarte (Arguello), a student activist born in the Dominican Republic and raised in New York City, who first served in East Harlem before transferring to the Lower East Side branch. Several others followed, including Myrna Martínez, a student activist and co-founder of UNICA, the Latinx student organization at Lehman College in the Bronx; and later Minerva Solla, a high school student from Manhattan's Chelsea neighborhood who joined the Young Lords Party in September 1970. Together, these women broke the gender barrier within the Young Lords, earning respect for their commitment and bravery under difficult and perilous conditions.

Childcare as Collective Responsibility

Initially, the Young Lords viewed childcare as an individual woman's responsibility, but we quickly came to recognize it was a societal issue requiring a collective solution. Without childcare, poor and working mothers found it difficult to hold jobs, attend school, or participate in activities outside the home. YLO mothers had a hard time balancing parental and political responsibilities. Babysitters were expensive and hard to find, often leaving mothers with no choice but to bring their children to the Young Lords' office—an unsustainable solution.

The Women's Caucus pushed for a better approach and persuaded the Central Committee. A childcare policy introduced in 1970, required officers to assign members, both men and women, to care for children during meetings, demonstrations, and other organizational activities. This policy enabled mothers to remain active in the movement and reinforced the idea that men shared responsibility for child-rearing and parenting. Communal childcare thus became a meaningful and significant practice within the Puerto Rican movement.

The childcare demand extended beyond the Young Lords. Across the country, feminists campaigned for federal legislation to establish quality, affordable day care. In 1971, however, President Nixon vetoed a bill that would have created a comprehensive national childcare system, stating that he would not commit "the vast moral authority of the national government to the side of communal approaches to childrearing over against the family-centered approach."[3] His veto ignited a conservative backlash that cast public childcare as a threat to the nuclear family, leaving generations of mothers, particularly working-class and women of color, without accessible, affordable childcare options to this day.

Challenging Sexual Objectification

Within the Young Lords Organization, the sexual objectification of women was a serious and persistent problem. The Women's Caucus demanded political consequences for demeaning and abusive acts against women—a highly controversial demand. Heated debates erupted as Young Lords grappled with entrenched beliefs about gender roles, male privilege, and accountability.

Some men scoffed at the idea that they should be held responsible for male chauvinism. Others refused to acknowledge the existence of structural inequalities. Many were unwilling to relinquish their favored positions and male advantages. Some dismissed the issue outright, calling it a political distraction or a "white women's thing." Others complained that women were gaining too much power—but rarely explained what they meant or feared.

Because women were not the majority in the YLO, the Women's Caucus sought allies. The first to support us were the youngest men—the teenagers. They worked alongside us daily, witnessed the risks we took, and learned about the history of women's oppression in political education classes. Most importantly, they committed to putting their revolutionary principles into practice. They joined the Women's Caucus in our journey of personal and political transformation. As socialists, they insisted that sexual objectification had no place in a revolutionary movement. "Women are comrades," they said. Their support proved critical.

Among the first to back us were Mark, Ramón, Benjy, Fi, Adrian, Carl, Ray, and others whose names I regret have faded from memory.

With their solidarity, the Women's Caucus achieved a major victory. Although not all members agreed, the general membership reached a consensus: sexual objectification and abuse of women would not be tolerated. All members, including Central Committee members, would be held accountable.

To handle abuse allegations, a process developed. A designated YLO officer would investigate the complaint, meet with the parties, and mediate to seek resolution. If needed, the matter could be brought before the general membership for discussion and possible disciplinary action. Consequences ranged from suspension and demotion to removal from leadership or expulsion, depending on the facts of the case.

Throughout 1970, the Central Committee disciplined, suspended, or demoted male members for demeaning or abusing women. Among those held accountable were Central Committee members: Juan González, Pablo "Yoruba" Guzmán, Felipe Luciano[4] and David Pérez. Juan "Fi" Ortiz, the youngest, was the only Central Committee leader not charged.

Palante and The Women's Caucus

In April 1970, the Young Lords Organization opened a second storefront in the Bronx. At the time, the borough was becoming home to the fastest-growing Puerto Rican population in New York City. The new branch mirrored the activities in East Harlem, with members focused on organizing efforts and "serve the people" programs. Under the leadership of Minister of Information Pablo "Yoruba" Guzmán, the Bronx office also served as the organization's communications center.

The YLO prioritized publishing an independent newspaper as indispensable to shaping political discourse, raising class consciousness, and attracting new members. In May 1970, *Palante* debuted as a bi-monthly, bilingual publication. Its masthead proudly carried the subtitle *Latin Revolutionary Service*, signaling its identity as both a Puerto Rican and Latinx voice. The final page of each issue was reserved for the 13-Point Program and Platform, reinforcing the organization's goals.

At its peak, *Palante* had a circulation of 10,000 to 15,000 copies per issue. As both an educational and organizing tool, *Palante* offered a wealth of international and local news, expressing solidarity with revolutionary movements across the globe. It reported on events in many countries, including Vietnam, Palestine, Cuba, Uruguay, Cambodia, Brazil, Trinidad, the Dominican Republic, the Basque Nation, Italy, Argentina, Panama, Mexico, Laos, India, Japan, Ceylon (renamed Sri Lanka in 1972), Bolivia, the Congo, Guatemala, Haiti, Colombia, Spain, the Philippines, Rhodesia (Zimbabwe), among others.

The newspaper also served as a crucial fundraising tool. Each member was responsible for selling copies and submitting receipts to the Ministry of Finance. On rare occasion, members facing severe financial hardships were allowed to keep a percent of their sales. In addition to individual sales, *Palante* was available at select newsstands, bookstores, bodegas, and other venues across the United States.

Recognizing the importance of *Palante*, the Women's Caucus pushed for the inclusion of more women-centered articles and women writers. Two articles published in 1971 are especially noteworthy for their early critiques of the corporate media's portrayal of women of color. Jenny Figueroa and Lulu Rovira examined how mainstream media reinforced systems of sexism, racism, and classism.

In "World of Fantasy," Figueroa, a cadre in the Information Ministry, denounced television as a tool of "brainwashing" that perpetuated gender roles and "enslaved minds." She deconstructs the racial and gender stereotypes embedded in Spanish-language television soap operas, or *telenovelas*, which glorified upper-class values, whiteness, and traditional gender roles. Figueroa emphasizes the marketing aspect, concluding that television "is a tool to sell us lies and try to make us believe those lies."[5]

In "Makeup and Beauty," Rovira, a cadre in the Economic Development Ministry, analyzed the relationship between capitalism and advertising in shaping beauty standards rooted in racism, ageism, and classism. "We are made to feel ugly, inadequate, and inferior, when we don't live up to the false standards of 'beauty,'"[6] she writes. Rovira critiques the ideals of whiteness, thinness, and youth, underlining the damaging psychological, emotional, and physical effects on Third World women.

Caucus members strengthened *Palante's* reach and ensured that women's voices and experiences remained part of the Young Lords' revolutionary narrative. Women also played vital roles in the production and distribution of *Palante,* contributing to layout, design, translation, outreach, circulation, and sales.

Fig. 6. Jenny Figueroa selling *Palante.* 1970.
(Courtesy: Michael Abramson)

Among the women members who wrote or worked on the production of the *Palante* newspaper were: Mecca Adai, Micky Agrait, Marta Arguello, Bernadette Baken, Iris Benítez, Lulu Carreras, Gloria Colón, Carmen Copeland, Aida Cruset, Jenny Figueroa, Gloria González, Mirta González, Beverly Kruset, Elsie López, Lulu Limardo, Iris López, Letty Lozano, Myrna Martínez, Nydia Mercado, Carmen Mercado, Raquel Merced, Connie Morales, Iris Morales, Denise Oliver, Luisa Ramírez, Isa Ríos, Olguie Robles, Gloria Rodríguez, Miriam Rodríguez, Heidy Ruiz, Becky Serrano, Lydia Silva, and Cleo Silvers.

The Formation of the Young Lords Party

On June 5, 1970, *Palante* broke startling news: the Young Lords in New York and Chicago had parted ways. The New Yorker group criticized the Chicago leaders for failing to provide consistent political guidance and not producing the *Y.L.O.* newspaper on a regular basis. In turn, the Chicago group accused the New York leaders of attempting to seize control. Unable to reconcile their differences, the groups separated. The Chicago organization remained the *Young Lords Organization*, while the New York chapter reconstituted itself as the *Young Lords Party* (YLP).[7]

In New York, the Central Committee remained intact: Felipe Luciano as Chairman, Pablo "Yoruba" Guzmán as Minister of Information, Juan González as Minister of Education and Health, and Juan "Fi" Ortiz as Minister of Finance. David Pérez assumed a new role as "Field Marshal," tasked with expanding the YLP by developing branches across the country. These national aspirations created opportunities for women.

In late June 1970, Denise Oliver was promoted to Minister of Finance, becoming the first woman on the YLP's Central Committee. Juan "Fi" Ortiz, former Finance Minister, was reassigned as Chief of Staff. Oliver, a cofounder of the Women's Caucus, had been among the thirteen persons arrested at the People's Church in 1969. Prior to her promotion, she served as Secretary of Communications from April to mid-June 1970, then as Information Captain.

Several other women were promoted during this period: Lulu Carreras became lieutenant of finance; Gloria Cruz (later known as Gloria González) was appointed lieutenant in the Health Ministry, and I was appointed lieutenant in the Education Ministry.

Fig. 7. *Palante* cover. *¡Liberación o Muerte!* June 5, 1970.

Leadership Crisis in the Central Committee

Following the split from Chicago, the Young Lords Party faced a serious crisis. On July 31, 1970, the *Palante* newspaper ran a dramatic headline:

> The Mafia has put out a $20,000 contract for the murder of Chairman Felipe.[8]

The article speculated that the murder contract was in retaliation for the Young Lords' campaign against heroin dealers in East Harlem. As a precaution, the Central Committee immediately assigned Felipe Luciano a 24-hour security detail for an indefinite period.

Just weeks later, a white hippie woman appeared at the East Harlem office. She extended an invitation to Luciano to attend a meeting that evening to discuss fundraising for the organization. He accepted the invitation, dismissed his security team, and asked Pablo "Yoruba" Guzmán to accompany him. Late that night, members of the Defense Ministry received phone calls at the Young Lords' offices alerting them that both men were missing, but efforts to locate them were unsuccessful.

Luciano and Guzmán returned the following morning. Later that day, they met with the other Central Committee members—Juan González, Denise Oliver, Juan "Fi" Ortiz, and David Pérez. Luciano gave no explanation for dismissing his security detail but disclosed that the woman who had invited him to the meeting drugged him and that he had sex with her. The Central Committee members were stunned by Luciano's disregard for the organization's security protocols—especially in light of the active death threat against him and the ongoing FBI and police surveillance of the Young Lords Party. Meeting privately with an unknown individual without notifying other members of the leadership or coordinating with the Defense Ministry constituted a serious breach. It violated basic principles of security and the collective accountability expected of those in leadership positions. His actions raised broader concerns about judgment, political discipline, and the responsibilities of those tasked with modeling revolutionary values. As a consequence, the Central Committee demoted Luciano from his position as chairman and called a general meeting to inform the membership of its decision.

On September 5, 1970, *The New York Times* reported Luciano's removal from the Central Committee, citing "male chauvinism, unclear politics, political individualism, and lack of development" as the official reasons for the demotion.[9] Although the YLP's press release stated Luciano would remain a member,[10] he ultimately choose not to return. A few Young Lords left with him, arguing that the demotion was too severe a penalty even though all members, regardless of rank, were expected to follow the same security protocols and rules of discipline.

The New York Times also reported that Luciano's demotion "was seen by informants as moving the Young Lords Party into an open nationalist position in relation to the struggle for the independence of

Puerto Rice."[11] This assertion surprised many members, as the organization had embraced the independence of Puerto Rico as a core principle from its inception. Yet the statement foreshadowed a significant political shift that would unfold later that year. The article also raised a pressing question: Who were the "informants" cited by *The New York Times*? Were these independent political observers or agents of state surveillance embedded in the movement?

In the chaotic aftermath, the Central Committee retired the title of "Chairman," replacing it with "Minister of Defense" as the highest rank within the Young Lords Party. Juan González assumed this new title. Guzmán, Oliver, Ortiz, and Pérez retained their positions. Gloria González (formerly Gloria Cruz) was promoted to the Central Committee as a second Field Marshal. A cofounder of the Health Revolutionary Unity Movement (HRUM), she had joined the Young Lords Organization in January 1970. On July 26, 1970, she and Juan González celebrated their wedding[12] in a ceremony officiated by Luciano and Oliver on the one-year anniversary of the New York chapter's founding.

From the start, the Women's Caucus had pushed for the appointment of women to the Central Committee. Denise Oliver's appointment in June marked a victory. However, Gloria González had refused to support or take part in the caucus. Oliver and González represented contrasting approaches to feminism. Oliver was a cofounder of the Women's Caucus and advocated a socialist feminist perspective, while González identified as a nationalist. Their differing views highlighted a crucial point—women in leadership positions, while important, was not enough to advance gender equality. Some were motivated more by personal ambition than by the collective advancement of women.

Meaningful progress for women's rights required leadership committed to collective action. For example, the Women's Caucus' sustained advocacy led to tangible organizational reforms. These included internal childcare policies, mechanisms to hold men accountable for sexual abuse, and reproductive rights campaigns. Additional victories involved enriching the political education curriculum with feminist texts, expanding *Palante's* coverage of women's issues, and promoting nonsexist and nonracist language. Collectively, these changes reshaped the Young Lords Party, advancing it toward greater equity and justice.

The Men's Caucus: Change from the Top to the Bottom

The Women's Caucus believed that if the men in the organization understood gender oppression and exploitation, they would join the fight to end male supremacy. After all, they had important relationships with mothers, sisters, cousins, friends, and partners. This belief led to formation of the Men's Caucus to explore the connections between capitalism and gender oppression and to raise consciousness about men's attitudes and behaviors toward women.

David "Pelu" Jacobs, a member of the Defense Ministry, described the challenge:

> "It's tough for someone who has been dealing a certain way with women, whose father was dealing with women a certain way ... and now they have to change."[13]

Richie Pérez, then captain in the Information Ministry, explained:

> "Male chauvinism is a problem every man has by virtue of being raised in this society. ... We recognize machismo is one of the biggest problems in making revolution."[14]

He wrote:

> We not only have to change the political structure of this country; we've also got to change everything else. Revolution means change from the top to the bottom, and that includes the way we deal with each other as human beings.[15]

Pérez's words highlighted the crucial link between personal and systemic change, emphasizing that the personal is political.

The "YLP Position Paper on Women"

Shortly after the one-year anniversary of the Young Lords' founding in New York, the Central Committee published the "YLP Position Paper on Women." The full-page centerfold appeared in the *Palante*[16] issue dedicated to *El Grito de Lares*—the 1868 armed uprising against Spain's colonial rule that launched Puerto Rico's national liberation struggle.[17]

The position paper represents a fusion of socialist, feminist, and nationalist ideologies. It reflects the political insights of the Women's Caucus and draws from a rich array of sources: caucus meetings, political education classes, exchanges with other feminists of color, community organizing campaigns, and feminist and socialist texts. Opening with an analysis of *triple oppression*, it asserts that Third World women face intersecting forms of subjugation—rooted in gender, race, nationality, and class. Identifying capitalism as the primary enemy, the paper emphasizes the leading and indispensable role of Third World women in advancing global social transformation. It declares:

> [T]he women's struggle is the revolution within the revolution. Puerto Rican women will be neither behind nor in front of their brothers but always alongside them in mutual respect and love.

Fig. 8. *Palante* cover. "YLP Position Paper on Women." 1970.

The position paper adopted the phrase "the revolution within the revolution" from a 1966 speech by Fidel Castro delivered at the Congress of the Federation of Cuban Women. At the time, 85 percent of Cuban women were homemakers, many uneducated and socially marginalized under a deeply patriarchal and racist system.[18] In response, the Cuban government launched wide-ranging programs to integrate women into the nation's economic and political life. By the mid-1970s, the government pledged:

> The participation of women in society must be in absolute equality with men, and so long as any vestige of inequality remains, it is necessary to continue working to achieve this objective of the revolution.[19]

Drawing on this idea, the Women's Caucus rejected the nationalist argument that women's concerns should wait until after the revolution. Instead, we insisted that the struggle for gender justice was ongoing, even within the context of socialism.

The "YLP Position Paper on Women" articulates a distinctly socialist feminist perspective. It critiques the oppressive institutions of marriage and the nuclear family, offering global examples to illustrate how patriarchal control is exercised and maintained. Drawing on Friedrich Engels's, *The Origin of the Family, Private Property, and the State,* the paper traces the historical subordination of women to the development of private property and the emergence of a privileged male class. Under capitalism, it argues, working-class women have been reduced to household slaves and child-bearing machines, whose primary role is to reproduce future generations of workers. By linking women's oppression to material and economic structures, the paper situates gender inequality as a fundamental feature of class society.

The position paper maintains that capitalism commodifies all people, compelling individuals to sell their labor—and in many instances, their bodies—in order to survive. It emphasizes that women of color are disproportionately pushed into the most exploitative sectors of the economy, where they are subjected to sexual harassment, abuse, and violence at the hands of employers and supervisors.

The paper concludes:

> The Central Committee of the Young Lords Party has is-
> sued this position paper to explain and to educate about
> the role of sisters in the past and how we see sisters in the
> struggle now and in the future.

Published in September 1970, the "YLP Position Paper on Women," marked a significant victory for Puerto Rican and African American socialist feminists within the organization. Through the sustained collective efforts of the Women's Caucus, the Young Lords Party—a revolutionary nationalist organization—officially endorsed a socialist feminist perspective. This marked a critical milestone in the Young Lords' ideological development and evolving commitment to gender justice.

The Women's Caucus and *The New York Times*

The Women's Caucus caught the attention of a reporter at the *New York Times*. At the time, it was highly unusual for the mainstream corporate media to cover the political work of young Puerto Rican, Latinx and African American women. On November 11, 1970, the *Times* published an article titled "Young Women Find a Place in High Command of Young Lords," featured in the *Food, Fashions, Family, and Furnishings* section, a space then typically reserved for "women's stories."[20]

The reporter interviewed four members of the Women's Caucus, offering a rare public platform to articulate our political commitments and organizing work. At the time, we were between the ages of eighteen and twenty-three—and deeply engaged in organizing and activism. We used the opportunity to express our goals: to serve our communities, build toward a socialist society, and fight for the equality of women of color.

Olguie Robles, an eighteen-year-old Education Ministry cadre from the Bronx branch, stated, "We are dealing with both male chauvinism and the passivity of the Puerto Rican woman," highlighting the internal struggles within the organization and with ourselves.

I added, "We do everything that the brothers do," emphasizing our equal participation in community organizing, leading campaigns, and engaging in all of the YLP's activities.

Martha Duarte (Arguello), a Defense Ministry cadre from the Lower East Side branch, drew a distinction between revolution and reform. "We don't believe in electoral politics," she explained. "It's the Band-Aid approach to a gaping wound."

Central Committee member Denise Oliver explained, "Revolution is not just guns and fighting. Right now, we're in an educational phase."

While the article wasn't the one we would have written, it confirmed what the "YLP Position Paper on Women" had already made clear: women of color were not just participants in the struggle but central to its leadership, vision, and political direction. The interview concluded with an unequivocal expression of our commitment to revolutionary change and social justice for all oppressed people.

7.
QUEER LIBERATION AND THE YOUNG LORDS PARTY

> We were all involved in different struggles,
> including myself and many other transgender people.
> But in these struggles, in the Civil Rights movement,
> in the war movement, in the women's movement,
> we were still outcasts. The only reason they tolerated
> the transgender community in some of these movements
> was because we were gung-ho; we were frontliners.
> We didn't take no shit from nobody.[1]
>
> —Sylvia Rivera, *Street Transvestite Action Revolutionaries*

On June 28, 1969, when police raided the Stonewall Inn in Greenwich Village, most of the Third World Left in the United States remained largely silent. Over the next six days, clashes between gay, lesbian, bisexual, and transgender activists and the police rocked the streets of New York City, marking a turning point in the struggle for LGBTQ+ rights. A new militancy emerged, dramatically increasing the visibility of the gay community, both in the United States and around the world.

Weeks later, on July 31, 1969, activists involved in the rebellion founded the Gay Liberation Front (GLF).[2] Among the cofounders were Marsha P. Johnson, an African American self-identified drag queen, and Sylvia Rivera, a Puerto Rican–Venezuelan transgender woman, who joined soon after. Their activism confronted not only homophobia and transphobia but also racism and class inequality.

Around the same time, on July 26, 1969, the Young Lords Organization launched its New York chapter with a rally at Tompkins Square Park in the East Village. In September 1970, the organization opened a storefront office in the Lower East Side—a multiethnic working-class neighborhood home to African American, Latinx, Asian, Jewish, and Italian communities. Many Young Lords were longtime residents and community organizers, which helped foster strong ties to the neighborhood.

As the Lower East Side branch grew, it attracted new members, including Puerto Rican lesbian and bisexual women who formed a Gay and Lesbian Caucus within the organization. Although archival documentation is scarce, this chapter seeks to recover and examine the Young Lords' relationship with the LGBTQ+ movement and trace the activities of the YLP Gay and Lesbian Caucus. By weaving together fragments of recollection and scattered historical accounts, it aims to prevent their total erasure.

Queer of Color Activism Confronts Racism and Homophobia

In 1970, several key events amplified the visibility of the U.S. queer liberation movement. Shortly after the formation of the Gay Liberation Front (GLF), Black, Latinx, and Asian gays and lesbians broke away to form the Third World Gay Revolution (TWGR), citing racism within predominantly white organizations as the primary reason. In an article published in *Come Out!* the TWGR wrote:

> Despite the many organizations emerging in the Gay Liberation movement, third world people haven't been able to relate to any of these. This is due to the inherent racism found in any white group with white leadership and white thinking.[3]

This declaration marked a turning point.

The TWGR called on the Third World Left to recognize the necessity of their inclusion into all left-wing revolutionary groups, demanding "immediate nondiscriminatory open admission/membership for radical homosexuals." They asserted:

> Our straight sisters and brothers must recognize and support that we, third world gay women and men, are equal in every way within the revolutionary ranks. We each organize our people about different issues, but our struggles are the same against oppression, and we will defeat it together.[4]

TWGR insisted that revolutionary change required directly confronting both racism and homophobia within the movement.

The TWGR's politics paralleled those of the Black Panthers and the Young Lords, emphasizing *triple oppression* by capitalism, racism, and sexism[5]—an analysis aligned with socialist feminists of color. In the same article, TWGR cited both the Young Lords' 13-Point Program—"We want the liberation of all Third World People"—and a pivotal speech by Huey P. Newton, Chairman of the Black Panther Party (BPP), titled "Letter to the Revolutionary Brothers and Sisters about the Women's Liberation and Gay Liberation Movements."[6] Delivered in New York on August 15, 1970, Newton's speech called for solidarity among Black, women's, and gay movements.

Newton's letter recognized homosexuals as an oppressed group and called for a broad coalition against the racist, patriarchal capitalist state. Historian Ronald K. Porter attributes Newton's evolving views on gender and sexuality to the influence of James Baldwin and Jean Genet.[7] Newton himself cites his time in prison, along with "talks with gay brothers,"[8] the Stonewall Rebellion, and LGBTQ+ activism as key to his shift in thinking.

Newton emphasized the need to "unite in a revolutionary fashion"[9] and urged respect for "all oppressed people." In this groundbreaking statement in 1970, he wrote:

> "[H]omosexuals are not given freedom and liberty by anyone. ... They might be the most oppressed people in the society."[10]

He challenged male revolutionaries to confront their insecurities and fears about homosexuality, openly acknowledging his own past "hangups," including a fear of lesbians that triggered anxieties about castration. Newtown attributed these reactions to the "conditioning process" in U.S. society[11] and concluded, "homosexuals are not enemies of the people," urging activists to eliminate derogatory terms such as "faggot" and "punk" from their vocabulary.[12]

Historians Joshua Bloom and Waldo E. Martin identify Newton's letter as a critical moment in securing support for gay rights from a national Black organization.[13] Despite its male-centric gaze, the letter helped raise awareness about the queer movement and sparked important debates within the New Left.

The Black Panther Party newspaper published Newton's letter alongside an announcement for the Revolutionary People's Constitutional Convention planned for the Labor Day weekend in Philadelphia in 1970. The event aimed to unify the U.S. radical left and draft a new version of the U.S. Constitution.[14] An estimated 12,000 to 15,000 activists attended,[15] including a delegation from the Young Lords Party, which included Pablo "Yoruba" Guzmán, Denise Oliver, myself, and other cadre. On the first night, approximately twenty Young Lords from the New York and Philadelphia branches provided stage security alongside members of the Black Panther Party. Among them was one of the youngest Lords, Mark Ortiz.

Fig. 9. Revolutionary People's Constitutional Convention. 1970.
Left to right: Iris Morales, Denise Oliver, and Pablo "Yoruba" Guzmán
(Courtesy: Michael Abramson)

During the convention, gay liberation activists—including white and people of color—entered the plenary, chanting, "Gay power to Gay people! Black power to Black people!"[16]

In his dissertation, "Freedom Indivisible: Gays and Lesbians in the African American Civil Rights Movement," historian Jared E. Leighton notes that while such moments of unity were powerful, they also exposed persistent tensions around homophobia, sexism, racism, and class. Leighton observes:

> It seems white gay men expressed more unequivocal sup-
> port of the BPP ..., while white lesbians had a more diffi-
> cult relationship with the Panthers. LGBT people of color,
> like Third World Gay Liberation, also ... experienced hos-
> tility from the Panthers.[17]

These complexities reveal that solidarity across movements was often as-
pirational, challenged by intersecting forms of oppression that activists
were still struggling to confront.

Following the convention, a group of white lesbians from New York
severed ties with the BPP, citing the cancellation of their workshop, derogatory remarks, and acts of male intimidation.[18] Third World Gay Revolution also voiced grievances, responding with a revised 16-Point Platform and Program, which declared:

> We believe that so-called comrades who call themselves
> "revolutionaries" have failed to deal with their sexist atti-
> tudes. ... Men still fight for the privileged position of man-
> on-the-top. Women quickly fall in line behind their men.[19]

This critique was likely aimed at the Black Panther Party. The revised
platform also advocated for the abolition of capital punishment, solidarity with women's liberation and demanded equal employment and decent housing.[20] It condemned state-sanctioned violence, called for the
abolition of the "fascist police force," and demanded the release of Third
World gay and political prisoners from jails and mental institutions.
TWGR's critique extended to heteropatriarchy, denouncing the "bour-
geois nuclear family" as a capitalist institution that perpetuates the oppression of homosexuality.

In summary, TWGR's "radical queer activism called for a reorder-
ing of society, including conventional family structures and capitalist
economic principles, such as private property."[21] The final point of the
16-Point Platform declared, "We want a new society—a revolutionary
socialist society."

The Young Lords Party and the LGBTQ Movement, 1970-1971

In 1970, Pablo "Yoruba" Guzmán, the Young Lords Minister of Information, began meeting with activists from the Gay Liberation Front,
the Third World Gay Revolution, and other emerging LGBTQ groups.

These conversations coincided with internal struggles, especially the demands of the Women's Caucus, which opened the organization to broader discussions about gender justice.

That year, women in the Lower East Side branch formed the Gay and Lesbian Caucus (GLC). They invited Guzmán to serve as adviser, recognizing his willingness to engage in dialogue around sexual orientation and gender identity issues. Gay, lesbian, and bisexual members joined the Young Lords Party for the same reasons as other members—drawn to its platform and demands for Puerto Rican rights. Like Puerto Rican feminists, LGBTQ activists found few organizations that addressed their concerns.

Within the YLP, queer members participated in and led community organizing campaigns, conducted door-to-door health testing, and represented the organization at public events. They sold the *Palante* newspaper and attended general meetings, political education classes, and protests. LGBTQ members served in the Defense Ministry, providing security for Central Committee members and other leaders and played key roles in the Information Ministry. While most LGBTQ members were not openly "out," neither were they closeted—occupying an in-between space of coexistence. One exception was Micky Agrait, a tenant organizer in the Health and Field Ministry in the East Harlem branch, who was the only openly gay member of the New York organization.

Around this time, Marsha P. Johnson and Sylvia Rivera founded Street Transvestite Action Revolutionaries (STAR). The group created a safe haven for LGBTQ youth, offering food and clothing, and support to those arrested, along with meetings and workshops for the gay and trans community. "STAR was for the street gay people, the street homeless people and anybody that needed help,"[22] Rivera explained.[23] She dedicated herself to the project, recognizing that trans-identified individuals remained heavily marginalized within both straight and gay communities and organizations.[24]

Although Rivera was not a YLP member, she was an ally. In an interview years later, she recalled marching with the Young Lords and over 10,000 others to the United Nations on October 30, 1970, demanding an end to colonialism in Puerto Rico and an end to police violence in U.S. communities. Rivera remembered proudly carrying the STAR banner, one of the first public displays of its identity.[25] This mass mobilization to the United Nations marked a historic moment of solidarity between Third World LGBTQ people and radical liberation organizations.

During this period in early 1971, the Young Lords Party released the book *Palante: The Young Lords*, a collection of essays and photographs edited in collaboration with photojournalist Michael Abramson. It featured articles by YLP members and striking black-and-white photographs. A powerful visual and political documentation of the organization's activism, the book quickly gained popularity.

In a section titled "Revolution Within the Revolution," Pablo "Yoruba" Guzmán wrote about the gay liberation movement and issues of sexual orientation and gender identity. Guzmán's article was the first public expression of solidarity with the queer liberation movement by a Young Lords Party leader, reflecting emerging relationships with organizations such as the Third World Gay Revolution and Street Transvestite Action Revolutionaries (STAR). Informed by conversations with members of the YLP's Gay and Lesbian Caucus and inspired by Huey P. Newton's 1970 statement on gay and women's liberation, Guzmán's essay marked a critical step toward aligning the organization with queer liberation.

Guzmán's begins by reflecting on the YLP's internal struggles around gender justice. He acknowledges the initial hostility toward the women's liberation movement and credits the Women's Caucus with advancing the organization's understanding of the oppression and exploitation faced by "Third World women." Guzmán explains that the debates with the Women's Caucus served as a critical precondition in moving the Young Lords Party to accept LGBTQ members. "The truth is that the idea of equality with gays was less acceptable than women's equality," he writes. His conclusion: "It's a lot quicker for people to accept the fact that sisters should be in the front of the struggle than saying that we're gonna have gay people in the organization."[26]

Guzmán critiques the deep-seated fear and hatred of gay people in society, particularly within communities of color. He describes the ways families perpetuate the belief that being gay is wrong, unnatural, or even evil. He writes:

"Being gay is not a problem; the problem is that people do not understand what gay means."

Guzmán argues that gender is not innate but a social construct—an identity shaped by learned behaviors and expectations to conform to narrowly defined roles and traits associated with "man" or "woman." Those who deviate from these norms are marginalized and labeled deviant. He states:

> Gender is a false idea, because gender is merely traits that have been attributed through the years to a man or a woman.

He challenges rigid gender roles, criticizing the view that masculinity equates to strength and femininity to weakness. He provocatively argues:

> We're saying that ... it would be healthy for a man, if he wanted to cry, to go ahead and cry. It would also be healthy for a woman to pick up the gun.[27]

Guzmán concludes that the binary gender categories—like "man" and "woman"—produce what he calls "half-people." He envisions a society liberated from this traditional binary, asserting that a society without rigid gender classifications is essential for individuals to become "whole" human beings. His argument anticipates contemporary understandings of gender as fluid and existing on a spectrum.

Scholar-activist Loretta Ross would later expand on the falsity of gender dualism:

> [T]he binary definitions of womanhood and manhood erect a false gender dualism that ignores the continuum of human experiences that include people who are lesbian, gay, bisexual, transgender, or gender nonconforming.[28]

At the time, terms like gender nonconforming or gender fluid were not yet widely used, but Guzmán's analysis foreshadows these frameworks.

Guzmán's essay sparked important conversations around sexual orientation and gender identity. He directly confronts the "homophobic" ideas within the organization and emphasizes that shared struggles against oppression unify revolutionary people and advance revolutionary goals. He concludes with an appeal to YLP members to support the queer liberation struggle, framing it as a liberatory force for humanity.

Despite Guzmán's efforts, LGBTQ issues remained absent from the YLP's political platform. However, documents suggest that LGBTQ members pressed for change from within. At the YLP's retreat in July 1971, gay members from the Puerto Rico branches spoke out against rising homophobia in the organization. The Central Committee responded:

> The biggest problem of this period has been the oppression of homosexual cadres in the Party. No one should oppress anyone else for sexist reasons. ...

Yet no action followed—no workshops, political education, or efforts to build alliances with queer organizations. Instead of addressing the issue directly, the Central Committee instructed the cadre "to write up their feelings."

> We ask those people that have a good understanding to write up their feelings and to give it in to high levels of the Party so we can study ... and in the future take a complete position.

This deferred approach dismissed the urgency of the matter. Worse still, the Central Committee proceeded to ban all "homosexual caucuses," including the newly formed group in Puerto Rico and the Gay and Lesbian Caucus in New York, which had been active for ten months.

Justifying the ban, the Central Committee claimed:

> Homosexual caucuses, just like women's caucuses, are not the solution for resolving this contradiction. Inside the Party, all contradictions are resolved by waging ideological struggle.[29]

This response failed to explain how "waging ideological struggle" would address the concrete realities of homophobia and marginalization faced by queer members. The shutdown of the "homosexual" caucuses marked a clear step backward—far removed from the solidarity Guzmán had urged just months earlier.

Six months later, in a December 1971 communiqué, the Central Committee made a brief reference to "a cadre at National [headquarters]" preparing a paper on *bisexuality*[30] for the July 1972 Party Congress. This brief mention suggests that some queer members continued to raise LGBTQ concerns to the Central Committee and advocated to bring these concerns to the general membership. However, the *bisexuality* document never circulated, and no further public discussion materialized.

Conclusion

The Young Lords' engagement with LGBTQ activism reflected a complex intersection of radical politics, gender justice, and queer liberation. Although Guzmán publicly advanced a transformative vision, the Central Committee's shifting political priorities in 1971 ultimately undermined the organization's commitment to LGBTQ rights and queer liberation.

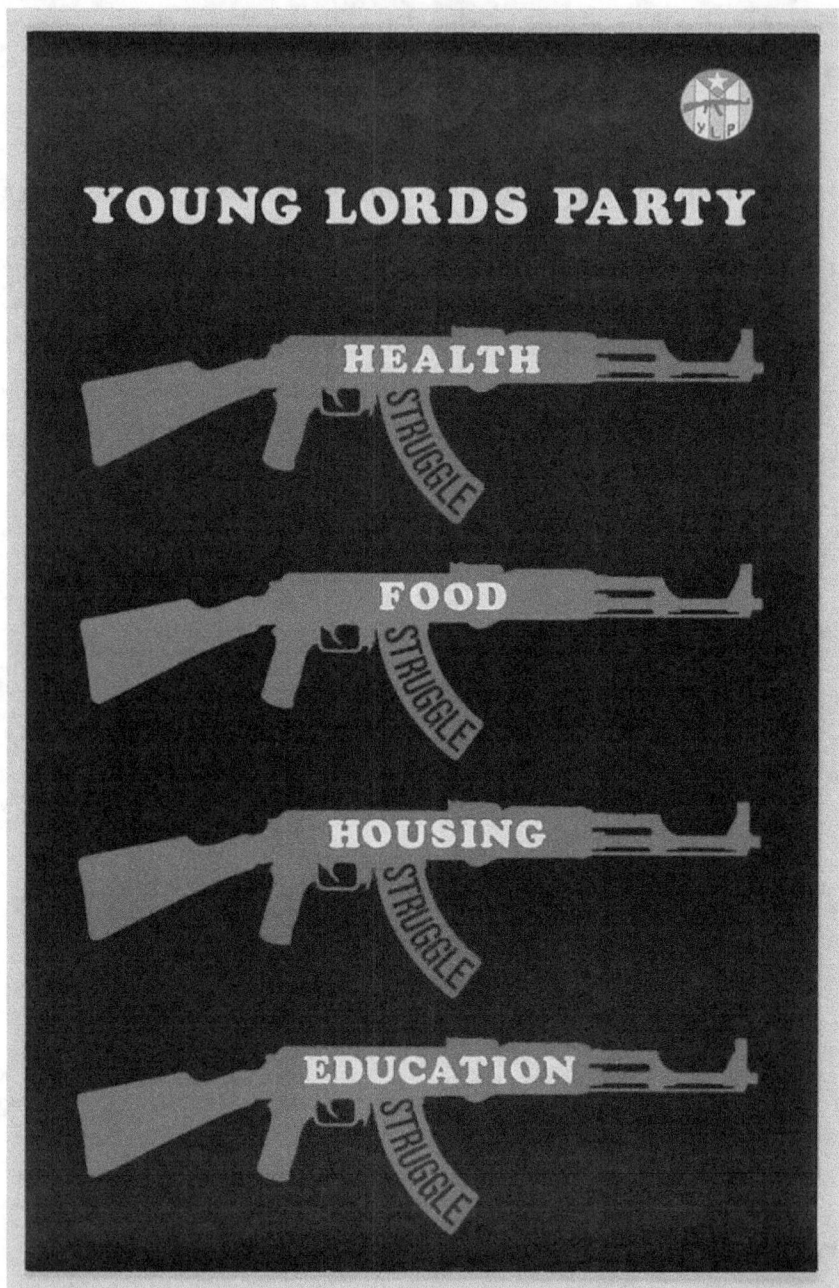

Fig. 10. Young Lords Poster. 1970.

PART III.
"WE DO NOT LIVE SINGLE-ISSUE LIVES"

There is no thing as a single-issue struggle
because we do not live single-issue lives.[1]

—Audre Lorde

In 1970, the Young Lords Party brought local, national, and international attention to the struggles of Puerto Ricans in the United States and highlighted the colonial status of Puerto Rico. The organization ignited widespread public discourse, gained significant popular support, and prompted policy and programmatic reforms. A key force behind this momentum was the Women's Caucus, which played a critical role in ensuring that gender justice and feminist concerns were included within the YLP's political agenda.

The following chapters focus on the activism of women in the Young Lords as leaders, strategists, spokespersons, and organizers. Women played significant roles in major YLP campaigns during that pivotal year, including protests at Lincoln Hospital; advocacy for prisoners' rights and criminal justice reform; and mobilizations in support of Puerto Rico's decolonization.

8.
POVERTY IS A HEALTH ISSUE:
PROTESTS AT LINCOLN HOSPITAL

> We want free publicly supported health care
> for treatment and prevention.[1]
>
> —10-Point Health Program, Young Lords Organization, 1970

From its beginnings in New York City, the Young Lords Organization fought for quality health care for poor people and working-class communities. Initiatives such as free breakfast programs and screenings for lead poisoning and tuberculosis provided vital services to low-income families and children. These efforts advanced the idea that poverty was, in fact, a public health issue.

In April 1970, the Young Lords opened an office on Longwood Avenue and Kelly Street to engage with the growing Puerto Rican population in the Bronx—a community suffering dehumanizing conditions: rundown housing, high unemployment, inadequate schools, police violence, and a severe lack of social services.[2] Health disparities were stark. Residents suffered disproportionately from infant mortality, tuberculosis, pneumonia, asthma, malnutrition, anemia, hepatitis, sickle cell anemia, and heroin addiction. At the time, the South Bronx was one of the poorest U.S. congressional districts. Public health services were rapidly deteriorating as vast medical empires expanded across New York City.[3]

This chapter examines the leadership of women in the movement for health care as a human right, focusing on their organizing role at Lincoln Hospital with the Young Lords in 1970.

Located at 141st Street and Bruckner Boulevard in the Bronx, Lincoln Hospital served approximately 400,000 primarily poor and working-class Puerto Ricans and African Americans.[4] Founded in 1839, the nine-story, 346-bed facility had functioned as a nursing home for Black people, many of whom had been enslaved prior to the abolition of slavery in New York.[5] By 1970, the building was in a state of severe disrepair: lead-based paint peeled off the walls, elevators frequently failed, and rodents and roaches ran across its floors. Though it had been condemned nearly thirty years earlier, Lincoln remained open, almost exclusively for poor people of color.[6] Neighborhood residents referred to it as "the butcher shop." Lincoln Hospital embodied everything wrong with the U.S. healthcare system.

In 1969, the New York State legislature set up the Health and Hospitals Corporation (HHC) to manage the budgets of eighteen municipal hospitals, including Lincoln. Under an affiliation agreement between the city and the Albert Einstein College of Medicine, Einstein's physicians provided medical services and supervised students, interns, and residents. Despite the multi-million-dollar contract, Lincoln remained one of the country's "worst urban hospitals."[7] While a steady stream of poor patients arrived at its doors, the physician-administrators prioritized testing equipment, procedures, and drugs, and securing city payments, rather than healing patients.

Lincoln Hospital was no stranger to worker and community protests. In 1969, a major dispute erupted in the hospital's mental health clinic. More than one hundred workers, mostly African Americans and Puerto Ricans, evicted the clinic's director[8] and ran the facility for nearly thirty days. They were supported by professional staff, Black Panther Party members, neighborhood service organizations, and local clergy.[9] The workers demanded better training, job upgrades, and greater worker participation in hospital administration.[10] They also opposed the hospital's growing reliance on psychotropic drugs to treat patients.[11] The takeover ended with the arrest of twenty-two activists and the firing of sixty-seven workers, most of whom were later reinstated.

In his memoir *White Coat, Clenched Fist: The Political Education of an American Physician,* Dr. Fritzhugh Mullan reflects that the most important outcome of the takeover was "the drawing together of people who were to be instrumental in subsequent events at Lincoln."[12]

Women's Organizing and Health Activism at Lincoln Hospital

In early 1970, when the HHC announced job freezes, service rollbacks, and deep budget cuts for Lincoln Hospital, to take effect on July 1, 1970,[13] workers and activists quickly mobilized. At the forefront of the resistance was the Health Revolutionary Unity Movement (HRUM), a network of hospital workers allied with the Young Lords and the Black

Panthers. HRUM's membership reflected the city's public hospital work-force—80 percent Puerto Rican and African American, and predominately women.

Cleo Silvers, HRUM cochair and a veteran of the 1969 mental health clinic takeover, helped organized the Think Lincoln Committee (TLC), uniting doctors and interns, other hospital employees, and neighborhood residents.

Fig. 11. Patient-Worker Complaint Table. Lincoln Hospital. 1970.

(Courtesy: Michael Abramson)

The TLC's approach emphasized direct action. One of its first initiatives was the creation of a patient-worker complaint table at the entrance to the hospital's emergency room. Activists greeted incoming patients, reinforcing the message that Lincoln Hospital existed to serve the people. TLC militants informed the newly hired hospital administrator, Dr. Antero Lacot, that the table's purpose was to address the grievances of patients and workers. Staffed by volunteers for up to eighteen hours a day,[14] the table ensured that grievances were handled promptly with hospital staff.[15] The TLC also circulated flyers and held rallies in surrounding Bronx communities to raise awareness of the impending budget cuts. These efforts culminated in a list of demands. Carl Pastor, a leading organizer in the Young Lords' Health Ministry and a member of HRUM, noted that the hospital administrators were fully aware of the grievances.[16]

HRUM's origins traced back to the Gouverneur Health Center in Manhattan's Lower East Side in 1969, which then employed 350 workers, mostly neighborhood residents. When administrators announced plans to lay off ninety-six workers, the response was swift. Gloria González (then Gloria Cruz), Valerie Laguer, and other workers at Gouverneur rejected their union's response to the layoffs. Inspired by the Dodge Revolutionary Unity Movement (DRUM)—a radical organization of African American auto workers in Detroit—they formed HRUM as a revolutionary alternative to the traditional union structures.[17]

Most HRUM members were African American and Puerto Rican women, though other people of color also joined. At Gouverneur, HRUM worked closely with I Wor Kuen (IWK), a Chinatown-based organization founded in 1969.[18] IWK initiated "serve the people" programs, including draft counseling, childcare, and a free clinic that provided preventive health care and door-to-door tuberculosis screenings. Their efforts pressured New York City's Health Department to open an X-ray unit in Chinatown in response to high TB rates.[19]

Around the same time, workers and health advocates at Metropolitan Hospital in East Harlem also mobilized against budget cuts. In 1969, the Young Lords joined these efforts and helped create a 10-Point Health Program. It called for community-worker control, free health care, pre-

ventive health services delivered door to door, and the hiring of local residents.[20] Gloria González represented HRUM at one of the initial meetings and began collaborating with the Young Lords on community
health projects.

As patient services deteriorated, so too did conditions for the over-
worked and underpaid staff.[21] To improve both hospital care and working conditions, HRUM expanded its presence across the city's public
hospitals and health clinics, creating workers' collectives at Lincoln, Metropolitan, Morisania, Fordham, and Greenpoint hospitals, as well as at
the Gouverneur and NENA Health Centers, among others.

HRUM adopted the 10-Point Health Program and published a
pamphlet titled *Ideology, History, Patients' and Workers' Rights*, outlining its goals and critiques:

> We are faced with fighting racism, the corrupt health sys-
> tem, the hospital administration, and the union leadership.
> At the same time, we must struggle with male chauvinism
> and female passivity in our own ranks.[22]

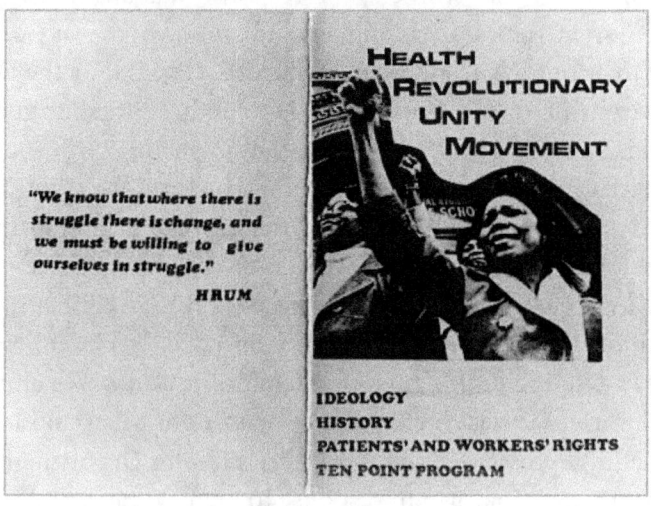

Fig. 12. Health Revolutionary Unity Movement pamphlet. 1971.

To build solidarity among workers and communities, HRUM also
launched a newspaper titled *For the People's Health*. The first issue,
printed in February 1970, had a run of 10,000 copies.

Kathy Larkin, an HRUM organizer and spokesperson, explained their approach to organizing: "We lay out what the problems are and challenge them to see the issues."[23] Given the predominance of women in the hospital workforce, HRUM highlighted the exploitation of "Third World women" at the intersection of class, race, and gender. The HRUM pamphlet stated:

> Our wages are lower than those of white women workers. Working in hospitals as clerks, aides etc. we take insults from racist supervisors (who are usually men) and male workers who, because of their machismo, see us as objects to be pinched, propositioned, and treated as mentally inferior.[24]

Third World women were disproportionately relegated to lower-paid roles, the "dead-end jobs," and faced systemic gender discrimination and harassment. In response, they demanded fair wages and "working conditions fit for human beings."[25] Recognizing that many women spent up to 50 percent of their wages on childcare, they also called for hospital-funded, community-worker-controlled daycare centers located in or near the hospital.[26]

HRUM's guiding principle was "worker-patient-community unity and control."[27] As they wrote:

> We believe that the duty of every health worker is to fight for decent medical care and the human rights of every patient receiving that care. Patients and workers should be able to aid and communicate with each other without fear of reprisal.[28]

As workers, mothers, women, and patients, HRUM members challenged the authority and practices of health institutions. Their vision of solidarity recognized that public hospital workers were caregivers and also patients themselves. They emphasized:

> We say, all workers must become patient advocates, that is, defend the rights of the patients against bad patient care and disrespect on the part of doctors and hospital administrators.[29]

This kind of day-to-day organizing at Lincoln Hospital, combined with HRUM's militancy, laid the groundwork for the hospital takeovers and protests that erupted in 1970.

The Lincoln Hospital Takeover

By July 14, 1970, Lincoln Hospital's administrators had failed to respond to the workers' demands. In response, the Young Lords' Central Committee, together with leaders from the HRUM and the Think Lincoln Committee (TLC), devised a plan to take over the hospital and dramatize the urgent situation. Security precautions were implemented to ensure that the details were not leaked to the police or the press.

At a special members' meeting, the Young Lords were informed of the plan. The group remained together until 4:00 a.m., when approximated fifty members loaded into the back of a truck headed to Lincoln Hospital. Willie Santiago, a District 65 union member and longtime supporter of the Young Lords, drove the truck.

Upon arrival, members rushed out of the back of the truck, with the security team leading the way. Others followed to hang banners from windows declaring, "Welcome to the People's Hospital, Bienvenidos al Hospital del Pueblo." A few headed to the roof to raise the Puerto Rican flag. The rest of us went to designated areas to conduct health screenings, hold political education classes, and set up daycare for children. Members of HRUM, the Black Panther Party, the Think Lincoln Committee, and hospital staff mobilized alongside the Young Lords in the occupation.

Approximately two dozen physicians from the Lincoln Pediatric Collective, including new interns and residents just two weeks into their posts, found themselves amid this extraordinary action. They, too, joined,[30] ensuring patient services continued uninterrupted.

In the hospital auditorium, a press conference brought together reporters, activists, workers, patients, and doctors. Two large banners hung at the back of the stage: "Lincoln Hospital Must Serve the People". (*El hospital tiene que servirle al pueblo*). At center stage, a table crowded with reporters' microphones awaited the speakers. Cleo Silvers and Gloria González, cochairs of HRUM, and Pablo "Yoruba" Guzmán, the YLP Minister of Information, presented the coalition's seven demands.

The first demand was "No cutbacks in services or jobs," followed by a call for the construction of a new Lincoln Hospital. Additional demands included a minimum wage for workers, a childcare center for patients and workers, door-to-door preventative health care programs, and a twenty-four-hour complaint table staffed by patients and workers. The final demand called for "*total self-determination*" and the establishment of an oversight board of community residents and workers.[31]

Throughout the day, representatives of TLC, HRUM, and the Young Lords negotiated with hospital officials, including Dr. Antero Lacot (hospital administrator), Sid Davidoff (Mayor John Lindsay's representative), and Health and Hospital's Corporation personnel.[32] By about 5:00 p.m., Dr. Lacot convened an emergency meeting with approximately one hundred medical staff members.[33] He announced that negotiations had broken down and that he had authorized the police to retake the hospital. At this point, nearly half of the physicians in the room walked out to join the activists.[34]

As police surrounded the building, someone suggested the Young Lords exit wearing the white smocks of hospital personnel. Accompanied by workers and doctors, the Young Lords left the building. However, just five blocks away, police recognized Pablo "Yoruba" Guzmán accompanied by fellow Young Lord Luis Pérez. Police chased them, fired shots, caught them, and charged them with possession of karate sticks. A judge later threw out the case, calling the charges "totally absurd."[35]

The Young Lords Party declared the hospital takeover a political victory. It demonstrated the power of worker-patient-community organizing. City and health officials agreed to two demands: no cutbacks in services and the implementation of preventative health screenings.[36]

Although the occupation lasted only twelve hours, it drew national and international attention to the appalling state of public health services and working conditions in Puerto Rican and African American communities in New York City. The action exposed the ongoing neglect and disregard of the health care needs of its most marginalized residents.

Demands for Legal and Safe Abortions

Less than a week after the Lincoln Hospital takeover, another protest erupted, this time in response to an abortion-related death. During the

1960s, abortion was illegal in all fifty states. According to a 1967 report, approximately 800,000 abortions were performed annually, the vast majority of them in unsafe, clandestine conditions.[37] The criminalization of abortion disproportionately harmed low-income women of color. Wealthy women could access safe abortions by paying private doctors exorbitant fees or traveling to countries where the procedure was legal. In contrast, poor and working-class women faced dangerous alternatives, often resorting to self-induced and sometimes fatal methods, including the infamous "clothes hanger" abortions.

In July 1970, New York State became the first state to legalize abortion. The new law allowed abortions up to twenty-four weeks of pregnancy and at any stage if the woman's life was at risk.[38] On July 20, Carmen Rodríguez, a thirty-one-year-old mother of two from the South Bronx, entered Lincoln Hospital for an abortion. Rodríguez was already a patient being treated for rheumatic heart disease,[39] a condition clearly noted in her medical records. However, the doctor performing the abortion failed to review her chart. Saline solution entered her bloodstream, causing fluid to accumulate in her lungs. She fell into a coma from which she never recovered, becoming the first person to die under New York's new abortion law.[40]

The community erupted in outrage. The Young Lords, HRUM, the Black Panther Party, and other advocates mobilized, shouting "Murder!" and demanding accountability. At a public meeting convened by administrator Dr. Antero Lacot, in an attempt to calm tensions, described Rodríguez's death as "medically acceptable."[41] This statement further inflamed the community.

Protesters demanded the firing of Dr. Joseph J. Smith, head of the Obstetrics and Gynecology Department.[42] Smith left reluctantly, accusing the Young Lords of creating a hostile work environment. In support of him, twenty-seven doctors and residents in the OB-GYN unit, walked out, temporarily shutting down the department.[43] Ten days later, they returned on the condition that activist groups be barred from the hospital. Administrators complied by obtaining a restraining order stipulating that any member of the Young Lords Party, the Health Revolutionary Unity Movement, or the Think Lincoln Committee would be arrested if found "interfering with patient care and medical services."[44]

Abortion rights were a deeply contested issue within the social justice movement. Most nationalist organizations opposed abortion. The Black Panther Party denounced it as a form of genocide,[45] until women in the organization successfully reframed it as a matter of health care and reproductive justice.[46] Similarly, Puerto Rican nationalist and pro-independence organizations rejected abortion as foreign and a form of colonial oppression.[47] The nationalist view called on Puerto Rican women to bear children to "save the nation" from genocide.

In contrast, the Women's Caucus pressed the Young Lords Party to support a woman's right to make autonomous decisions about her reproduction. The caucus emphasized that the decision to carry a pregnancy to term belonged solely to the woman, free from the interference by the government, church, parents, husband, or boyfriend.[48] Furthermore, we viewed abortion as a necessary option in a society where women bore the financial, social, emotional, and spiritual responsibilities of raising children, while being relegated to low-wage jobs with no support for childcare or housework.

New York's 1970 abortion reform expanded legal rights, but lawmakers failed to address the life-threatening disparities faced by women of color in public institutions. Without access to affordable, quality health care, the legal right to abortion was meaningless, as demonstrated by the case of Carmen Rodríguez. The Women's Caucus included the right to abortion in the broader demands for safe, quality health care for poor and working-class women of color.

Drawing from the ideologies of both feminists of color and nationalists, the caucus advocated for reproductive justice.[49] Feminist politics emphasized a woman's right to control her reproduction, while nationalist politics championed self-determination. Together these ideas forged a liberatory vision rooted in the needs of women of color and poor communities.

The Women's Caucus envisioned abortion services under community control, overseen by of a board of caring neighborhood residents, hospital workers, and medical professionals. In a *Palante* article, Gloria Colón, from the YLP's Education Ministry, outlined the criteria for community-controlled abortion services:

> We believe that abortions should be legal if they are com-
> munity-controlled, if they are safe, if our people are edu-
> cated about the risks, and if doctors do not sterilize our sis-
> ters while performing abortions.[50]

Colón's warning was warranted. Women of color, both in the United States and Puerto Rico, had long been subjected to involuntary and co-erced sterilization procedures, as discussed in Chapter 5.

Historian Jennifer Nelson, in her article "Abortions under Commu-nity Control," interviews Olguie Robles, a former Young Lord and mem-ber of the Women's Caucus. Robles confirmed the Young Lords' stance on abortion, noting that poor women need genuine reproductive options and that most women would not choose abortion if they had the re-sources to raise children.[51] The idea—that poverty limits reproductive choice—was echoed in the "YLP Position Paper on Women," which con-cluded, "Change the system so that women can freely be allowed to have as many children as they want."[52]

The Women's Caucus believed that a socialist society would pro-vide the material support—health care, childcare, housing, and in-come—necessary to support women and their children. Reproductive freedom, we believed, was impossible without economic justice.

The Lincoln Detox Program: From Protest to Practice

A few months after Carmen Rodríguez's death, another protest erupted at Lincoln Hospital—this time demanding drug addiction ser-vices. Just a year earlier, in 1969, President Richard Nixon had declared a "War on Drugs" in a message to Congress, labeling drug abuse as pub-lic enemy number one. He reported: "New York City alone has records of some 40,000 heroin addicts, and the number rises between 7,000 and 9,000 a year."[53] Instead of increasing treatment services, both the state and federal governments responded with punitive policies and measures, such as mandatory sentencing and no-knock warrants, that dispropor-tionately and adversely harmed African American and Puerto Rican communities.

In response to the growing heroin crisis and rising overdose deaths, grassroots activists across New York City mobilized. Young people un-der the age of sixteen were dying from overdoses at the rate of one a week,[54] with youth of color most affected. Yet despite the urgency, there were no hospital programs dedicated to serving them.

Frustrated by the city's inaction, a group of African American women founded Mothers Against Drugs (MAD) to fight the heroin epidemic. At the time, I was a teacher at the Academy for Black and Latin Education (ABLE), an independent storefront school rooted in the principles of Black Power and self-determination.[55] Many of our students were addicted to heroin. The school's director, Dave Walker, approached the local hospital seeking treatment services but was turned away.

In December 1969, a twelve-year-old boy named Walter Van Der Meer died from an overdose in the bathroom of a Harlem tenement on West 117th Street. He became the youngest recorded heroin fatality in New York City. His death sent shockwaves through the community.

Outraged by the continued indifference of city officials, police, and healthcare institutions, ABLE and MAD joined forces. In early January 1970, they occupied the Office of Community Psychiatry at St. Luke's Hospital, demanding adolescent treatment services. After four days, the sit-in ended with a joint statement from hospital administrators and community activists, announcing the creation of a twenty-eight-bed detoxification center for adolescents—the first such program in the city.[56]

In the South Bronx, the heroin epidemic had reached catastrophic levels, affecting one in four residents.[57] In response, neighborhood activists, along with the Young Lords, the Black Panthers, HRUM, and former addicts, formed the South Bronx Drug Coalition (SBDC). On November 10, 1970, they occupied the sixth floor of Lincoln Hospital's Nurses' Residence—marking the third major protest at the hospital that year.

Following negotiations, the activists succeeded in establishing the Lincoln Hospital Detox Program, which would go on to treat thousands of individuals over the next eight years. The program became internationally recognized for its innovative and community-centered approach, combining acupuncture-based detoxification with political education and consciousness-raising. It stood in sharp contrast to the state's punitive policies and emerged as a powerful example of grassroots, community-controlled health care rooted in the lived experiences and needs of the most affected populations.

Pediatrics Collective Demands Community-Worker Control

While the South Bronx Drug Coalition's takeover was still in progress, another crisis surfaced in Lincoln's Pediatrics Department. This conflict revealed deep divisions between Dr. Arnold Einhorn, the department head, and approximately thirty resident doctors and interns, members of the Pediatrics Collective.[58] This group, composed predominantly of Jewish physicians, was committed to developing community-based health care programs aligned with the principles of medical justice and grassroots accountability.

In early November 1970, administrators from the Albert Einstein College of Medicine announced plans to hire Dr. Helen Rodríguez Trías, a pediatrician and women's rights advocate from Puerto Rico, as the assistant director, with the intention that she would eventually lead the department. Dr. Einhorn opposed the transition, prompting the Pediatrics Collective to call for his resignation. They cited his "inability to administer the department and his resistance to community-worker control."[59]

In response, several Jewish organizations protested Einhorn's removal, alleging that he was the target of ethnic discrimination because he was Jewish. However, a civil rights investigation conducted by the city concluded that the dispute was not based in antisemitism but stemmed from "fundamental and irreconcilable disagreement over philosophy and goals."[60]

Radical Health Advocacy and Patients' Bill of Rights

The 1970 protests at Lincoln Hospital reflected a broader national debate over the state of medical care in the United States. In response to systemic neglect and patient mistreatment, HRUM, the Young Lords, the Black Panthers, and allied doctors collaborated to develop a Patients' Bill of Rights.

The document outlined a set of expectations for the doctor-patient relationship. It affirmed that all patients be treated with respect, informed about diagnoses and treatment options, and granted access to their medical records. The original version also demanded on-site, hospital-funded day-care centers and preventative health programs.[61]

Today, a version of the Patients' Bill of Rights is posted in hospitals throughout the country, though often watered down from the radical, community-driven vision that first inspired it.

At the core of the Lincoln Hospital struggles was the conviction that health care is a human right. African American and Puerto Rican women played a vital role, insisting that those most affected by hospital policies and practices—patients, workers, and community residents—should have a decisive voice in governance and setting priorities. Lincoln Hospital became "one of the first thin threads of a sustained struggle to achieve worker-community control within a health institution."[62]

While the protests led to some internal reforms, the overwhelming structural inequalities and entrenched power hierarchies remained largely untouched. The actions at Lincoln exposed the urgent need for a total overhaul of the expanding "medical industrial complex."[63] Despite progress in some areas, the core issues of health care inequality persist— and the demand for health equity remains as urgent today as it was in 1970.

9.
UPRISINGS AGAINST NEW YORK CITY CRIMINAL JUSTICE SYSTEM

And, if I know anything at all,
It's that a wall is just a wall
And nothing more at all.
It can be broken down.[1]

—Assata Shakur, "Affirmation," 1987

The call for "law and order" by politicians in the 1960s triggered a get-tough-on-crime politics that exploded into a nationwide fervor for incarceration,[2] ultimately making the United States the world's leading jailer.[3] By 1970, New York City jails were overflowing with poor and working-class African Americans and Puerto Ricans, who made up approximately 85 percent of the jail population.[4] Most were charged, but not convicted, of any crime, held behind bars largely because they could not afford the exorbitant bails.[5]

The brutality and violence of the criminal justice system were central concerns to low-income communities. Jail overcrowding was a critical issue. For instance, the Manhattan Detention Center for Men, known as "the Tombs," was designed to hold a maximum of 932 men but was operating at 213 percent capacity.[6] Even the Board of Corrections acknowledged that people were confined in inhumane conditions, "caged like animals,"[7] evidencing the city's disregard for African American and Puerto Rican lives. As a result of these conditions, the walls separating social movements from prisoners' struggles "grew increasingly permeable."[8]

Most New Yorkers, however, gave little thought to the realities of life inside the city's jails.[9] At the time, male detainees were held at five facilities: the Manhattan Detention Center; two Queens Detention Center branches in Long Island City and Kew Gardens; the Brooklyn House of Detention; and Rikers Island. Women were confined at the Women's House of Detention, known as "the House of D."

This chapter explores jail and community protests across New York City in 1970. It traces the development of the emerging prisoners' rights movement and highlights the contributions of feminists of color who challenged both state violence and gender oppression within the criminal legal system.

The Women's House of Detention: Fixture of State Violence

From 1932 to 1974, the Women's House of Detention was a fixture of state violence and repression in New York City. Black feminist Audre Lorde described it as "a defiant pocket of female resistance, ever-present as a reminder of the possibility, as well as the punishment."[10] Located at the intersection of Greenwich Avenue, West Tenth Street, and Sixth Avenue, the eleven-story facility incarcerated poor and working-class women—most of them women of color—for crimes of survival, poverty, and desperation. Among its detainees were mothers, lesbians, sex workers, and political activists, young and elderly.

Over the course of its history, the House of D held numerous high-profile political activists. In 1950, Rosa Collazo and Carmen Torresola were incarcerated for nearly two months on $50,000 bail each,[11] accused of conspiring with their husbands—Puerto Rican Nationalists Oscar Collazo and Griselio Torresola, who had attempted to assassinate President Truman. According to historian Olga Jiménez de Wagenheim, both women were released in December 1950 after the prosecution failed to build a case.[12] However, following the 1954 nationalist-led attack on the House of Representatives, they were arrested again and convicted under the Smith Act—a statute criminalizing advocacy for the overthrow of the U.S. government.[13] Collazo was sentenced to six-years; Torresola to four. Both were later transferred to the Alderson Federal Prison in West Virginia, where they joined fellow nationalist Lolita Lebrón.[14]

In 1951, the House of D also held other prominent activists including Claudia Jones, a Black socialist feminist, and Elizabeth Gurley Flynn, a labor organizer and founding member of the American Civil Liberties Union. Both leaders of the U.S. Communist Party's Women's Commission were detained under the Smith Act for so-called "un-American activities." That same year, Ethel Rosenberg was also held at the House of D during her trial for espionage.

Two decades later, Black Panther leaders Afeni Shakur and Joan Bird were held on $100,000 bail each after their April 2, 1969, arrest in the case known as "the Panther 21." Charged with 156 counts of "conspiracy" to bomb subway and police stations, department stores, railroads, and the New York Botanical Gardens, both women were eventually acquitted of all charges. Their imprisonment drew national attention, sparked widespread protests, and further highlighted the plight of political prisoners. Frequent demonstrations in front of the jail forged solidarity between those detained inside and the activists on the outside.

On June 28, 1969, while Shakur and Bird were still incarcerated in the House of D, police raided the Stonewall Inn. What followed was an uprising led by "a mix of queens, gay men, and lesbians, most of them people of color, and many of them street kids."[15] In solidarity, some detainees at the House of D set fire to their few belongings and threw them from the barred windows while chanting "Gay power! Gay power!" according to Arcus Flynn, an early member of Daughters of Bilitis, one of the first lesbian organizations in the United States.[16] Later that year, the Gay Liberation Front organized around-the-clock protests outside the jail from Christmas through New Year's Day, calling for "peace, freedom, and the rights of all peoples."[17]

On March 7, 1970—International Women's Day—the Women's Caucus of Youth against War and Fascism (YAWF) led a rally in Union Square Park to reclaim the day's socialist feminist origins[18] by highlighting "the struggle of the most oppressed women,"[19] as YAWF member Deirdre Griswold later explained. Speakers included Flo Kennedy, a well-known African American feminist activist, and Iris Benítez, an information lieutenant in the Young Lords Organization. Benítez denounced the police killing of Antonia Martínez, a university student shot days earlier in Puerto Rico during protests against the U.S. Reserve Officers' Training Corps (ROTC). "The role of police and prisons are the same in Puerto Rico as in the United States," she declared, "to oppress poor and working people."

Following the rally, members of the Young Lords' Women's Caucus joined marchers heading downtown. "Marching from the rally to the House of Detention drew attention to the plight of poor and working-class women, in particular, and to women political prisoners,"[20] Griswold emphasized. Protesters carried huge banners demanding free and legal abortions, equal pay for equal work, an end to job discrimination, and freedom for women political prisoners. Outside the House of D, over a thousand demonstrators chanted, "Free our sisters! Free ourselves!"[21] In response, incarcerated women raised their fists through the barred windows in solidarity with the demonstrators below.

In the months that followed, demonstrations at the House of D continued. The jail became an important site—and symbol—of political resistance. In June 1970, marking the first anniversary of the Stonewall Rebellion, a coalition of gay, lesbian, trans, and supporters marched past the jail in solidarity with incarcerated women.[22] The following month, the Gay Liberation Front organized another protest against police harassment, culminating once again at the House of D.[23]

These actions brought together African American and Puerto Rican activists, white feminists, LBGTQ organizers, revolutionary nationalists, and incarcerated people in a shared demand to dismantle the oppressive systems of policing and incarceration.

City Jail Rebellions and the Fight for Justice, 1970

On the morning of August 10, 1970, a protest broke out inside the Tombs, New York City's notoriously overcrowded and brutal jail.[24] Inhumane living conditions and severe overcrowding had produced a full-blown human rights crisis. Although Mayor John Lindsay had received a scathing report about jail conditions, he had taken little action to remedy the situation.[25]

Prisoners at the Tombs outlined a long list of grievances: vicious daily beatings by guards, moldy and rotten food, vermin-infested cells, substandard medical care, inadequate legal representation, delayed trials, excessive bail, and restricted access to legal books.[26] Detainees also reported that guards made sexual slurs and lewd propositions to their mothers, wives, sisters, and girlfriends during visits. Furthermore, the jail lacked adequate bathing facilities, and showers were rare.[27]

The immediate catalyst for the uprising was the brutal beating of a Black detainee by three white guards.[28] In response, 225 men took five guards hostage.[29] Rejecting the narrative that the beating was the result of a few "bad apples," prisoners asserted that racial violence was endemic to the prison system.[30] Many identified with the politics of the Black Panther Party and the Young Lords. Inside the Tombs, they formed the Inmates Liberation Front (ILF), which soon emerged as a leading force in the uprising. Victor Martínez, its cofounder, later joined the Young Lords Party and affiliated the ILF as a "people's organization."

Fig. 13. Young Lord at rally in support of prison rebellions. 1970.
(Courtesy: Michael Abramson)

The protests soon spread to other city jails. As historian Heather Ann Thompson notes:

> More than 900 men at the Queens House of Detention in Kew Gardens, along with hundreds more at the dreaded Brooklyn House of Detention for Men and a group of young people on Rikers Island had also launched their own protests.[31]

On October 1, 1970, the Queens House of Detention in Long Island City erupted in protest. Demonstrators echoed grievances raised at the Tombs and added demands: more Spanish-speaking staff, access to the *Palante* and *Black Panther* newspapers, and the release of Afeni Shakur, then still held at the Women's House of Detention. Supporters gathered outside the Queens House of Detention in solidarity.

Among the leaders of the Queens protests were nine Black Panther Party members held in connection with the Panther 21 case.[32] They insisted that the criminal justice system imposed excessively high bail on poor and working-class prisoners and demanded that a judge come to the jail to hear bail reduction cases.[33] In an extraordinary development, three state Supreme Court justices arrived, acknowledged the inequities in bail practices, and released thirteen detainees that day.[34] Among them was Gilbert Jiménez, who later joined the Young Lords Party and organized with the Inmates Liberation Front.[35]

Despite this judicial victory, Police Commissioner Patrick V. Murphy and Mayor Lindsay ordered a violent retaking of the jails. By October 6, the uprisings had been forcibly suppressed. Once detainees were back in confinement, guards retaliated brutally against those who had participated in the protests.[36] Yet the horrific jail conditions that sparked the uprisings remained unaddressed.

Young Lords in the Tombs and Community Protests

On October 14, shortly after the jail uprisings, undercover narcotics agents arrested two Young Lords, Julio Roldán and Bobby Lemus. Accused of setting a fire in the vestibule of the East Harlem building where they lived, they were charged with first-degree arson. The arrests were part of a broader pattern of police harassment against the Young Lords, as described in Chapter 14. While in custody, Roldán and Lemus were abused by the police, denied access to their attorney, and processed without regard for their legal rights. The judge imposed $1,500 bail on each, and both were sent to the Tombs.

Before the Young Lords could raise bail, jail officials reported that Roldán had been found hanged in his cell, labeling the death a "suicide." It was one of several suspicious jail "suicides" reported by the police that year. The Young Lords, other activists, and community members be-lieved that Roldán had been murdered and immediately took to the streets in protest. As expected, the New York City Board of Corrections ruled the death a suicide,[37] despite the jail's responsibility for his safety. However, a pathologist hired by the Roldán family found evidence of

physical trauma consistent with a beating,[38]

Fig. 14. *Palante* cover. December 11, 1970.

More than 2,000 people marched through East Harlem in a funeral procession and protest. Representatives from Third World Left organi-zations served as pallbearers, including members of the Black Panther

Party, the Puerto Rican Student Union, Movimiento Pro Independencia, I Wor Kuen,[39] Justicia Latina, and Los Siete de la Raza.[40] The march led Roldán's casket to the People's Church on 111th Street and Lexington Avenue. Young Lords, armed with carbines and automatic weapons, entered the church with two hundred supporters[41] and opened the doors to the public. Thousands came to pay their respects.

Protestors issued two demands to the city: that it fund a defense center at the People's Church and that it allow local clergy to investigate jail conditions. Although the church's new pastor provided space for the Inmates Liberation Front to offer free legal services to the community, the city refused both demands, showing little political will to reform the prison system.

Fig. 15. Justicia Latina activists at Julio Roldán's funeral. 1970.
(Courtesy: Michael Abramson)

Anticipating a police raid on the church, the Young Lords' Central Committee formed a special squad of Young Lords to remain in the building and defend against the assault. Several men assigned to the squad called it a suicide mission and resigned from the organization.

However, the three women assigned to the squad remained until the end. The truth is, we were poorly equipped and inadequately trained.

As police surrounded the church, Mayor Lindsay's negotiators offered amnesty on the condition that no weapons would be found when the police entered.[42] With help from neighborhood residents, the Young Lords successfully removed all firearms, averting a bloodbath. The second takeover of the People's Church ended peacefully in early December 1970.

Conditions at the Women's House of D and the Bail Fund

Mecca Adai, a leading cadre in the Young Lords Party's Information Ministry, wrote an urgent appeal in *Palante* highlighting the dire conditions within the Women's House of Detention. She wrote:

> For the past few months, newspapers and magazines all over the country have been writing articles about the prisons. … [W]e can see that in every article the author deals only with what's been happening inside the concentration camps for men. No attention has been paid to our sisters who are being held inside of the Women's House of Detention. …

> [W]e write articles in *Palante* to educate our people about our sisters and to explain that we must fight for the liberation of all our people—not just for half of our population.[43]

The majority of women detainees at the House of D were African American or Puerto Rican, poor and working class, like their male counterparts in New York City jails. Most were incarcerated simply because they could not afford the $100 to $1,000 bail—which, for them, amounted to no bail at all.[44]

Adai chronicled the distinct forms of gendered and racist punishment that women faced from arrest through imprisonment. Lacking adequate legal representation, many saw their children placed in the foster care system. Inside the jail, women faced sexual and racial violence, exploitation, and degradation. Basic toiletries such as toothpaste and soap were often withheld; some were forced to trade sex for these necessities. Detainees labored in the jail's kitchens and laundries for wages of only two to ten cents an hour. Administrators deliberately promoted racial divisions among detainees, exacerbating conflict within the jail.[45] Adai also emphasized the lack of educational programs and support services.

Throughout 1970, several political prisoners were detained at the House of D, including Black Panther Party leaders Afeni Shakur and Joan Bird, held for ten and fifteen months, respectively. Angela Davis was also detained there for nine weeks between October and December 1970 while awaiting extradition to California on kidnapping and murder charges. Their cases garnered international publicity and highlighted the conditions faced not only by political prisoners but also by poor and working-class women of color.

Shakur described her experience at the Women's House of D in an article for *Palante*,[46] detailing the systemic cruelty and scorn poor women of color faced in the judicial system. Class-based, racist, and sexist assumptions drove the process at every step—from arrest and booking to court appearances and assignment of legal aid attorneys.[47] Shakur urged activists to organize "brigades of women" on the outside to build connections with detainees and advocate for their rights. Her vision of an "inside-outside" strategy became central to the prisoners' rights movement.[48]

Angela Davis also wrote about her time in the Women's House of Detention, emphasizing that "women's prisons have held on to oppressive patriarchal practices" and forms of state-sanctioned violence against women that receive little attention.[49] Specifically, Davis denounced the mandatory strip search—the internal examination of a woman's body cavities—explaining that a woman's refusal to submit landed her in solitary confinement.[50]

On December 20, 1970, a major protest in front of the Women's House of D, drew hundreds of African American, Puerto Rican, Asian, and white women. The rally called for bail reform, educational programs, and the rights of women political prisoners. Black Panther Joan Bird, recently released from the jail, led the crowd in songs and chants. "Hey Hey, Ho, Ho, House of D has gotta go," and "The rich set the bail, the poor go to jail!" Members from the Young Lords' Women's Caucus led chants in Spanish.[51] Inside the prison, women, including Angela Davis, waved down to the crowd in solidarity.

Fig. 16. Young Lords lineup for march. 1970

(Courtesy: Michael Abramson)

Speakers included women from the Black Panther Party, the YAWF, the Young Lords, I Wor Kuen, and the Puerto Rican Student Union.[52] They described the appalling jail conditions and demanded rights for incarcerated women. A new initiative was announced: a fund for women held on bail amounts under $500.[53]

Cheers erupted when a bail fund representative declared, "This morning, we secured the release of two detainees."[54] The Women's Bail Fund grew from a coalition of "Third World and White women," including members from the Black Panther Party, the Young Lords Party, the Anti-Imperialist Women's Collective, and Youth against War and Fascism.[55] For six months, the coalition had raised funds, circulated public information about injustices at the House of D, maintained contact with women inside the prison, and created legal information resources in English and Spanish.

The protests revealed how race, class, and gender intersect in the carceral system—and demonstrated the radical potential of collective resistance. As historian Tony Platt observes, "One important legacy was the successful effort to make the prison cell into an outpost of a broader agenda for social and economic equality."[56] Women activists advanced a vision of justice and solidarity that transcended prison walls.

Mass incarceration continues to disproportionately affect Black, Latinx, and Indigenous communities, who comprise over two-thirds of the incarcerated female population.[57] Historian Emily L. Thuma, author of *Our Trials*, notes that by 2019, the rate of women's imprisonment had increased eightfold since the 1970s.[58] Despite this staggering growth, incarcerated women remain largely invisible in public discourse and policy,[59] echoing Adai's warning from decades ago about the erasure of women in prison and their struggles for justice.

The 1970 jail uprisings and community protests in New York City constituted a bold, organized critique of racialized poverty, gendered punishment, and carceral power. The inside-outside organizing model they helped to pioneer remains foundational to contemporary movements for prison abolition and social justice.

10.
FREE PUERTO RICO NOW!
ORGANIZING WITH STUDENTS

> Unless we act now, we may be the last
> Puerto Ricans on this planet.[1]
>
> —Puerto Rican Student Union, 1970

Equal access to education was at the forefront of the national civil rights movement. The landmark 1954 U.S. Supreme Court ruling in *Brown v. Board of Education* declared the segregation of schools based on race unconstitutional, and the Civil Rights Act of 1964 prohibited discrimination in education. Yet despite these laws, access to public higher education for African American and other students of color remained largely inaccessible.

In New York City, educators, parents, community activists, students, and progressive politicians waged campaigns to open doors to higher education. During the 1960s, nearly one million African Americans and Puerto Ricans migrated to the city.[2] However, the student population at public universities failed to reflect the changing demographics. In 1961, the City University of New York (CUNY), the nation's first free public university system, was still 94 to 97 percent white and largely middle class.[3] The situation at the City College of New York (CCNY), located in Harlem, was "especially dissonant, having an almost entirely white student population."[4]

By the mid-1960s, the education rights movement had gained momentum. Public university officials began to discuss how to recruit "economically and educationally disadvantaged"[5] students. CCNY's Faculty Council agree to admit some New York City high school graduates who did not meet traditional admission criteria but were believed to have potential for successful college work.[6]

In the fall of 1965, CCNY launched a pilot "pre-baccalaureate" program, a five-year initiative where the first year would focus on remediation courses. The program enrolled 113 African American and Puerto Rican students from low-income neighborhoods, including myself.

Among my classmates were Henry Arce, Eduardo "Pancho" Cruz, Francine Covington, Khadija DeLoache, Mary McRae, Cenen Moreno, Louis Reyes Rivera, and Sekou Sundiata—each of whom would go on to make important contributions in the arts, politics, and community leadership. Our first professors included passionate and dedicated educators such as Allen Ballard, Toni Cade Bambara, Barbara Christian, Addison Gayle, and Anthony Penale.

The "pre-bac" program offered low-income students of color a long-denied opportunity for a college education. However, at the end of its first year, the program faced elimination due to budget cuts. In response, administrators and faculty mobilized, arranging for buses to Albany to petition the legislature for continued funding. Eager to ensure the program's survival, students rallied behind the cause. I was among five students chosen to speak before legislators in defense of the program.

Our collective advocacy proved successful. Not only did the legislature restore funding, but it expanded the program to other CUNY senior colleges. This victory led to the creation of SEEK (Search for Education, Elevation, and Knowledge)—a major step forward in the struggle for educational equity.

SEEK opened the doors of higher education to the first generation of Puerto Rican students in New York City in historically significant numbers. Most from working-class families were the first in their households to attend college. To navigate the university system, Puerto Rican students formed advocacy organizations. At City College, I joined Henry Arce, Eduardo "Pancho" Cruz, and others to form Puerto Ricans Involved in Student Action (PRISA) in the spring of 1968. At Lehman College, Hildamar Ortiz and Myrna Martínez cofounded UNICA in 1969.[7] Puerto Rican students joined forces with African American students to demand increased admission of students of color, the establishment of Puerto Rican and African American studies, and the hiring of African American and Puerto Rican professors.

On April 22, 1969, a coalition of African American and Puerto Rican students at City College walked out of classes, renamed the institution "Harlem University," and occupied the campus for two weeks. The demands included the creation of a "School of Black and Puerto Rican studies" and admission policies "reflective of the city's high school population." Similar protests quickly spread throughout the CUNY system, sparking sit-ins and rallies at Brooklyn College, Queens College, Queensborough Community College, Bronx Community College, and the Borough of Manhattan Community College.[8] African American and Latinx communities rallied in overwhelming support of the students' demands.

By July 1969, negotiations with CUNY administrators led to a groundbreaking policy: open admissions.[9] The Board of Higher Education guaranteed every New York City high school graduate a seat at a CUNY college. The agreement also mandated the establishment of Black and Puerto Rican studies programs across all twenty-five campuses in the largest urban university system in the United States.

The Rise of the Puerto Rican Student Union (PRSU)

By the fall of 1969, Puerto Rican student groups across New York City were coordinating efforts across campuses to address educational issues and raise awareness about politics in Puerto Rico. That November, Puerto Rican student and community groups gathered at St. Mark's Church in the Lower East Side to support Edwin Feliciano Grafals,[10] a member of the *Movimiento Pro Independencia* (MPI), who had been sentenced to one year in prison for resisting induction into the U.S. army.

At the same time, students at the University of Puerto Rico (UPR) held protests at the ROTC building in San Juan, denouncing Grafals' sentence and the broader injustice of Puerto Rican men being drafted into the U.S. military—while many college men in the United States received deferments. Seven students were arrested during those demonstrations.[11]

In response, Puerto Rican activists in New York mobilized in support. Mirta González, a Young Lord in the Information Ministry, reported in the *Y.L.O.* newsletter:

> "A number of Puerto Rican organizations formed a committee to publicize and defend the struggle and repression against the freedom fighters on the island."[12]

Under the name "Puerto Rican United Front," the ad hoc group organized fundraising for the arrested students, sent dozens of protest telegrams to Puerto Rico's colonial government and to UPR officials, issued a joint press release, and circulated information throughout the United

States. The committee included representatives from several organizations: L.U.C.H.A [13] (New York University), PRISA (City College), UNICA[14] (Lehman College), and United Puerto Rican Students (Rutgers University–Newark), along with the MPI and the Young Lords Organization.

Fig. 17. *¡Despierta Boricua!* Graphic, *Palante*. 1970.

These cross-campus organizing efforts laid the foundation for a growing Puerto Rican student movement. In December 1969, more than one hundred students from fifteen colleges and universities across the New York metropolitan area convened for a two-day conference. At that gathering, the Puerto Rican Student Union (PRSU), or *La Unión Estudiantil Boricua,* was born.[15]

The mission of the PRSU was threefold: to advocate for the rights of Puerto Rican college students, to organize in defense of Puerto Rican communities in the United States, and to support Puerto Rico's independence movement. During the conference, participants heard reports of the Young Lords' takeover of the People's Church in East Harlem. In a show of solidarity, a contingent of PRSU members went to join the occupation. When it ended, ten PRSU members were among those arrested.[16]

In March 1970, the PRSU opened a storefront office on East 138th Street in the Bronx. Carrying out its commitment to student–community unity, members worked alongside local residents to clean and transform an abandoned lot across the street. The space, named *La Plaza Borinqueña*, became a site for political and cultural events.

In the years that followed, PRSU members remained active in broader movements for justice. They organized campaigns around tenants' rights, access to health care, and police brutality,[17] while also leading educational initiatives on Puerto Rico's colonial status and the struggle for independence.

Campaign to Support the Independence of Puerto Rico

From the outset, the Puerto Rican Student Union and the Young Lords Organization maintained a close, collaborative relationship. Many Young Lords had been active in early Puerto Rican student struggles, and the PRSU was among the first organizations to support the Young Lords. They were united by a commitment to social justice and Puerto Rico's national liberation.

In the fall of 1970, the PRSU and the Young Lords organized two major initiatives to build momentum for Puerto Rico's independence struggle: the first Puerto Rican student conference in the United States and a mass demonstration at the United Nations.

Hildamar Ortiz and I served as lead coordinators of the student conference, representing the PRSU and the YLP, respectively. Held at Columbia University on September 23-24, the two-day event drew more than 1,000 students.[18] A central aim was to encourage the formation of "Free Puerto Rico" or "Liberate Puerto Rico Now!" committees at high school and colleges across the country.

Flavia Rivera, of *La Federación Universitaria Pro Independencia de Puerto Rico* (FUPI), delivered the keynote address, reporting on student struggles in Puerto Rico. Denise Oliver of the Young Lords' Central Committee spoke about the role students have historically played in liberation movements.

Puerto Rican and African American women activists co-led workshops on Puerto Rican history and culture, women's roles in revolutionary movements, political prisoners, Third World solidarity, education and media, and socialism. On the conference's final day, I announced that several "Liberate Puerto Rico Now!" had been formed at various schools and reminded participants of the forthcoming demonstration to the United Nations.[19] After the conference, attendees marched to *La Plaza Borinqueña* to rally for independence.

Fig. 18. Puerto Rican Student Conference. September 1970.
Hildamar Ortiz and Iris Morales make opening remarks.
(Courtesy: Michael Abramson)

On Friday, October 30, 1970—twenty years after the 1950 Jayuya uprising—thousands gathered at 125th Street and Lexington Avenue in Harlem to march to the United Nations on 47th Street. With 10,000 marchers, the demonstration brought international attention to Puerto Rico's colonial status. A broad coalition took part, including the Black Panther Party, *El Comité, El Frente Estudiantil Revolucionario Dominicano,* FUPI, the Gay Liberation Front, the Health Revolutionary Unity Movement, I Wor Kuen, Justicia Latina, MPI, *Resistencia Puertorriqueña,* STAR, Third World Gay Liberation, Third World Women's Alliance, Youth Against War and Fascism, among others.

The march raised three core demands: an end to colonialism in Puerto Rico, an end to police brutality in local communities, and the release of Puerto Rican Nationalist political prisoners: Oscar Collazo, Lolita Lebrón, Rafael Cancel Miranda, Andrés Figueroa Cordero, Irvin Flores Rodríguez, and Carlos Feliciano. As noted earlier, Collazo was sentenced to life imprisonment for the 1950 attempt on President Truman. Lebrón, Cancel Miranda, Figueroa Cordero, and Flores Rodríguez received sentences of up to seventy-five years for the 1954 attack on the U.S. House of Representatives. [20] Feliciano, accused in a series of New York bombings, was later acquitted in 1975.

The choice of October 30 for the demonstration was deeply symbolic. As described in Chapter 2, in 1950, the Nationalist Party had launched coordinated uprisings in eleven towns—including Jayuya, Peñuelas, Utuado, Ponce, San Juan, Mayagüez, Arecibo, and Naranjito[21]—to demand Puerto Rico's independence and draw global attention to the archipelago's colonial status. In Jayuya, Nationalists seized the police station, and Blanca Canales raised the Puerto Rican flag in the town plaza, proclaiming the Republic of Puerto Rico.

The U.S. and Puerto Rican governments responded with overwhelming force. President Truman declared martial law. Army and Air Force military planes, artillery, and ground forces bombarded Jayuya, crushing the revolt.[22] More than twenty-three Nationalists were killed, and many others wounded or arrested.[23]

In a public broadcast, Puerto Rico's Governor Luis Muñoz Marin declared support for the U.S. intervention and denounced the uprising as "a conspiracy against democracy helped by the Communists."[24] Blanca Canales was sentenced to life imprisonment plus sixty years by the District Court of Arecibo and the U.S. Federal Court in San Juan to be served at Alderson Federal Prison in West Virginia.[25]

While at Alderson, Canales met Claudia Jones, a Trinidad-born Black feminist, anti-imperialist, and U.S. Communist Party member. Jones's FBI file described her as an "enemy of the state."[26] Jones had been fighting deportation since 1948 and had been detained at various locations, including Ellis Island and the Women's House of Detention in New York City. In 1955, she was deported to London, where she continued her activism until her death.[27]

During their time at Alderson, Jones and Canales developed a friendship grounded in their anti-imperialist beliefs and shared political commitments. Jones wrote a poem dedicated to Canales, titled *For Consuela—Anti-Fascista*.[28] It opens with the following verse:

> It seems I knew you long before our common ties—
>   of conscious choice
> Threw under single skies, those like us
> Who, fused by our mold
> Became their targets, as of old.

The poem concludes with these lines:

> We swear that we will never rest
> Until they hear not plea
> But sainted sacrifice to set
> A small proud nation free
>
> O anti-fascist sister—you whose eye turn to stars still
> I've learned your wondrous secret—source of spirit and
>   of will
> I've learned that what sustains your heart—
>   mind and peace of soul
> Is knowledge that their justice—can never reach its goal.

As scholar Carole Boyce Davies notes, the poem "recognizes the power of women in leadership positions in the political struggle for radical social change" and highlights the solidarity between Jones and Canales as Caribbean sisters engaged in a shared "politics of decolonization."[29]

In 1956, Blanca Canales was transferred to a prison in Puerto Rico. She was released in 1967 after receiving a pardon from Governor Roberto Sánchez Vilella. Until her death in 1996, Canales remained a steadfast advocate for Puerto Rico's independence.[30]

Fig. 19. United Nations demonstration. October 30, 1970.

(Courtesy: Michael Abramson)

PART IV.
Nationalisms and Feminisms

Río Grande de Loíza! … Great river.
Great flood of tears. The greatest of all
our island's tears save those greater
that come from the eyes of my soul
for my enslaved people.[1]

—Julia de Burgos, "Río Grande de Loíza," 1938

11.
"Rebellion Rushin' Down the Wrong Road"[1]

> [W]e have to think of two analyses because
> we have to think of two struggles which are
> interrelated and at the same time not related…
> In other words, we have to make one analysis
> for the Puerto Rican nation that includes Puerto Rico…
> then another one for the Puerto Ricans who are
> struggling in the United States.[2]
>
> —Pablo "Yoruba" Guzmán, Minister of Information,
> Young Lords Party, 1971

The Young Lords Party closed 1970 with a remarkable record of victories in the fight for social justice. Over the course of the year, the organization's political ideas and direct-action strategies gained widespread support, leading to the creation of new chapters and affiliated groups across the northeastern United States—including in New York, Pennsylvania, Connecticut, Massachusetts, and New Jersey. Through community organizing, bold protests, strategic alliances, and savvy media engagement, the Young Lords reshaped public discourse, influenced policy, and sparked reforms in Puerto Rican communities across the United States.

Reflecting on these activities, Minister of Information Pablo "Yoruba" Guzmán wrote "Why a Young Lords Party?" in *Palante's* December 1970 issue. He concludes:

> There would be no Young Lords Party if there were no capitalism and no racism. Since both exist, a force has arisen to stamp both evils out. We also are on the move against a force just as deadly: machismo.[3]

Guzmán's statement underscored that the Young Lords Party emerged in response to systemic oppression. By naming machismo "a force just as deadly" as capitalism and racism, he affirmed that sexism was also a primary concern. His analysis—linking capitalism, racism, and machismo as interconnected systems—echoed the perspectives of U.S. socialist feminists of color and marked a break with nationalist frameworks that treated the liberation of women as a secondary priority. Notably, this marked the first time a Central Committee member had endorsed this position, and it reflected Guzmán's own political growth and evolution. His statement energized the liberatory hopes of Puerto Rican and African American women members.

Around this time, in late December 1970, the Central Committee—composed of Juan González, Pablo "Yoruba" Guzmán, David Pérez, Juan 'Fi' Ortiz, Denise Oliver, and Gloria González—held a retreat to evaluate the Young Lords' activities since that September and to chart a course for the year ahead. As the first major meeting following Felipe Luciano's demotion and Gloria González's promotion, the retreat carried heightened importance.

Over eight days, the group met and produced a twenty-two-page document titled *Report of Central Committee Evaluation and Retreat*. In it, Field Marshal David Pérez summarized the key decisions made.[4] First, the Young Lords Party would open branches in Puerto Rico. Second, it would shift the focus of U.S. organizing toward developing "people's organizations."

This chapter examines the change in the Young Lords' priorities and the consequences for gender and racial justice organizing.

The "Divided Nation" Debate

The Central Committee retreat centered on two critical questions: What role should Puerto Ricans in the United States play in Puerto Rico's independence struggle? And what should be the relationship of the Young Lords Party to Puerto Rico?

Field Marshal Gloria González took the lead and presented the concept of a "divided nation." She theorized that Puerto Ricans constituted one nation, geographically separated, with one-third exiled in the United States severed from the two-thirds living in Puerto Rico.[5] According to González, the divided nation needed to be reunited, and she proposed establishing YLP branches in the archipelago for this purpose. The idea of Puerto Ricans as one people—who were divided—had powerful nationalist appeal.

In her section of the retreat report, González wrote that the Central Committee had first considered opening branches in Puerto Rico during the summer of 1970. She stated that Juan González and Juan "Fi" Ortiz had traveled to the archipelago in August "to begin preparations to unite the nation."[6] However, in an account in the *Palante* newspaper, Juan González and Ortiz contradicted her version. They wrote:

> The purpose of this trip was to make a formal and official contact with other political parties, push the student conference [September 23], and get a better sense of the realities of the political situation in Puerto Rico.[7]

Hence, as far as the Young Lords membership and general public were aware, the trip was exploratory—intended to gather information about the political situation in Puerto Rico. This made it all the more surprising when Gloria González revealed in her report that the Central Committee had, in fact, secretly (*clandestinamente*) voted in September to begin preparations for the YLP expansion to the archipelago.[8]

At the retreat, Juan González, Gloria González, and Pérez pushed for opening YLP branches in Puerto Rico. Guzmán, Oliver, and Ortiz replied, "The people of Puerto Rico will lead the struggle for national liberation." They emphasized that the Young Lords had zero experience in Puerto Rico and insisted that the role of the Young Lords was to organize with Puerto Ricans in the United States.

Unlike the proponents—who were born in Puerto Rico—Guzmán, Ortiz, and Oliver were U.S.-born and raised: Afro-Boricuas and African Americans who identified with the Black freedom movement and U.S.-based social justice struggles. In addition, during their visits to the archipelago, they encountered anti-Black racism, class elitism, and gender bias—even within the pro-independence movement. "How will the Young Lords Party tackle these issues?" they asked. Clarification about the fight against racism in Puerto Rico was a consideration for them.

Gloria González responded that the YLP would focus on organizing Puerto Rico's most exploited sectors: "the working class, the poor, the lumpen, *the jíbaro*, and the Afro-Puertorriqueño."[9] She maintained that Puerto Rico's working class lacked revolutionary leadership, and that pro-independence organizations, such as the Movimiento Pro Independencia (MPI) and the Puerto Rican Independence Party (PIP), were largely led by members of the middle and upper classes. González argued that the Young Lords could fill this leadership vacuum and "reunify the nation."[10] However, she offered no explanation of what "reunification" would entail or how the U.S.-based organization would bridge two different realities—one rooted in colonial subjugation, the other lived within the colonizer's borders.

Beneath the surface, the debate also raised a struggle over identity—about who counted as authentically Puerto Rican—a question debated across the Puerto Rican Left. A form of "linguistic chauvinism also emerged, privileging Spanish over English"[11] as a marker of authenticity. Notably, González's four-page explanation of the "divided nation" was written in Spanish—which many Young Lords could not read. As the only Central Committee member to write in Spanish, she positioned herself as the "most authentic" Puerto Rican among the leadership, introducing a narrow nationalist position into the debate. In her view, a "real" Puerto Rican would support the Young Lords' move to the archipelago.

When the Central Committee members voted, the outcome was to open YLP branches in Puerto Rico. David Pérez's report presented the result as a consensus and affirmed the "new political lines," but this did not tell the whole story. In fact, the vote had ended in a tie: three in favor, three opposed. Juan González, as Minister of Defense and the highest-ranking member, cast the deciding vote in favor to proceed with establishing YLP branches in the archipelago. Guzmán, Oliver, and Ortiz—despite their strong objections—accepted the outcome, deferring to an interpretation of democratic centralism put forward by the proponents, arguing that the highest-ranking member held the authority to break a tie. However, democratic centralism does not inherently grant this tie-breaking right, which must be decided by the organization.

The decision left a bitter aftertaste and opened a Pandora's box of internal conflict. Why move forward with such a consequential step without full consensus? Given the split vote, why not consult the general membership or delay allowing time for deeper investigation and evaluation? What urgency justified this rush—especially from an organization barely a year and a half old? And ultimately, whose interests did this move serve? These questions remained unresolved and unanswered.

Internal Struggles with Male Chauvinism Continue

While the debate over expanding to Puerto Rico dominated the December 1970 retreat, the Central Committee also held extended discussions on male chauvinism and the role of women within the organization. This was not surprising, given ongoing tensions with the Women's Caucus and the first-time participation of two women—Denise Oliver and Gloria González—on the Central Committee.

The retreat report acknowledged that male chauvinism persisted across the organization. It cited low number of women officers and admitted several women with clear leadership potential had not been promoted—though it offered no explanation for why. The report vaguely declared, "Extra efforts must be made to educate sisters out of passivity and prepare them to become officers." Yet it failed to define what those efforts would entail—and in practice, none materialized.

The Central Committee also admitted that the *Palante* newspaper reflected a male-dominated perspective. One member remarked, "A normal working woman would find little to interest her"—highlighting the need to expand the paper's focus. Seeking to push the conversation further, Denise Oliver introduced the concept of "sexism," defining it as an ideology rooted in the belief that men are inherently superior to women. In response, the Central Committee agreed to revisit and discuss the meaning of sexism in future meetings—but took no other action.

Meanwhile, the retreat report reprimanded members for failing to adequately study the "YLP Position Paper on Women" and instructed cadres to memorize entire sections and be prepared to discuss them.[12] The position paper reflected the foundational role of the Women's Caucus in pushing the Young Lords Party in a more progressive direction. Caucus members had advanced women's rights, created space for feminist organizing, and played an important role in recruiting and developing new cadres.

Throughout 1970, the Central Committee responded to nearly all ten demands put forth by the Women's Caucus—except one: the right of women to caucus. Given the caucus's significant contributions, it was surprising to read in the report that it had been disbanded. The Central Committee wrote, "The female caucus is not the right solution.... Separate caucuses are not the answer."[13] With that statement, both the Women's and Men's Caucuses—spaces vital for political discussion, organizing strategy, and collective growth—were dismantled. Many Young Lords credited these caucuses with expanding their understanding of gender oppression and aiding both personal and political transformation. Nonetheless, the Central Committee made the decision without consulting the general membership.

The homosexual caucuses eventually met face the same fate the next year. In retrospect, it appears that the proponents of the Puerto Rico project sought to eliminate internal groupings that might challenge or complicate their political objectives.

Ironically, the Central Committee's retreat report included a section titled "Democratic Centralism." It emphasized general membership meetings and open dialogue as "the core of democracy in the Party"[14] and stressed the importance of involving the rank and file in debate and decision-making. In practice, however, the Central Committee bypassed these participatory processes, excluding the general membership from critical decisions. Rather than open dialogue and debate, the leadership imposed its agenda from above. Unilateral decisions—such as the expansion to Puerto Rico and the disbanding of the Women's and Men's Caucuses—directly contradicted the democratic values the leadership claimed to uphold. These actions ran counter to the principles of democratic centralism, which were intended to promote unity, active engagement, and shared decision-making.

The Central Committee's clandestine and unilateral actions profoundly undermined the integrity of the Young Lords Party. Though the retreat report was filled with lofty rhetoric and ambitious declarations, it was riddled with contradictions, vague commitments, and a lack of concrete plans. These decisions—and omissions—set the organization on a precarious course.

Emerging Authoritarian Leadership in Central Committee

Following the retreat, the Central Committee convened a general membership meeting in early January 1971 and distributed the *Report of the Central Committee Evaluation and Retreat* to every Young Lord. We had been anxiously awaiting it. On that cold, overcast day, I couldn't help but wonder if a storm was coming.

The most striking announcement in the report was the decision to open Young Lords Party branches in Puerto Rico. It was presented as a fait accompli—with no acknowledgment of dissent within the leadership or the arguments raised against the move. Instead, Central Committee members merely asked the cadre, "What do you think about the plan to open branches in Puerto Rico?"

A flood of thoughts raced through my mind: the long history of U.S. colonialism in Puerto Rico, the struggles of the Nationalist Party, the sacrifices of past generations. I imagined many Young Lords shared similar thoughts and feelings, given our deep connection to Puerto Rico. Some immediately embraced the idea of opening branches in Puerto Rico, romanticizing it as a direct confrontation with U.S. colonialism. A few even suggested that the organization shut down and relocate to Puerto Rico. But many others, myself included, disagreed. We believed that the Young Lords' primary mission was to fight for the rights of Puerto Ricans living in the United States and continue to advocate for the end of colonialism in Puerto Rico.

Most of us expected a discussion—not a rushed poll. We had questions: Why was the Central Committee pursuing this direction? How would it affect our organizing efforts in the United States? What would it mean to operate branches in two countries? Would the Young Lords in Puerto Rico follow the 13-Point Program or create their own? Where would funds for the expansion come from? How would the Young Lords collaborate with organizations in Puerto Rico? What strategies would the Central Committee adopt to combat racism in Puerto Rico? How would the YLP continue advancing women's rights? Who would be assigned to go? And when would the move occur?

All Young Lords were unequivocally committed to the decolonization of Puerto Rico. Our concerns about the Central Committee's decision to open branches in Puerto Rico stemmed from how many questions remained unanswered. Despite the gung-ho attitude, no concrete plan was offered for how the move would unfold. The process felt rushed and disorganized. Without adequate information, we were left confused and unable to fully grasp its implications—or stakes—of what this shift meant for the future of the Young Lords Party.

Carlos Aponte, a captain in the Education Ministry and a highly respected member since January 1970, asked the Central Committee about the decision. Aponte—a 25-year-old Vietnam War veteran trained as a medic—had previously organized with the Peace and Freedom Party and the Black Panthers in California.

Shortly after the retreat report circulated, the Central Committee summoned more than fifty members to a special meeting. It quickly became clear that the focus was on Aponte—not to answer his questions, but to put him on trial.

Aponte was subjected to an intense interrogation that probed every corner of his life—his childhood, military service, political activism before joining the Young Lords, his record as a member, and even his relationship with his wife.[15] Gloria and Juan González led the charge, accusing Aponte of being a police informant and claiming he had received training at a CIA base. The so-called "evidence" amounted to little more than insinuation, name-calling, character attacks, and guilt by association. They cited his four years in the Air Force, his attendance at early meetings of the Puerto Rican Student Union, and even his travel to Cuba as supposed proof of his betrayal.[16]

At the conclusion of the interrogation, the Central Committee expelled Aponte from the Young Lords Party and labeled him "one of the highest-level agents" in the organization.[17] His photograph and biography were published in the *Palante* newspaper, with those of other alleged agents.[18]

Shocked and humiliated, Aponte wrote a twelve-page letter to the Central Committee vigorously refuting the allegations and criticizing the lack of evidence and the methods used against him.[19] He outlined his contributions to the movement—first as a student, then as a community organizer in all three Young Lords' branches in New York City—and requested a people's trial to clear his name. The Central Committee denied his request.[20] Years later, Juan González expressed regret for the leading role he played in what he called "the sham trial."[21]

The vicious grilling of Aponte sent shockwaves through the organization and the political movement. It provoked anxiety, seeded mistrust, and fueled fear among the cadre. Many began to worry that asking questions could result in being branded an informant. While we understood that the move to Puerto Rico was a major shift, few of us grasped the full extent of its consequences once implemented. Even fewer of us foresaw that it was merely the first step in a tsunami that would fundamentally reshape the Young Lords Party.

Around this time, the book *Palante: The Young Lords Party* was published, including an essay by Minister of Information Pablo "Yoruba" Guzmán[22] that discussed the relationship between the Puerto Rican struggles in the United States and those in Puerto Rico. Guzmán argued for analyzing the specific conditions of each separately—one analysis for the Puerto Rican nation and another for Puerto Ricans in the United States—to shape the organization's strategy accordingly. Many of us assumed this essay reflected the Central Committee's approach. However, we later learned that Guzmán's proposal was rejected by the Puerto Rico project proponents.

Restructuring the Young Lords Party: A Shift in Focus

From January to July 1971, the Central Committee focused on the move to Puerto Rico, which was named *Ofensiva Rompe Cadenas,* or the "Break the Chains Offensive." Minister of Defense Juan González outlined its goal: "The slogan we should remember is 'Consolidate the base' (U.S. branches) to 'prepare the front' (Puerto Rico)."[23]

During this period, the *Palante* newspaper expanded its coverage of Puerto Rico's history and politics to deepen awareness of colonial conditions. In the first issue of 1971, *Palante* named Luis A. Ferré—Puerto Rico's governor and founder of the pro-statehood New Progressive Party—as "Pig of the Year."[24] The article denounced Ferré for exploiting the people of Puerto Rico, declaring, "You are doing nothing but selling our people down the drain." It cited his millionaire status, extensive banking and business interests, and the 35 percent unemployment rate under his tenure.

To further contextualize the struggle, *Palante* launched a thirteen-part series titled "History of Borikén," tracing the archipelago's evolution from its Indigenous origins through Spanish colonization and the enslavement of Indigenous and African peoples. It examined pivotal events such as the Spanish-Cuban-American War, when 18,000 U.S. troops invaded Guánica, Puerto Rico on July 25, 1898.[25] Spain soon ceded Puerto Rico to the United States, which swiftly imposed policies to "Americanize" the population and manufacture consent for colonial rule,[26] including making English the official language.

From 1900 to 1946, U.S. politicians, military officers, and appointed governors ruled Puerto Rico, parading their contempt for the people while enabling U.S. corporate exploitation of its land and resources. In 1917, Congress passed the Jones Act, making Puerto Ricans U.S. citizens subject to the military draft, yet denying Puerto Ricans the right to vote in presidential elections or elect congressional representatives.

Fig. 20. *Palante* newspaper. "Why Rebellion?" 1971.

U.S. colonial policies intensified poverty. In 1930, the Puerto Rican Nationalist Party elected Pedro Albizu Campos—an Afro-Boricua and Harvard Law School graduate—as president. Under his leadership, the party intensified demands to end U.S. colonial rule. In retaliation, the Puerto Rican government, backed by the United States, passed Law 53, known as the Gag Law (*Ley de la Mordaza*), to crush the pro-independence movement. The law criminalized the display of the Puerto Rican flag, singing patriotic songs, speaking, writing or public assembly in favor of independence. Violators faced up to ten years in prison, fines up to $10,000, or both. Hundreds of activists were arrested.

These legacies were foundational to the Young Lords Party's commitment to Puerto Rico's liberation and to *Ofensiva Rompe Cadenas.*

The move to Puerto Rico required a major shift in political focus, financial resources, and personnel. With whirlwind speed, the Central Committee restructured the Young Lords Party—shuffling people into new assignments, shutting down "serve the people" programs, and abandoning local offices across U.S. neighborhoods. Cadres were redirected to a newly created unit—the Committee to Defend the Community—which had no physical location. The East Harlem office, once a vibrant hub of Young Lords activity was closed. People in the community began to ask, "Where are the Young Lords?"

Gloria González defended the drastic cutbacks, explaining, "In order for us to move forward in one area—preparing for the move to Puerto Rico—we had to sacrifice in the area of community work."[27]

The shift strained the YLP's already limited finances and volunteer base. Disillusioned, members began to leave the organization rather than take part in what they viewed as a misguided policy. For some, it felt like "a rebellion rushin' down the wrong road."

As the Young Lords' activities waned in the United States, other organizations filled the void. The Movimiento Pro Independencia (MPI), originally focused on building support for Puerto Rico's independence movement within the United States was influenced by the Young Lords' earlier organizing.[28] MPI leaders began to reconceptualize their mission[29] and made what they described as "a strategic decision" to begin organizing for the rights of Puerto Ricans living in the United States, while continuing to support the independence movement in Puerto Rico.[30]

12.
THE WOMEN'S UNION AND THE 12-POINT PROGRAM

> Whenever any people are victims of abuse,
> it's only natural that they fight against it.
> The Third World Woman, as the most
> oppressed person in the world today,
> is no exception.[1]

—The Women's Union, *La Luchadora*, 1971

Throughout 1971, as *Ofensiva Rompe Cadenas* unfolded in Puerto Rico, the Young Lords in the United States focused on building "people's organizations"—independent, democratic entities designed to bring together diverse constituencies around shared interests. This strategy was rooted in the belief that revolutionary change required broad, organized participation across multiple sectors, such as labor, health, education, criminal justice, and others where people united to fight for collective goals. Within these organizations, the role of Young Lords cadre was to advance revolutionary politics, cultivate new leadership, and help grow the broader social justice movement. Field Marshal David Pérez described these groups as "the mass movement the Party leads," adding, "If we serve, guide, and protect them, they will definitely follow us."[2]

Among the most significant YLP-affiliated peoples' organizations were the Health Revolutionary Unity Movement (HRUM) and the Puerto Rican Student Union (PRSU), discussed in earlier chapters. HRUM and PRSU connected the Young Lords Party to thousands of healthcare workers and working-class students. Both were independent networks with distinct leadership structures and political priorities. Young Lords who participated in these organizations engaged in their political work while promoting the Party's broader agenda.

The Inmates Liberation Front (ILF), a leading force in the 1970 jail uprisings in New York City, also affiliated as a people's organization. Pérez described the ILF as "the organizing group of the lumpen,"[3] emphasizing that "the two most important parts of Puerto Rican society were the lumpen and the workers."[4] The YLP defined the *lumpen* as those discarded by capitalist society: the unemployable, incarcerated, drug-addicted, and welfare dependent.[5] Although the ILF's relationship with the Young Lords Party was short-lived, it had a notable impact in raising awareness of specific injustices affecting incarcerated people.

Alongside these existing groups, the Central Committee prioritized creating new people's organizations. Many were proposed, with establishing a "Workers' Federation" in New York City—focused on organizing workers in factories and other workplaces identified as the political priority. On the Central Committee, Gloria González assumed this responsibility. I was assigned to create a Women's Union (WU) as a people's organization.

This chapter traces the founding of the Women's Union and its evolving relationship with the Young Lords Party.

Confronting Gender, Racial, and Class Oppression

During the 1960s and 1970s, African American women and Latinas in the United States faced severe economic, social, and political conditions, highlighting the urgent need for a movement addressing gender, racial, and class oppression. Government officials and corporate media alike vilified poor and working-class women of color, portraying them as burdens on the welfare system and unfit to lead their families or communities.

In 1965, Assistant Secretary of Labor Daniel Patrick Moynihan released his controversial report, *The Negro Family: The Case for National Action*,[6] which quickly gained influence across the mainstream political spectrum.[7] According to historian Chong Chon-Smith, Moynihan argued that the root cause of cyclical poverty in Black urban communities was the absence of nuclear families and the growing dependence on welfare programs.[8] Moynihan described "unstable" Black family structures as producing a so-called "tangle of pathology"—a set of conditions manifested in delinquency, joblessness, school failure, crime, and fatherlessness.[9] Ultimately, he blamed the African American "matriarchy" as the primary obstacle to racial advancement.

Moynihan's assertions reinforced racialized, class-based narratives used to justify conservative attacks on working-class and poor Black

146

communities.[10] Along with other officials, he promoted stereotypes of African American women and Latinas as welfare-dependent, lazy free-loaders, and unfit mothers. Corporate media amplified these portrayals, blaming women of color for failed parenting, raising unemployable workers, and perpetuating generational poverty.

Black feminists swiftly condemned Moynihan's conclusions, denouncing the report as racist, sexist, and rooted in capitalist ideology. They demanded greater economic opportunities for both African American women and men. Civil rights activist Pauli Murray blasted Moynihan's claims about African American "matriarchy," calling them "a grave disservice to the thousands of Negro women in the United States who have struggled to prepare themselves for employment in a limited job market."[11]

The National Organization for Women (NOW) similarly rejected Moynihan's report, stating:

> People are poor for one reason—the economic system in the United States is not structured to eliminate poverty, and it is not intended to be. It depends upon a cheap reserve of labor—extracted primarily from women and minorities and especially minority women.[12]

Decades later, anthropologist and activist, Susan Greenbaum revisited the report in her essay "Where's the Obituary for the Moynihan Report?" In her critique, she wrote:

> The Moynihan Report was misguided in conception and defective in its research. It survives today only because it feeds the narrative that poor people cause their own problems, and the economy is not to blame.[13]

Despite sustained critique from scholars, activists, and feminist organizers, the ideas embedded in the Moynihan Report continue to shape public discourse and influence racial, gender, and class inequality in policymaking.

Building a Feminist People's Organization: The Women's Union

Organizing for the Women's Union began in East Harlem in early 1971, with Young Lords distributing flyers throughout the neighborhood. I served as lead organizer, while Gloria González was appointed liaison since she was the sole woman on the Central Committee after Denise Oliver's resignation that February. The *Palante* newspaper had briefly noted Oliver's departure but omitted any mention of her opposition to the Young Lords Party's expansion to Puerto Rico.

Oliver's resignation critically altered the balance of power within the Central Committee. A faction composed of Juan González, Gloria González, and David Pérez began driving decision-making, often overruling Pablo "Yoruba" Guzmán and Juan "Fi" Ortiz. Oliver's departure also weakened the organization's feminist politics. As the only socialist feminist on the Central Committee, Oliver had advanced perspectives that were increasingly sidelined after her exit.

Gloria González, by contrast, had refused to join the Women's Caucus and ultimately voted to disband it. Given this history, I was skeptical of her commitment to fight for women's rights. However, her involvement in forming the Women's Union was minimal because she was in Puerto Rico opening Young Lords' branches.

I advanced the Women's Union according to the proposed framework for a people's organization: independent, with its own leadership, political priorities, and membership. By April 1971, an outreach committee included Elsie López, a lifelong *independentista* and East Harlem resident and Yvonne Dominguez, a Puerto Rican student activist from the Bronx. Our aim was to organize and advocate for the concerns of Puerto Rican and other women of color.

As Kimberly Springer notes in *Living for the Revolution*, Black women's organizations of the era addressed the intersection of race, gender, and class, building alliances to advance a broader social justice movement. She writes that these groups:

> "…sought to attain visibility and allies for a movement that encompassed race, gender, and class questions of social justice through their activities and myriad other traditional ways of organizing of the time period.[14]

Similarly, we envisioned the Women's Union as a militant, activist organization.

However, tensions with the YLP Central Committee emerged almost immediately, centered on questions of political autonomy and who would determine the group's priorities. Although she was not involved in the WU's daily work, González attempted to steer its political direction. Most notably, she ordered the WU to establish a daycare center in East Harlem.

Childcare had long been a recurring demand of women in the Young Lords. During the 1969 People's Church takeover, the Young Lords called for "a free day-care center for the mothers of the community," alongside free breakfast programs. Similarly, during the 1970 occupation of Lincoln Hospital, the list of demands included "the establishment of a childcare center for patients and working parents at the hospital." The Women's Caucus had also fought for—and won—an internal policy mandating that childcare be provided at political meetings and events, recognizing that mothers needed this support to fully participate in the organization's activities.

Acknowledging the importance of childcare, WU members agreed to follow González's directive. However, the Central Committee provided no material support—no funding, staffing, political guidance, or logistical resources. Without the necessary infrastructure and backing, the project soon stalled.

Nonetheless, the Women's Union continued organizing political education workshops and meetings that attracted a cross-section of Puerto Rican, Latinx, and African American women—students, mothers, homemakers, workers, and activists. It brought together revolutionary nationalists, socialists, and feminists committed to advancing women's rights and social justice. Members drafted a 12-Point Program and rules of discipline, joined protests, and launched a bilingual newspaper.

As the Women's Union expanded, the early tensions with the Central Committee over priorities gave rise to an even more fundamental question: What was the mission of the Women's Union? That question—and the political battles it sparked—is the focus of the chapters that follow.

The 12-Point Program: A Socialist Feminist Agenda

The Women's Union's 12-Point Program articulated a radical vision that fused socialist, feminist, and revolutionary nationalist principles. At its core was a clear declaration: "Equality for women—down with machismo and sexism." Grounded in the lived experiences of working-class and marginalized women of color—including welfare mothers, street sex workers, drug-addicted women, and incarcerated women,[15] the program centered the concept of triple oppression," emphasizing class, race, and gender. This framework was central to the WU's political analysis and organizing work.

Among the most urgent demands in the 12-Point Program were full employment and equal pay, highlighting the stark wage disparities faced by women of color compared to both men and white women. The program also called for "day-care facilities provided by the work institution," recognizing that the lack of affordable childcare posed a major barrier for mothers seeking to work, study, or take part in activities outside the home. In its absence, most women relied on informal networks of family, friends, neighbors, and even strangers—arrangements that were often unstable and unpredictable.

Welfare mothers, particularly African American and Latina women, were vilified by politicians and the corporate media. Portrayed as parasites and scapegoated for the country's financial troubles, they became targets in coordinated campaigns to dismantle social services and impose punitive work requirements.

The 12-Point Program critiqued the state's treatment of welfare recipients, especially women of color. Point 5 stated:

> We want an end to the present welfare system; community-worker boards must be established in all welfare centers to [e]nsure the protection of women and their needs.[16]

Members of the Women's Union joined protests at welfare centers, demanding increased state resources desperately needed for childcare, education, healthcare, employment, and other vital services.

Mainstream feminist organizations did little to resist the attacks on welfare mothers. As scholar bell hooks later wrote:

> The most profound betrayal of feminist issues has been the lack of mass-based feminist protests challenging the government's assault on single mothers and the dismantling of the welfare system.[17]

Her critique underscored how divisions of class and race within the feminist movement left poor women of color without needed solidarity.

The Women's Union also called attention to systemic, state-sanctioned violence. Point 8 called for the release of political prisoners and prisoners of war, specifically denouncing "the sexual brutalization and torture enforced on sisters by prison officials." Point 7 condemned sexual abuse committed by U.S. military personnel. At the time, the U.S. military occupied 13 percent of Puerto Rico's land and conducted bombing and training operations on the islands of Vieques and Culebra.[18] WU members cited cases of assaults on women by U.S. soldiers that went unpunished.

Point 11 affirmed a women's right to self-defense: "We believe in the right to defend ourselves against rapes, beatings, muggings and general abuse."

In keeping with reproductive justice struggles discussed in Chapter 4, the program also demanded "an end to the experimentation and genocide committed through sterilization, forced abortions, contraceptives, and unnecessary gynecological exams," practices that disproportionately targeted women of color.

Point 10 demanded "a true education of our story as women," reflecting the importance of historical consciousness and political literacy in movement building.

Several WU demands mirrored those in the YLP's 13-Point Program. Point 1 declared, "We want the liberation of all Puerto Ricans— liberation on the island and inside the U.S." The final point affirmed a shared goal, "We want a socialist society."

La Luchadora: Newspaper of the Women's Union

The Women's Union produced a bilingual English-Spanish newspaper titled *La Luchadora* ("The Fighter"), conceived as both an educational and organizing tool. The inaugural issue, released in June 1971, addressed a foundational question: "Why a Women's Union?" The answer was clear:

> Because as women, we best understand our own oppression and can organize ourselves for our liberation, always remembering that we will not be free until all our people are free.[19]

Written by women of color—many of whom had participated in the WU workshops—the newspaper reflected nationalist and socialist feminist perspectives, ideologies shaping the political discourse among women activists of color during this period.

Central to many articles was the concept of triple oppression. In the article "House Slave," for example, the writer explains how layered systems of domination shape daily life:

> First, we are oppressed because we are poor. ... Then we are oppressed because of our nationality and/or race. Finally, we suffer because we are women, and women are considered inferior to men.[20]

This analysis resonated deeply with members of the Women's Union and readers of *La Luchadora*.

Fig. 21. *La Luchadora* cover. 1971

In another article, "Women Workers," a garment factory worker recounted her experiences under triple oppression. Assigned the most grueling and lowest-paid jobs, she worked in unsafe, unsanitary conditions and endured racial discrimination, manhandling, and sexual abuse. She condemned the International Ladies' Garment Workers' Union for failing to advocate for its 450,000 members—80 percent of whom were women. Her struggles continued at home, where she was responsible for cooking, cleaning, and caring for her family. She wrote:

> Fathers, husbands, and brothers, who are also worked like slaves, take out their anger on women. Workers, women and men, must fight united to create a new society that does not exploit anyone.

Her conclusion called for unity with oppressed men in the broad struggle to end the exploitation of all people.

Another article, "Machismo," addressed the oppression of women of color in the home and workplace, reaching a similar conclusion: "Women must educate our men so that they will join us in the struggle to end machismo."[21]

La Luchadora also echoed Marxist feminist thought, offering sharp critiques of the nuclear family and unpaid domestic labor. One article stated:

> The modern individual family is founded on the open or concealed domestic slavery of the wife.[22]

In the piece titled "House Slave," domestic work is described as a form of invisible labor:

> Our role is to deal with the housework like a servant. We live in a world of dishwashing, ironing, cooking, mopping, sweeping, and taking care of children. We do the same jobs over and over again.[23]

The article asserted that housework was not recognized as "real work" because it was performed by women in private homes.

In addition to addressing gendered labor and domestic inequality, *La Luchadora* also included articles on Puerto Rico's anti-colonial movement, the role of women in the struggle for independence, and reproductive rights. Between June and August 1971, the Women's Union produced three issues, helping to circulate radical feminist ideas both within the movement and in the community. The paper sparked critical conversations about the lived realities of poor and working-class women of color. *La Luchadora* underscored the essential role of feminist thought in advancing both national liberation and gender equality.

Feminism in Action: The Women's Union through Mid-1971

By mid-1971, the Women's Union was deeply involved in political education and social justice organizing. Workshops centered on the herstories of women of color, examining how systemic oppression and colonialism shaped communities, identities, and self-perceptions. A central question guiding these sessions was: How do colonialism and oppression affect our perception of ourselves and communities? Drawing on Frantz Fanon's concept of "colonized mentality," WU members explored how oppressed people internalize sexist and racist ideologies— beliefs continually reinforced by systems of power.

Alongside educational efforts, the WU engaged in direct action and coalition-based activism. Members joined protests against the U.S. war in Indochina, mobilized to stop public assistance cuts, challenged poor working conditions confronting women of color, and distributed materials for the "Third World Health Workers' Conference." On International Women's Day, the WU demonstrated at the Women's House of Detention demanding the rights of incarcerated women. On May Day, WU members marched carrying the "Unión de Mujeres" banner.

Fig. 22. Unión de Mujeres banner. *Palante.* 1971.

By the time the Women's Union was formed, the Young Lords' Women's Caucus had already established working relationships with women in the Black Panther Party, the Student Nonviolent Coordinating Committee, the Third World Women's Alliance, the Brown Berets, the Puerto Rican Student Union, I Wor Kuen, and others. With the creation of the WU, participants sought to deepen and expand these connections—particularly with women in the Puerto Rican left, such as the Movimiento Pro Independencia (which later became the Puerto Rican Socialist Party) and El Comité, which had formed in the summer of 1970 on Manhattan's Upper West Side.[24]

Puerto Rican women were actively engaged in the radical movement and often first connected at cultural events, demonstrations, and protests in support of Puerto Rico's independence. It was through these gatherings that I met and formed lifelong friendships with El Comité members Carmen Martell and Diana Caballero. As collaborations among Puerto Rican organizations grew, so did conversations among women about confronting male supremacy.

Like other nationalist movements of the era, the Puerto Rican left was male-dominated. Women were generally relegated to administrative and logistical roles. As one male member of the Puerto Rican Socialist Party later reflected:

> The women were presumed to be responsible for following through on the detailed plans; the men specialized as the ideologues, the strategic thinkers.[25]

Moreover, the prevailing belief was that addressing sexism was unnecessary in a movement that was focused on colonial and class oppression.[26]

Puerto Rican women activists pushed back. In 1972, El Comité formed a Women's Commission "to facilitate the participation of women in the organization."[27] Similarly, when the Puerto Rican Socialist Party launched its U.S. branch in 1973, Digna Sánchez, the only woman on its Political Commission,[28] introduced a political education program that, in her words, "reaffirmed feminist principles in support of reproductive rights and challenged the patriarchal underpinnings of our culture."[29] These efforts sought to ensure that feminist perspectives were not only acknowledged but actively integrated into the organizing work.

Women's Conference and Critique of *Palante* Editorial

In April 1971, the Women's Union joined activists from the Black Workers' Congress, El Comité, I Wor Kuen, and the Puerto Rican Student Union to attend the Indochinese Women's Conference in Toronto, Canada. Our delegation participated to express transnational solidarity and to protest the U.S. escalation of the Vietnam War. At the conference, six women from Vietnam, Laos, and Cambodia—having journeyed through war-ravaged regions—shared firsthand testimonies and called for the immediate and total withdrawal of U.S. forces from Indochina.[30] They also urged attendees to join upcoming protests in Washington, D.C.[31]

Gloria González and I attended the Indochinese Women's Conference as representatives of the Young Lords Party and the Women's Union. The gathering brought together approximately 1,000 North American women from across the spectrum of the U.S. women's liberation movement. Attendees reflected a range of economic classes, races, nationalities, ages, sexual orientations, and political ideologies—differences that gave rise to sharp and contentious debates on racism, classism, and homophobia within the movement.

Upon returning to New York, González and I gave a full report to members of the YLP leadership. Recognizing the significance of the international gathering, the Central Committee—composed of Gloria González, Juan González, David Pérez, Pablo "Yoruba" Guzmán, and Juan "Fi" Ortiz—decided to publish an editorial in *Palante* titled "Position on Women's Liberation."[32]

The editorial begins by categorizing the U.S. women's movement into three broad ideological sectors. On the right, it situates middle- and upper-class white feminists whose primary goal is equality with men within existing capitalist and patriarchal structures, largely ignoring class and race. In the center, the article identifies "liberals and reformers," who advocate for legislative reforms to improve women's status. On the left, it locates anti-capitalist and anti-imperialist feminists[33] who view the primary global struggle as one between capitalism and socialism.

The Central Committee members aligned the Young Lords Party with this third, left sector.[34] Despite the editorial's title, "Position on Women's Liberation," it fails to articulate any meaningful connection to anti-capitalist or anti-imperialist feminist frameworks. Instead, it veers into vague commentary about "the negative things inside all of us,"[35] reducing gender oppression to interpersonal conflict—men and women simply "struggling with each other."[36] In contrast, socialist feminists of color located gender oppression within structures of patriarchy, capitalism, and colonialism,[37] interconnected systems of domination to be confronted together.

By fixating on individual behavior while sidestepping any materialist or institutional critique, the Central Committee effectively disclaimed the 1970 "YLP Women's Position Paper. This foundational document recognized the systemic oppression and exploitation of women and called for gender justice to be fully integrated into the organization's revolutionary nationalist agenda. In its place, the Central Committee advanced a narrow nationalist framework that relegated women's liberation to a post-revolutionary afterthought.

What emerges in the editorial is a rhetorical nod to women's liberation masking a profound ideological rollback. It reveals a Central Committee unwilling to recognize the systemic oppression of women as a political reality—or to accept its responsibility, as a revolutionary body, to fight for the liberation of all oppressed people. The article exposes profound internal divisions over the meaning and urgency of women's liberation—conflicts that would erupt publicly and take an increasingly regressive turn at the Young Lords Party's July 1971 retreat.

Fig. 23. U.S. Imperialism. *Palante* cover. July 24, 1971.

13.
FROM REVOLUTIONARY TO NARROW NATIONALISM

a deep remembering of what was,
she survives all.[1]

—Aja Monet, "the ghosts of women once girls," 2017

The Vietnam War continued to dominate foreign policy. Antiwar sentiment surged worldwide. In the United States, more than 750,000 people protested in Washington, D.C. on April 24, 1971, in what became "the largest-ever demonstration opposing a U.S. war."[2] Two months later, the release of the Pentagon Papers—a top-secret Department of Defense study—revealed that successive presidents had lied to the public about the extent of U.S. involvement in Vietnam, further escalating public condemnation of the war.[3]

On the domestic front, economic issues such as poverty, high food prices, and inflation took center stage. Unemployment reached staggering levels, particularly in communities of color. In response, the Nixon administration imposed a freeze on wages and issued an anti-strike order, provoking mass resistance. Thousands of workers took to the streets under the rallying cry: "Freeze War, not Wages."

Meanwhile, in Puerto Rico, the U.S. military continued its operations on the islands of Vieques and Culebra, among other locations. Resistance against the military presence intensified,[4] particularly over the Navy's continued use of Culebra as a primary bombing range. University students organized walkouts and demonstrations against the military draft and ROTC programs on campuses. The colonial police, backed by U.S. politicians, corporations, and troops, launched a wave of repression against the pro-independence movement, raiding activists' homes and carrying out arrests across the archipelago.

Amid this volatile political climate, the Young Lords Party launched *Ofensiva Rompe Cadenas*, the initiative to establish a presence in Puerto Rico. On March 21, 1971, Young Lords arrived in the archipelago. Gloria González, Juan González, Richie Pérez, Deputy Minister of Information, and others joined eighty nationalists in a march through the city of Ponce. The date marked the anniversary of the 1937 Ponce Massacre, when police opened fire on a peaceful demonstration, killing eighteen people and seriously wounding over two hundred.[5]

From January to July 1971, the Central Committee focused on expanding operations to Puerto Rico. Under Gloria González's direction, two offices eventually opened: one in Aguadilla in the northwest and another in Santurce in the northeast.

Ofensiva Rompe Cadenas involved a major restructuring and reassignment of cadres to support the move to Puerto Rico and the shift to developing people's organizations in the United States. Local branch offices and "serve the people" programs were shut down. At the same time, a national headquarters opened on 117th Street and Third Avenue in El Barrio, staffed by selected members reassigned from the closed branches. The Puerto Rico project stretched already scarce resources and led to a steady stream of resignations of members who disagreed with the new direction. Among those who left during this time were key women officers, including Denise Oliver, Connie Morales, and Letty Lozano.[6] These departures signaled growing internal tensions.

Which Direction Forward? Between Frontlines and Fault Lines

In July 1971, the Central Committee—Juan González, Gloria González, David Pérez, Pablo "Yoruba" Guzmán, and Juan "Fi" Ortiz—expanded their midyear retreat into an organization-wide convening to evaluate the political work of the prior six months. Members were eager to participate, seeing an opportunity to shape the Young Lords Party's future. Young Lords from East Harlem, the Bronx, the Lower East Side, Philadelphia, Bridgeport, Aguadilla and Santurce, Puerto Rico gathered at their respective branch locations. Cadre and chapter leaders submitted written reports outlining their political activities, concerns, and recommendations.

The obvious question looming over the July retreat was simple: "*Should the organization continue its work in Puerto Rico?*" From the moment the Central Committee proposed opening branches in the archipelago, it triggered internal conflict and marked a turning point in the YLP's politics and practices. The effort to establish a presence in Puerto

Rico while simultaneously building multiple people's organization's in the United States had created significant and complex challenges.

Given the challenges faced, the cadres expected a full and honest report from the Central Committee on the status of the Puerto Rico project, along with an open discussion about whether the work there should continue. It is crucial to emphasize that the Young Lords Party emerged from the material conditions faced by Puerto Ricans in the United States. Members had joined to fight the injustices Puerto Rican encountered in U.S. communities while also supporting the national liberation of Puerto Rico.

The YLP's expansion into the archipelago was fracturing the organization and draining its already limited resources. It became increasingly clear that attempting to managing branches in Puerto Rico from a headquarters in East Harlem was unsustainable. Many of us, myself included, hoped the Central Committee would refocus the organizing efforts in the United States, strengthening the work already established in Puerto Rican communities where the Young Lords had deep roots. But that was not what happened.

The Central Committee met, reviewed all the branch and cadre reports, and released a forty-nine-page document titled the *July 1971 Retreat Paper*. The central question—whether to continue the political work in Puerto Rico—was conspicuously absent from its pages.

Instead, the Central Committee issued three major declarations. First, they praised and celebrated the Young Lords' move to Puerto Rico as a historic and vital step toward Puerto Rico's independence. Second, they proclaimed that the national liberation struggle of Puerto Rico would now be the Young Lords Party's *primary* mission. Third, they announced plans to hold a national YLP Congress in 1972. These declarations imposed the Central Committee's position, presenting it as a unified view, rather than engaging in honest dialogue and collective political reflection with the membership.

Regarding the move to Puerto Rico, the retreat report boasted:

> This [*Ofensiva Rompe Cadenas* or the Break the Chains Offensive] was the most important offensive in our history, beginning the reunification of the Puerto Rican nation. The greatest impact was felt on the front [Puerto Rico].[7]

The claim that *Ofensiva Rompe Cadenas* had initiated the reunification of the Puerto Rican nation was, at best, an extravagant exaggeration—and at worst, political theater or outright fabrication. It conveyed a sense of progress intended to rally enthusiasm among members while masking the serious difficulties facing the YLP's organizing work.

Framing the move as historic allowed the Central Committee to justify prioritizing the struggle for Puerto Rico's independence while relegating the organizing efforts in U.S. communities to a secondary role. The *July 1971 Retreat Paper* made this shift explicit, affirming the intent of *Ofensiva Rompe Cadenas:* that the U.S. branches were to serve as a support base for operations in Puerto Rico—referred to as "the front."

Finally, the Central Committee's announcement of a national congress in 1972 hinted at the possibility of greater clarity ahead. In the immediate, however, its failure to face the problems inherent in the politics and implementation of the "divided nation" notion only intensified existing divisions.

Meanwhile, in the archipelago, Puerto Ricans watched the Young Lords' arrival with a mix of curiosity and skepticism. The main independence organizations—the Movimiento Pro Independencia and the Puerto Rican Independence Party—criticized the Young Lords as arrogant and politically immature for claiming they would lead a revolutionary movement in Puerto Rico. They viewed the Young Lords as outsiders, unfamiliar with local conditions, language, culture, and the complex dynamics of the anti-colonial struggle. Some activists even accused the Young Lords of acting as "imperialist" intruders.

The YLP members who were sent to Puerto Rico as organizers also raised serious concerns. They faced severe challenges: scarce resources, minimal organizational guidance, and disorientation in a new political context. Some members did not speak Spanish fluently and had never lived in Puerto Rico. As frontline organizers, they bore the brunt of severely underfunded branches, often going without basic necessities—including food. Strategies and tactics that had worked in the United States failed to gain traction in Puerto Rico. By July 1971, the cadres were demoralized, exhausted, and increasingly doubtful of the project's viability.

Still, the Central Committee ignored the criticisms and the mounting hardships on the cadres. It pushed forward, insisting that the national liberation work in Puerto Rico would be the Young Lords' top political priority.

Silencing Gender and Racial Justice Organizing

The rapid shift in the Young Lords Party's political direction in 1971 led to widespread confusion and frustration among the rank and file. New structures and assignments created uncertainty. When cadres sought concrete guidance, the Central Committee's responses were vague and inconsistent.

In the *July 1971 Retreat Paper,* the Central Committee placed the blame for this confusion on the membership, claiming the cadres were excessively focused on the issue of sexism.[8] This charge was both surprising and perplexing, particularly given that most Young Lords were men not actively engaged in gender justice organizing.

The Central Committee then outlined what it described as the Young Lords Party's "correct political priorities":

> The biggest contradictions are the division of the nation
> and the division between classes. Then come the divisions
> of sex and race.[9]

This framing marked a notable shift from the organization's earlier stance. Just six months prior, the *Palante* newspaper had published the "YLP Position Paper on Women," which treated the struggles against racism, poverty, and gender oppression as coequal and interconnected. That document affirmed that women's emancipation was integral to human liberation—not in conflict with, but inseparable from, Puerto Rico's national liberation struggle.[10]

In contrast, the *July 1971 Retreat Paper* relegated gender and racial justice struggles to secondary concerns. It labeled the rapid growth of the Women's Union as a "political mistake"[11] and canceled plans to establish a women's organization in Puerto Rico.[12] The Central Committee did not officially disband the Women's Union in New York. Instead it redirected its efforts toward three vaguely defined tasks: 1) organizing "women workers and lumpen," 2) developing "day care centers," and 3) distributing *La Luchadora.*[13]

These sweeping directives—overly broad in scope and issued without political guidance, strategic support, or material resources—did not appear less like a plan to strengthen the Women's Union. In fact, the absence of clarity and institutional backing showed a lack of genuine commitment to gender justice. At the same time, reports of homophobia within the organization were ignored, and the homosexual caucuses were abruptly disbanded[14] without discussion.

Most shocking was the Central Committee directive to end public discussion of sexism:[15] "Too much time had been given to sexism. This was incorrect,"[16] the retreat report stated. This abrupt reversal contradicted the *The Ideology of the Young Lords Party,* which had previously identified sexism as key struggle.[17] The report reverted to the earlier framing of "machismo and passivity,"[18]—a formulation that obscured the structural nature of male dominance as discussed in Chapter 3,

Similarly, the struggle for racial justice was deprioritized. Despite assurances from Gloria González, the Young Lords Party failed to follow through on its pledge to organize Afro-Puertorriqueños in Puerto Rico, When members reported rising anti-Black racism within the YLP, the Central Committee again attributed tensions to an overemphasis on sexism.[19]

Still, members pressed for clarity: "What does racial justice organizing as secondary to nation and class look like?" African Americans, who comprised approximately 20 percent of the membership, raised this question. The report's only reply was to suggest that African Americans learn Spanish "to do better organizing,"[20] a patronizing response that prompted further resignations. Likewise, the Health Revolutionary Unity Movement, composed of African American and Puerto Rican healthcare workers, rejected the "divided nation" line, insisting that its organizing was rooted in the United States, not Puerto Rico.

The Central Committee's articulation of "correct political priorities" exposed a profound ideological divide. Its claim that the Women's Union had grown "too quickly" reflected an underlying belief that national and women's liberation were mutually exclusive. It presumed that advancing women's rights would dilute support for Puerto Rico's independence—ignoring the reality that socialist feminists within the YLP were actively fighting colonialism, capitalism, racism, and patriarchy as interconnected systems of oppression.

More broadly, the Central Committee treated struggles for gender and racial justice as distractions—issues to be postponed until after Puerto Rico's independence was achieved. The Women's Union, by contrast, viewed these struggles as integral to anti-colonial organizing. At stake were two fundamentally different—and ultimately irreconcilable— visions of liberation.

The July 1971 retreat could have served as a moment of honest collective reflection and strategic recalibration. Instead, the Central Committee squandered the opportunity, defaulting to a rigid, top-down approach and failing to develop a differentiated strategy for organizing in Puerto Rico versus the United States—despite recommendations from members like Pablo "Yoruba" Guzmán and veteran cadres and allies.

Despite the mounting challenges, the Central Committee insisted that the failures of the Puerto Rico expansion stemmed primarily from insufficient funding.[21] Its refusal to confront the ideological limitations of its narrow nationalist politics, paired with increasingly authoritarian decision-making, marked a departure from the inclusive, intersectional activism that had once energized the Young Lords Party.

The Women's Union After the July 1971 Retreat

Despite the Central Committee's criticism of the Women's Union as an example of "incorrect" priorities, we continued our work much as before. We believed, naively, that we could carry out our political work independently of the Central Committee's pronouncements and involvement.

From the July retreat through December 1971, the Women's Union facilitated political education workshops and produced the July and August issues of *La Luchadora*. Members also participated in major protests across New York City. In September, following the uprising at Attica Correctional Facility in upstate New York, WU members marched in solidarity for twenty-five consecutive days. We condemned Governor Nelson Rockefeller's brutal assault on prisoners and demanded his indictment for the death of forty-three people.[22]

When the city announced a new wave of budget cuts—including firing teachers, reduced funds for supplies, and the elimination of discounted student transit fares—WU members joined the Third World Students' League and 2,000 students to protest outside the Board of Education.[23] In November, about 400 students, including members of the Puerto Rican Student Union and the Women's Union, attended a conference at Princeton University to advocate for the admission of Puerto Rican working-class students.[24]

Despite the pushback from the Central Committee, the Women's Union continued with an intersectional, grassroots approach to organizing that contrasted with the narrowing politics of the leadership.

The Gendered Limits of Anti-Colonial Politics

The *July 1971 Retreat Paper* did not explain why the Central Committee so adamantly opposed public discussions of sexism. In retrospect, several reasons become clear. First, most Central Committee members were nationalists who did not view struggles for gender and racial justice essential to Puerto Rico's independence struggle. Second, dismantling the systemic oppression of women of color—and confronting male domination—was not a cause they genuinely embraced. Most showed little interest in learning the herstories of women of color. Finally, proponents of the Puerto Rico expansion, obsessed with taking leadership in the pro-independence movement, feared that revolutionary socialist feminist perspectives would not be welcomed. On that point, they were not entirely mistaken.

In 1970s Puerto Rico, feminist movements faced significant hostility. Scholars have noted that feminism was widely viewed across the political spectrum "as an external, foreign, colonial imposition, and/or a contagion influence"— a threat to traditional values and gender roles.[25] As Puerto Rican Socialist Party member Carmen Vivian Rivera recalled, feminists were often dismissed as an outgrowth of the white U.S. women's movement or as "an aberration spawned by the yanqui radical left."[26]

In this context, women's rights were seen as a distraction.[27] Few organizations publicly addressed racism, heterosexism, or heteronormativity.[28] Women advocating for gender justice were expected to affirm heterosexuality and prioritize class struggle above all else in order to be taken seriously by men.

According to feminist scholar María I. Bryant, nationalist, socialist, and independence parties in Puerto Rico "privileged the struggle for national liberation and relegated women's and/or feminist activism to secondary status."[29] In her study of *Claridad*, Puerto Rico's leading pro-independence newspaper, Bryant found that "the rhetoric of liberation and self-determination rarely made reference to women or addressed the question of the nation from the perspective of women."[30]

Still, feminists in Puerto Rico organized with determination. They fought for improved education, labor rights, and reproductive freedom—including abortion and maternity leave—and against domestic violence, sexual harassment, and sexist media representations. Theirs was a dual militancy: as women and as *independentistas* struggling to end U.S. colonialism.

Pro-independence organizations in Puerto Rico often insisted that women's issues could be addressed after colonialism was defeated. But global history suggests otherwise. Across Africa, Asia, Latin America, and the Caribbean, women's contributions to anti-colonial and nationalist movements have rarely translated into lasting gains for women once independence was achieved.[31] Numerous studies show that without an explicit and sustained commitment to gender equality from the outset, women's rights are often sidelined—or even rolled back—in the post-colonial period.[32]

As scholar Ranjoo S. Herr writes in her essay "The Possibility of Nationalist Feminism":

> [E]ven when national independence is achieved, the tension between nationalism and feminism continues. Although male nationalists have encouraged the participation of feminists in nationalist struggles by promising that feminist issues will be addressed once these struggles succeed, feminists have often been betrayed in the end.[33]

Global feminist experiences affirm the need to pursue gender and nationalist goals simultaneously.[34] Postcolonial examples demonstrate that women's oppression endures even under socialism[35]—and racism persists as well. The struggles for gender and racial justice must continue as long as inequality exists.

Crushing Dissent And Consolidating Narrow Nationalism

By the fall of 1971, the Young Lords Party was in deep crisis. Several Central Committee members were away from New York: Pablo "Yoruba" Guzmán was in China as part of a U.S. delegation; Juan González was on a speaking tour in Hawai'i; and Gloria González was in Puerto Rico overseeing the new branches. Upon Guzmán's return, Central Committee members David Pérez and Juan "Fi" Ortiz informed him of serious organizational problems, particularly, the continuing decline in membership. Nearly sixty members had left the New York organization during the weeks Guzmán was away.[36]

In response, Guzmán drafted a paper titled "Our Present Situation: Statement, Analysis and Suggestions," dated November 10, 1971.[37] He circulated it to the Central Committee—Ortiz, David Pérez, Juan González, Gloria González (now using the name Fontanez)—and to the national staff, including Richie Pérez, Juan Ramos, Benjy Cruz, Huracán Flores, and me. Drawing on insights from his experience in China, Guzmán proposed a full membership discussion on the difficulties and called for a "rectification movement" grounded in internal democracy, critical reflection, and organizational renewal. Ortiz, Richie Pérez, Ramos, and I supported his proposal, convinced that the rank and file were eager for the open dialogue that had been denied at the July 1971 retreat. We urged for a rethinking and redesign of the Puerto Rico project.

In a follow-up letter dated November 14, 1971, Guzmán sent a second report to González and Fontanez,[38] emphasizing, "[O]ur situation is bad, both in Puerto Rico and the U.S. ... Many departures of important Party people. ... Demoralization reigns."

Before González and Fontanez returned to New York, Guzmán, David Pérez, and Ortiz took preliminary steps to address the crisis. They decided to transfer members out of the Women's Union to the weaker people's organizations in an effort to strengthen them. Guzmán later claimed he had secured consensus from both the New York central and national staffs to do so.[39]

David Pérez called me to a meeting to inform me of the decision. I strongly opposed removing members from the Women's Union. Pérez insisted, "The Women's Union was supposed to be the last priority but developed faster than the Workers' Federation, which was supposed to be first." I reminded him that I had been tasked with organizing the Women's Union. He accused me of caring more about women's issues than those of workers. "Women are also workers," I replied, "and face issues like childcare, reproductive rights, sexual violence, and others that aren't solely fought at the workplace. Our members include homemakers, working-class students, workers, and welfare mothers." Pérez repeated that the Women's Union had grown too quickly and concluded, "We don't have the resources." He ended the conversation, conflating a lack of political vision, commitment, and funding as justification for "withering away" the Women's Union.

When González and Fontanez returned to New York, they pulled the Central Committee members into a closed-door meeting, rejecting Guzmán's call for a general membership meeting. After three weeks, the Central Committee released a twenty-five-page document titled *"Communiqué of the Central Committee,"*[40] announcing Juan González, Gloria Fontanez, and David Pérez as the new "Executive Committee" of the Young Lords Party—consolidating their control.

The communiqué reaffirmed the "divided nation" line and accused supporters of the rectification movement of violating "democratic centralism" by engaging in political discussions with the rank-and-and file. As punishment for initiating these conversations—and for "thinking about forming two organizations, one in Puerto Rico and another in the United States,"[41]—the Executive Committee demoted Guzmán, Ortiz, Richie Pérez, Ramos, and me from our leadership positions and reassigned us away from our home branches. Ramos, cofounder of the Philadelphia branch, was sent to Aguadilla, Puerto Rico; and Ortiz to El Caño in Santurce, Puerto Rico. Guzmán and I were sent to Philadelphia.[42] My reassignment abruptly ended my work with the Women's Union.

The Executive Committee crushed the rectification movement. Its actions alienated many veteran cadres and supporters who had grown disillusioned with the leadership's antidemocratic methods and narrow nationalist politics.

In January 1972, I arrived at the Young Lords' storefront at Third and Diamond Streets in North Philadelphia and joined the local cadre and steering committee—composed of Pablo "Yoruba" Guzmán, Michael Rodríguez, and Gloria Rodríguez. With the transfer of Juan Ramos, the branch lost a longtime and respected leader, along with members who had looked to him for guidance. Nonetheless, we struggled to keep the branch going. Over the next three years, we organized with migrant laborers, factory and hospital workers, and university students. We also worked in coalition with the Black Panther Party and Yellow Seeds, a local Asian organization.[43]

During this period, we faced constant surveillance and harassment from the Philadelphia Police Department, led by former police commissioner and right-wing mayor Frank Rizzo.

In 1973, both Guzmán and Michael Rodríguez were imprisoned. Guzmán was sentenced to two years for refusing induction into the U.S. Army. Rodríguez was convicted of machine gun possession, the result of a frame-up by a federal agent from the Bureau of Alcohol, Tobacco, and Firearms. While incarcerated in federal prisons in Florida and Virginia, respectively, neither man received a visit or letter from any Executive Committee member.

In Philadelphia, Gloria Rodríguez and I continued to lead the branch—the only YLP branch headed by women. We received no financial support or strategic guidance from the national organization. In retrospect, we were better off, away from the Executive Committee's incessant ideological infighting, power grabs, and dogmatic politics.

Narrow Nationalist Control of the Women's Union

In early 1972, after my transfer to Philadelphia, the Executive Committee relaunched the Women's Union under the direct control of Gloria Fontanez and realigned its mission to conform to the YLP's priorities. This shift violated the autonomy originally envisioned for people's organizations and disregarded the revolutionary principle that women must lead their own liberation struggles—before, during, and after a socialist revolution.[44]

The Women's Union's primary objective was reframed as providing support for Puerto Rico's independence. Gender-specific concerns—

such as reproductive rights, access to health care, protection from gender-based violence, and workplace equity—were deferred, to be addressed after Puerto Rico's independence had been achieved.

The Women's Union's 12-Point Program and its intersectional feminist platform were abandoned. Members were instructed to stop using the term *sexism*, which identified systemic oppression, and instead adopt the language of *machismo and passivity*, which emphasized individual behaviors. This change marked a retrenchment into nationalist frameworks that socialist feminists within the YLP had challenged from the outset—and had explicitly rejected more than two years earlier.

In line with this narrow nationalist agenda, the Executive Committee assigned the Women's Union a new set of tasks: (1) establish a childcare center for activists living in the Lower East Side, (2) produce and distribute *La Luchadora* newspaper; and (3) organize advocacy efforts for the release of Lolita Lebrón from prison.[45] However, each initiative quickly faltered. The childcare project was shut down within three months[46] due to conflicts with city agencies over permits.[47] *La Luchadora* was never published again. As for the campaign to release Lolita Lebron, the Women's Union held a film screening and discussion in March 1972, but no further actions followed.[48]

By year's end, the Women's Union had ceased to exist.

The Women's Union and Radical Feminism in the Diaspora

The Women's Union marked a pivotal moment in the political history of the Puerto Rican diaspora. At a time when revolutionary nationalist movements marginalized women's concerns, the WU advanced a decolonial, socialist feminist vision rooted in lived experience and collective struggle. This radical feminism emphasized that gender justice was inseparable from struggles to dismantle systemic oppression. Puerto Rican feminists—shaped by the intersecting legacies of colonial displacement, migration, labor exploitation, and racial and gender violence—brought these lived realities into their political activism.

The Women's Union emerged in dialogue with a wider current of Third World feminism. In the early 1970s, African American, Chicana, Asian American, and Indigenous women were developing intersectional frameworks that critiqued capitalism, empire, heteropatriarchy, and internal hierarchies within radical movements. Drawing strength from these feminist interventions, the WU positioned its work within an internationalist and anti-imperialist tradition.

One of the Women's Union's central contributions was its dedication to developing feminist consciousness among both activists and community members. Through political education workshops, it introduced feminist theories, organizing practices, strategies, and herstories that resonated with the lived experiences of Puerto Rican, Latina, and other women of color. Its bilingual newspaper, *La Luchadora,* and 12-Point Program articulated demands that remain deeply relevant today: equal pay, access to childcare, reproductive justice, an end to gender-based state violence, and the liberation of Puerto Rico.

The Women's Union created vital entry points for Puerto Rican and other Latinas to participate in revolutionary politics, often for the first time. By linking everyday struggles, such as machismo in the home and workplace, to broader movements against police violence, labor exploitation, military occupation, and colonialism, the WU promoted a cohesive vision of resistance that was at once local, national, and international. Collaborations with feminist collectives, anti-imperialist networks, and citywide coalitions provided opportunities for women to grow as organizers, theorists, and militants.

From its inception, the Women's Union operated within significant constraints. Organized under the patriarchal hierarchy of the Young Lords Party, it lacked the autonomy, resources, and political backing to fully pursue organizing from a feminist perspective. When the Central Committee explicitly suppressed gender-based work, the WU was left structurally weakened and ideologically marginalized. This moment laid exposed the limitations of advancing feminist agendas within movements that fail to make space for gender justice and underscored the ongoing challenge of reconciling feminist ideals with nationalist politics. It also affirmed the necessity of making gender justice fundamental to any revolutionary struggle.

Although short-lived, the Women's Union represents a vital and overlooked chapter in the feminist history of the Puerto Rican diaspora and U.S. social justice movements. It was a moment when women demanded a "revolution within the revolution," insisting that without gender and racial justice, there could be no true liberation. Its socialist feminist politics helped seed a path for future generations, paving the way for more inclusive and intersectional forms of struggle.

The End of the Young Lords Party

I was organizing with the Young Lords Party in Philadelphia on March 21, 1972—the one-year anniversary of the organization's expansion to Puerto Rico. Writing in *Palante*, Minister of Defense Juan González reflected on its significance:

> We began to make clear that our goals are not just to fight
> for decent health care, against unemployment, racism, po-
> lice brutality and indecent housing. We made it clear that
> we are fighting principally for the freedom of the colony of
> Puerto Rico."[49]

González admitted that the Young Lords Party's expansion to Puerto Rico had led to serious setbacks: office closings, irregular publication of *Palante*, erratic community programming, and widespread resignations. He attributed these difficulties to the "impatience of some leaders, the youthfulness of members, and the lack of working-class consciousness."[50]

Notably absent was any recognition of the flawed "divided nation" political line—or how it weakened the YLP's influence and capacity to mobilize Puerto Rican communities in the United States.

In the same article, González announced plans for a Young Lords Party Congress later that year, describing it as an opportunity "to establish the beginning of true democracy in the organization" and to take "a new step in the struggle for national liberation and socialism for Puerto Rico and the United States."[51] Yet, given the Executive Committee's suppression of internal dissent, these promises rang hollow.

Unexpectedly, just a few months before the planned congress, Juan "Fi" Ortiz and Juan Ramos, key leaders of the Party's work in Puerto Rico, joined other cadres in proposing that the branches on the archipelago be shut down. Their experience had convinced them that the organization's primary focus should return to fighting for the rights of Puerto

Ricans in the United States. Gloria Fontanez reacted with outrage, accusing them of betraying the Puerto Rican nation and its people.

Nevertheless, on May 20, 1972, Ortiz, Ramos, and most of the Puerto Rico cadre resigned, forcing the closure of the Puerto Rico branches. Although many of us had already heard from members on the archipelago about growing tensions, we learned of the resignations through *Palante*. In a full-page attack, the Executive Committee labeled the departing Young Lords "splitters" and accused them of "factionalism."[52]

In this way, the Puerto Rico project ended in bitterness and disgrace.

Just weeks later, two nights before the scheduled Young Lords Party Congress, the Executive Committee abruptly reversed its position on the "divided nation" framework. In a hastily arranged meeting with Young Lords in the United States, they admitted it had been a political error. For many veteran cadres, including myself, the timing of this admission appeared to be a last-minute maneuver to retain control of the organization ahead of the congress.[53]

Since the introduction of the "divided nation" line in late 1970, Juan González, Gloria Fontanez, and David Pérez had consistently refused to heed internal critiques.[54] Yet those warnings had been frequent and emphatic. From the outset, Pablo "Yoruba" Guzmán, Denise Oliver, and Juan "Fi" Ortiz had raised serious objections to the proposal to open YLP branches in Puerto Rico, arguing that it lacked a clear strategy and failed to account for the distinct political conditions in the archipelago and the diaspora.

In early 1971, Carlos Aponte questioned the organization's new direction, and the Central Committee responded by accusing him of being a police agent. Six months later, at the organization-wide retreat, numerous members—including feminists, African Americans, HRUM workers, and LBGTQ cadres—voiced their opposition to the "divided nation" line. Still, no changes were made.

By late 1971, with membership in rapid decline, Guzmán, Ortiz, Richie Pérez, Juan Ramos, and I called for a full-membership evaluation of the Puerto Rico project. In retaliation, the Executive Committee demoted us from leadership roles and reassigned us to other branches. Disillusioned by the YLP's increasingly authoritarian practices and narrowing nationalist vision, many members left the organization during this period.

Juan González later admitted that he and Gloria Fontanez bore primary responsibility for implementing these damaging policies—and for the expulsion of dissenting members.[55] The mass resignations in Puerto Rico just prior to the 1972 Party Congress marked the final effort to correct what was the Young Lords Party's central political and strategic mistake.

The YLP Congress took place from June 30 to July 3, 1972, in the South Bronx. It was attended by cadres and representatives from people's organizations. A new crop of members supported changing the organization's name to the Puerto Rican Revolutionary Workers Organization (PRRWO) and confirmed Gloria Fontanez, Carmen Cruz (Fontanez's cousin), and Juan González as the new Executive Committee.[56]

After the Party Congress, the Executive Committee released a position paper. Regarding the "divided nation" concept, it stated:

> Originally, we felt that the Puerto Ricans in Puerto Rico and the U.S. together made up a divided nation, and that one party must be built to serve the interests of the workers of this divided nation. This was wrong. The Puerto Rican nation is not divided; it is in Puerto Rico.[57]

The paper also addressed the long-standing question: "What is the relationship of Puerto Ricans in the United States to Puerto Rico's national liberation struggle?" The answer echoed the stance that Pablo "Yoruba" Guzmán had advocated a year earlier:

> Revolutionaries who feel their work is primarily the national liberation of Puerto Rico should be there, living among the people, working, raising families, learning the conditions there as they unite with other revolutionaries to build the party of the proletariat in Puerto Rico.[58]

But by then, it was too late to revive the Young Lords Party.

Ironically, despite their relentless push to establish branches in Puerto Rico, none of the Executive Committee members chose to relocate to the archipelago to build the very organization they had so fervently insisted upon.

At the time of the Young Lords Party Congress, I was still in Philadelphia. I returned to New York City in late 1974 and formally resigned at a meeting in early January 1975.

The end of the Young Lords Party illustrates the dangers of consolidating too much power in a small leadership group. It reflects a pattern in social movements: unaccountable leadership suppresses internal democracy, isolates dissent, and, in doing so, hastens organizational decline.

In the years that followed, the Puerto Rican Revolutionary Workers Organization turned inward. At the helm, a power-hungry and frenzied Gloria Fontanez led a reign of repression against anyone who disagreed with her. Dissenters faced intimidation, purges, and physical violence. Fontanez betrayed the revolutionary movement, the Women's Caucus, and the Women's Union. But she did not act alone. She was supported by a mix of misinformed and inexperienced youth, opportunists, and undercover police.

By 1976, the PRRWO had faded into history a cautionary tale of political sectarianism and authoritarian leadership.

After the Young Lords: Paths of Activism and Resistance

The Young Lords Party marked a new chapter of Puerto Rican militancy in the United States. It championed the rights of Puerto Ricans, galvanized a grassroots movement, and inspired a generation. Counterintelligence operations and internal political conflicts contributed to its eventual demise. In my earlier book *Through the Eyes of Rebel Women: The Young Lords, 1969–1976,* I detail the conditions and decisions that led to the organization's decline.[59]

The end, however, was not a single moment or event. Members' experiences varied. Members left at different times and went their separate ways. Everyone came to terms with their involvement in their own way. Many former members continued the struggle for economic and social justice, women's rights, and the decolonization of Puerto Rico.

Former women members took part in committees to free Puerto Rican political prisoners and joined activists in the 1977 takeover of the

Statue of Liberty, demanding the release of Puerto Rican Nationalists in prison since the 1950s. Others joined efforts to free another generation of Puerto Rican political prisoners, released in 1999. Many more participated in the movement to expel the U.S. Navy from Vieques.

Women from the Young Lords also helped found and lead the National Congress for Puerto Rican Rights. Many continued organizing against police violence, standing with victims' families, and demanding justice and accountability.

Former Young Lords remained active in labor and the working-class movements. Sonia Ivany, the first woman member to join the New York chapter, later become president of the New York City Labor Council for Latin American Advancement. Minerva Solla served as a national organizer with 1199 SEIU (United Healthcare Workers East), and Cleo Silvers as a national organizer with the Black Workers' Congress.

Many became educators and college professors—Denise Oliver, Martha Duarte (Arguello), Gloria Rodríguez, and Diana Caballero among them—teaching courses in anthropology, women's and gender studies, Caribbean history, psychology, bilingual/multicultural education, and related topics. Others continued in community work: Olguie Robles provided counseling for Puerto Ricans and African Americans in drug rehabilitation programs, and Letty Lozano worked with urban youth programs. Several, such as Nydia Mercado, become medical doctors working in local communities. Some became lawyers and judges, including Myrna Martínez, Gloria Colón, Marlin Segarra, and myself. Still others founded organizations focused on women's health, such as Elba Saavedra; on women's spiritual and personal development, such as Gloria Rodríguez; or on producing educational media, as I have done.

Wherever life took us, many of us remained grounded in the values that brought us to the Young Lords in the first place. We continued to advocate for Puerto Rico's decolonization and engaged with the social justice efforts of Puerto Rican, Latinx, African American, Indigenous, and Asian communities. We stood with workers, youth, educators, and fellow activists in the fight for a just and humane society. Whether in classrooms, courtrooms, clinics, labor halls, or in the streets, we carried with us the revolutionary ideals, feminist principles, and collective spirit of solidarity that defined our activism in the Young Lords Party.

PART V.
RECKONING WITH THE PAST

A search for keys in past history to help
explain our time—a time that also makes history—
on the basis that the first condition for
changing reality is to understand it.[1]

—Eduardo Galeano, Open Veins of Latin America, 1973

14.
STATE SURVEILLANCE, POLICE VIOLENCE, AND THE ENEMY WITHIN

By all indications, domestic covert operations
have become a permanent feature of U.S. politics.
... [I]n the name of protecting our fundamental
freedoms, the FBI and the police systematically
subvert them.[1]

—Brian Glick, *The COINTELPRO Papers*, preface 1990

To understand the challenges of social justice organizing in the United States, it is essential to examine the intertwined histories of policing, race, and class. Ruling and financial elites have long opposed those seeking freedom and justice. As the historian Carmin Maffea notes, "Southern slave owners used slave patrols to maintain their 'private property'; the Northern bourgeoisie used the police to repress strikers and send them back to work."[2]

During the 1960s and 1970s, the U.S. government and law enforcement agencies deployed an array of violent tactics—including surveillance, sabotage, and the suppression of democratic and human rights—to crush social justice movements. This chapter focuses on the Federal Bureau of Investigation's Counterintelligence Program (COINTELPRO) and the New York City police department's covert operations against the Young Lords Organization and its members. From the outset, the Young Lords were subject to police surveillance, infiltration, harassment, and fabricated criminal charges. The FBI and New York's notorious Red Squad ran parallel operations, using informants, infiltrators, special undercover agents, and provocateurs to destroy the organization from within.

Many of the political police who infiltrated the Young Lords were Puerto Rican, African American, and Latinx, men and women who showed up at the Young Lords' offices and events posing as friends, nationalists, comrades, and "servants of the people." Behind their smiling faces and seemingly shared commitments were individuals tasked with undermining the aspirations of Puerto Rican revolutionaries and community organizers.

The full extent of counterintelligence activities against the Young Lords remains largely unknown and undocumented, even decades after the organization's decline. Key questions persist: What role did state-sponsored counterintelligence operations play in the Young Lords' move to Puerto Rico? How did covert actions contribute to dismantling the New York organization and the suppression of racial and gender justice organizing? Most troubling of all, what role did the political police play in the violence inflicted on members during the organization's later years? These questions are not only historical—they speak directly to how repression reshapes movements, obscures truths, and silences demands for justice.

COINTELPRO: Counterintelligence Program

The FBI launched the Counterintelligence Program, widely known as COINTELPRO, in 1956 with the explicit goal of destroying the Communist Party of the United States.[3] To fuel Cold War anxieties and intensify the "Red Scare," the FBI worked closely with media outlets to spread damaging information about the party[4] and circulate dossiers identifying alleged communists.

By the 1960s, however, COINTELPRO had expanded far beyond its original anti-communist objectives. The FBI redirected its efforts toward destroying the New Left, focusing on anti–Vietnam War activists and the Black liberation movement. Among the many targets was the Young Lords Organization founded in Chicago in 1968. The group's revolutionary ideology, grassroots mobilization, and close alignment with the Black Panther Party brought it under immediate FBI scrutiny.

José "Cha Cha" Jiménez, the YLO's founder, and Fred Hampton, leader of the Chicago Black Panther Party, became friends while both were imprisoned. Their collaboration gave rise to the Rainbow Coalition—a multiracial alliance of activists united against poverty, racism, and U.S. imperialism. The coalition also included the Young Patriots, a group of white working-class southerners based in Chicago. The FBI viewed this interracial solidarity as a serious threat and, as Bureau files later revealed,was "quite active in sabotaging it," with the explicit aim of "driving a wedge" into the movement.[5]

In 1969, FBI Director J. Edgar Hoover declared the Black Panther Party "the greatest threat to the internal security of the United States."[6] Hoover laid the foundation to destroy the organization and its members.[7] An earlier internal memorandum instructed agents in fourteen field offices to "submit imaginative and hard-hitting counter-intelligence measures aimed at crippling the Black Panther Party," framing these efforts in the language of "gang warfare" and "attendant threats of murder and reprisal."[8] These directives resulted in tactics, ranging from petty harassment to political assassinations[9]—most infamously, the killings of Black Panther leaders Fred Hampton and Mark Clark as they slept in their beds in Chicago on December 4, 1969.[10]

By the time the Young Lords' chapter formed in New York City on July 26, 1969, the political police had heavily infiltrated the Chicago YLO. It was not surprising then that FBI informants attended the Young Lords' inaugural rally in New York City's Tompkins Square Park and submitted reports to their handlers. When the Young Lords Party expanded to Puerto Rico, COINTELPRO's scrutiny intensified. The FBI had a long history of surveilling Puerto Rico's anti-colonial movements, dating back to the 1930s, when it devised a program to dismantle the Puerto Rican Nationalist Party.[11] In the 1960s, Hoover ordered agents to gather intelligence on pro-independence leaders[12] aiming to exploit what the Bureau characterized as "inherent factionalism" in such movements.[13]

COINTELPRO's existence remained secret until 1971, when a group of antiwar activists broke into an FBI office in Pennsylvania and retrieved more than 1,000 classified documents. They mailed these materials to major newspapers,[14] exposing the FBI's far-reaching government-sanctioned surveillance and criminal activities against a broad cross section of progressive organizations and individuals.[15]

New York City Bureau of Special Services: "The Red Squad"

In addition to the FBI's operations, the New York City Police Department operated its own counterintelligence division: the Bureau of Special Services—known as "BoSS" or "the Red Squad." Functioning as a municipal political police force, BoSS agents were specifically trained in undercover surveillance and subversion.[16]

Between 1968 and 1970, the Red Squad expanded its ranks from sixty-eight to ninety officers. These undercover agents employed tactics designed to destabilize social movements from within—spreading misinformation, sowing division, and creating confusion in the movement.[17] They encouraged illegal activity and instigated violence,[18] even arranging elaborate frame-ups using fabricated evidence.[19]

One of the most notorious examples was the case of the Panther 21. In 1969, twenty-one members of the New York chapter of the Black Panther Party were falsely accused of plotting to blow up police stations and department stores. After more than two years of legal proceedings, the case ended in a complete acquittal. "A jury took just ninety minutes to decide they were not guilty on all 159 counts."[20] Although the verdict acquitted all defendants, the case inflicted lasting damage on the Harlem chapter of the Black Panther Party, exhausting its resources and derailing its community organizing work.

State Repression and the Tactics of Political Policing

COINTELPRO and the New York Police Department's Red Squad employed deliberate and ruthless tactics to crush grassroots resistance. In a 1967 memorandum, FBI Director J. Edgar Hoover instructed agents to "expose, disrupt, misdirect, discredit, or otherwise neutralize" the social justice movement.[21] The FBI's objective was explicit: to destroy revolutionary organizations by any means necessary.

To carry out this mission, agents infiltrated the Young Lords Organization and compiled intelligence files. These included copies of internal reports, news clippings, speeches, flyers, transcripts of the *Palante* radio program, articles, correspondence, bank account records, and photographs. Federal and local agents engaged in illegal activities such as wiretapping, bugging, mail tampering and breaking into offices and homes—all without warrants or regard for constitutional rights.[22]

The *Palante* newspaper documented repeated instances of state violence, including police raids and firebombing of Young Lords offices in the Bronx and other cities such as Newark, Philadelphia, Bridgeport, and

El Caño, Puerto Rico. Hoover's overarching strategy was to "divide, con-quer, and weaken" radical movements, by immobilizing organizations, and demoralizing members.

To that end, the FBI and NYPD agents conducted sustained psy-chological warfare. Agents appeared unannounced at members' homes to intimidate, and contacted family members, employers, and neighbors to spread rumors and discredit activists. Intelligence files—each assigned a case number—contained political histories, physical descriptions, and personal data, including family details, to identify vulnerabilities. Organ-izational leaders were singled out and targeted for heightened surveil-lance.

COINTELPRO agents were skilled at exploiting internal political divisions. They noted points of conflict, fueled leadership rivalries, and seeded mistrust. Some infiltrators stole organizational funds and blamed others to provoke infighting.[23] Accusations of members being inform-ants became frequent, and some leaders weaponized such claims to sup-press dissent. These tactics fostered a climate of fear and suspicion that undermined organizational unity.

The Young Lords sought to educate members and the public about political policing and published articles in *Palante* on "security con-sciousness," detailing the use of police surveillance and "bugging" de-vices."[24] FBI files confirm extensive intelligence-sharing across agencies in the United States and Puerto Rico.[25] Informants combed through press and radio content, submitting clippings and reports.

When I obtained my FBI file through the Freedom of Information Act, I discovered that it contained *Palante* articles and other documents, though most were heavily redacted, leaving only fragments of visible text. The file's opening date was particularly revealing—it predated the New York Young Lords chapter's founding and my membership by seven months. A notation identified "Mexico City" as the point of origin—linked to my travel to Cuba—and indicated that ten copies had been dis-tributed to various federal agencies, including the New York field office.

The FBI's harassment of Young Lords was constant. Members were routinely arrested, physically assaulted, and charged with fabricated crimes. In February 1971, *Palante* published "Repression against the

Young Lords," which documented a staggering list of arrests in the organization's first eighteen months.[26] Agents stopped members at all hours—in the streets, on subways, while distributing flyers or selling *Palante*. Demonstrations frequently ended in members being beaten or detained by the police. Charges ranged from inciting to riot, resisting arrest, and obstruction of government administration, to arson, weapons possession, and flight to avoid prosecution.

Fig. 24. Philadelphia Young Lords at New York protest.
(Courtesy: Michael Abramson)

Bogus criminal charges served strategic purposes: draining the organization's resources through mounting legal fees, exhausting members physically and emotionally, and deterring others from exercising the right to protest. These state-sanctioned attacks disrupted the Young

Lords' community work and weakened the group's capacity for sustained action.

Police violence was ever-present. In East Harlem, undercover police arrested Julio Roldán and Bobby Lemus on charges of arson for allegedly setting a fire in the building where they lived. Both were detained at the Tombs. Days later, officials claimed Roldán had hanged himself though evidence suggested he had been beaten.

COINTELPRO's influence intensified internal debates, particularly around the move to Puerto Rico. As discussed in Chapters 11 and 13, this period provided fertile conditions for infiltration and division. By 1971, the YLP's hierarchical structure allowed little space for open debate. Authoritarian practices took hold in the leadership. Members of the Central Committee began accusing others—particularly those with differing political views—of being informants or agents. Unfounded accusations eroded trust, destabilized the group, and hastened its decline. Although rank-and-file members were led to believe the allegations, actual infiltrators likely remained hidden and unexposed.

COINTELPRO's impact was devastating. Constant surveillance, harassment, and repression left many former Young Lords suffering from what we now recognize as post-traumatic stress disorder (PTSD). The psychological toll—from repeated arrests, betrayals, and internal conflicts—led to burnout, paranoia, and disillusionment. Internal dissension, fueled by accusations and name-calling, further eroded morale. As comrades were lost to arrest, violence, or defection, many of us carried the emotional burden and trauma of watching a once-vibrant organization collapse under the weight of coordinated repression. Our spirits were wounded.

Activists Challenge Police Surveillance

In 1971, a class-action lawsuit challenged the New York Police Department's longstanding practice of surveilling activists and infiltrating political organizations. The city settled the case with a consent decree known as the Handschu Agreement, which prohibited police "from investigating political and religious groups unless there was 'specific information'" linking them to criminal activity.[27]

Following the attacks of September 11, 2001, however, the NYPD escalated its surveillance of Muslim communities and sought broader powers to monitor a wider range of individuals and organizations. In response, two lawsuits were filed that successfully established "minimum safeguards" to protect Muslims from discriminatory surveillance.[28]

A separate 2016 lawsuit filed by civil liberties advocates revealed the existence of 520 boxes of surveillance records and photographs that the New York Police Department had previously claimed were lost. These boxes contained files on prominent African American leaders such as Malcolm X and Martin Luther King Jr.; organizations including the Black Panther Party, the Nation of Islam, the Congress of Racial Equality, the Young Lords, and others; as well as on anti—Vietnam War protests and other demonstrations.

Upon hearing of the "discovery," Pablo "Yoruba" Guzmán, former Minister of Information for the Young Lords Party, expressed skepticism about the value of these records. He wrote:

> We would be most interested in discovering who they sent in to infiltrate us—who were the undercovers and who was subverting what we were doing. But we're not going to find out who the turncoats were, who the agents were. They're going to redact all that.[29]

Guzmán's prediction proved correct. The 520 boxes of sanitized files revealed nothing new. They offered no information about the identities of undercover agents or informants planted within the Young Lords. For decades, members have speculated about the identity of paid agents in the organization, but the files provided no new insights into the political police's covert actions to dismantle the organization.

COINTELPRO did its job. In the end, only a few self-designated "leaders" remained in the organization, resorting to gangster tactics and violence against anyone who disagreed with them.

The U.S. government's systematic program and campaign helped destroy grassroots political movements. Yet despite these severe setbacks, activists have continued to organize and fight for economic, racial, and gender justice—demonstrating the enduring resilience and adaptive power of grassroots movements despite sustained state repression.

15.
"THE PAST DOES NOT EXIST INDEPENDENTLY FROM THE PRESENT"

> We have to keep walking, even if we are short of breath, even if we are tired, even if there are stones in the road, even if we do not see the end. Because a revolution is precisely that. It is to climb as high as you can to touch the clouds in your hand.[1]
>
> —Zuleica Romay Guerra, Director Afro-American Studies, Casa de las Américas, Havana, 2021

History is often portrayed as a linear progression, seamlessly moving from one set of events and ideas to the next. But the experiences of women in the Young Lords reveal a more layered and contested reality. Our *herstory* emerged from contradiction and complexity, shaped by the intersecting forces of colonialism, migration, racism, sexism, and poverty. As women of color, we understood our struggle as part of a much longer history, rooted in the legacies of slavery and colonialism in the Americas.

Women joined the Young Lords to fight for the rights of Puerto Ricans in the United States and for the national liberation of Puerto Rico. While we organized campaigns for immediate reforms, our vision extended beyond any single political achievement. Victories and setbacks were part of our trajectory. At the heart of our work was a commitment to structural transformation—and to socialism.

Our activism was grounded in the lived experiences of working-class and marginalized Puerto Rican, Latina, and African American women. The herstory of women in the Young Lords is a story of transformation, shaped through everyday acts of resistance, collective struggle, and radical imagination. We believed in the power of oppressed people to change society.

Between 1969 and 1972, feminists within the organization challenged a nationalist ideology molded by male supremacist ideas and practices. In this effort, we connected with African American, Chicana,

Latina, Asian, and Native feminists—learning from their histories, philosophies, and organizing traditions. Most of us had not studied nationalist or feminist theory in academic settings, nor had we been part of the white women's liberation movement. Our politics developed through grassroots organizing—rooted in community needs, lived realities, and revolutionary ideals.

The struggle for gender justice in the Young Lords unfolded in distinct phases, reflecting a battle of ideas with real consequences for women's lives.

Early Feminist Organizing—The Women's Caucus

In 1970, the women members of the Young Lords Organization formed a caucus to confront the glaring contradiction between the group's stated commitment to the liberation of all oppressed people and its internal practices. The YLO's 13-Point Program endorsement of "revolutionary machismo" revealed a fundamental inconsistency. While it asserted, "We want equality for women," it reduced the substance of gender oppression to "bad male attitudes and behavior." This framing allowed the organization to preserve patriarchal norms, avoiding any commitment to dismantling the structural foundations of women's oppression.[2]

The Women's Caucus challenged the Young Lords to confront gender inequality and to broaden their nationalist agenda to include feminist concerns. Like African American and other U.S. feminists of color, caucus members embraced the concept of triple oppression, which identifies gender, race, and class as interlocking systems of domination. This analysis pushed the organization beyond a narrow nationalist perspective, insisting that any meaningful struggle for liberation must confront the multiple, overlapping structures of power that shape the lives of Puerto Rican and other women of color.

The advocacy of the Women's Caucus culminated in the "YLP Position Paper on Women," which advanced a distinctly socialist feminist analysis. The document's call for "a revolution within the revolution" made clear that gender justice was not a diversion from the movement's goals—it was central to them. The position paper affirmed that true liberation required the dismantling of all systems of oppression, including patriarchy.

Gender studies scholar Kristie Soares has underscored the significance of the Women's Caucus, writing:

> [T]he feminist restructuring of 1970 was one of the most successful examples of feminist organizing within the decolonial movements of the time, in that it introduced a focus on gender rather than a distraction from it.[3]

This moment of feminist intervention marked a critical turning point within the organization, signaling the potential for a more expansive, inclusive vision of liberation.

Yet despite the important gains of the Women's Caucus, the fight for gender justice within the Young Lords Party remained deeply contested. The expanded liberatory vision faced serious internal challenges. At the end of 1970, in an unexpected and consequential decision, the Central Committee unilaterally disbanded the Women's Caucus. This action raised critical questions about the organization's ongoing commitment to socialist feminist politics.

The shutdown of the Women's Caucus marked both a setback and a defining challenge: How would the Central Committee confront the growing contradiction between its nationalist framework and the feminist advances that had begun to take root?

The Women's Union: Between Nationalism and Feminism

In 1971, feminist struggles within the Young Lords Party entered a second phase. That year, the Central Committee declared that the organization's principal mission was to support Puerto Rico's anti-colonial struggle and launched *Ofensiva Rompe Cadenas*. This political shift reoriented the organization's strategic priorities, particularly in the diaspora. As part of its plan to build "people's organizations" in the United States, the Central Committee approved the formation of the Women's Union (WU). It developed as a vehicle for advancing an intersectional socialist feminist politics. The WU organized political education workshops, published a bilingual newspaper (*La Luchadora*), and took part in protests.

Its 12-Point Program articulated a radical vision that linked women's liberation to anti-imperialism, anti-racism, and class struggle—attracting members who sought a political home for women's rights.

However, the Central Committee moved to take direct control of the Women's Union, redefining its mission as subordinate to the goal of Puerto Rico's national liberation. Rather than support feminist organizing, the leadership redefined the WU's purpose as an auxiliary body. Women's issues, the Central Committee argued, could be addressed after the revolution, once Puerto Rico achieved independence.

This shift subverted the original purpose of the Women's Union, which had been to organize around the specific needs and conditions of Puerto Rican women in the diaspora, particularly in relation to gender, race, class, and migration.

Feminist Organizing: Carrying the Struggle Forward

The activism of feminists in the Young Lords was part of a broader surge of radical organizing led by women of color. From the 1960s through the mid-1970s, the activism of African American, Latina, Chicana, Puerto Rican, Asian, and Native women forged a vital bridge between earlier herstories and future movements for gender and racial justice. Feminist thought and practice continued to evolve, shaping new generations of intersectional activism.

In 1974, Black feminist lesbian socialists formed the Combahee River Collective, whose 1977 Combahee River Collective Statement remains foundational to Black feminist and socialist political theory and organizing. That same year, women within the Puerto Rican Socialist Party played a key role in establishing the Committee to End Sterilization Abuse. In 1975, members of El Comité–MINP (*Movimiento de Izquierda Nacional Puertorriqueño*), formed the Latin Women's Collective.

By the 1980s, Chicana feminists were producing a rich body of writing that expanded the theoretical and political foundations of women of color feminism. A landmark in this tradition was the 1981 anthology *This Bridge Called My Back: Writings by Radical Women of Color*, edited by Cherríe Moraga and Gloria Anzaldúa.

These efforts continue to resonate with—and inspire—new generations of activist feminists of color.

Reckoning with the Present

Revisiting Herstories: The Young Lords Party was originally written during the global COVID-19 crisis. This revised edition retains the discussion of the pandemic's impact because it so starkly illuminates the longstanding structural inequalities that remain relevant to feminist and social justice organizing.

While millions lost their lives and the poor plunged into further poverty, the wealth of billionaires—overwhelmingly white men entrenched in global capitalist systems—soared. They further enriched themselves through the intensified exploitation of labor, especially the undervalued and often invisible labor of women.

COVID-19 revealed the compounding burdens that women bear, underscoring the centrality of their labor to social and economic survival.[4] A study of the Organisation for Economic Co-operation and Development (OECD) highlighted that women are overrepresented in healthcare systems, continue to bear the majority of unpaid household labor, and face disproportionately high risks of economic insecurity and violence during times of crisis and quarantine.[5]

Even before COVID-19, women performed the vast majority of the world's unpaid care work. The crisis dramatically intensified this burden,[6] magnifying the ongoing neglect of socially reproductive work—childcare, domestic work, eldercare, and other forms of unpaid work. These forms of labor are essential to the functioning of society, yet they are overlooked and undervalued.

In the United States, Latina, Black, Indigenous, and immigrant women were the hardest-hit pandemic victims—particularly women without college degrees.[7] Existing health disparities were compounded by other systemic inequities, including workplace discrimination, rollbacks in reproductive rights, high incarceration rates, and attacks on immigrant families, among others. These realities reflect the enduring legacies of racial and ethnic injustice rooted in European imperialism and colonization across the Americas.[8]

In Puerto Rico, COVID-19 heightened the ongoing humanitarian crisis. Still under U.S. rule, the oppression of Puerto Rican women "cannot be separated from the colonial experience."[9] The intersection of colonialism, capitalism, and patriarchy continues to assert control over both the archipelago and women's bodies.[10] During the pandemic, gender violence rose—including state-sanctioned brutality, domestic violence, and sexual harassment in the streets and workplaces. As feminist scholar Marisol LeBrón emphasizes, the struggle against gender-based violence is "part of a larger constellation of structural forces that harm women and limit life chances."[11] Puerto Rico's femicide rate remains one of the highest in the Americas.[12]

Amid the global COVID-19 crisis, activists managed to open spaces for collective action throughout 2020. The far-reaching impacts of the pandemic galvanized millions to demand bold and transformative change. As state and institutional responses failed, communities mobilized, creating grassroots networks of mutual aid and political action. Black Lives Matter gained renewed urgency in responding to state-sanctioned killings of Black people. Feminist movements worldwide pushed for reproductive justice, racial equity, and economic rights. [13] In Latin America, feminist victories such as the legalization of abortion in Argentina, Mexico, and Colombia marked significant milestones in the fight for gender justice.[14]

COVID-19 laid bare the extreme concentration of wealth and power across the world, emphasizing the urgent need to redirect resources toward human needs and structural transformation. The current capitalist, profit-driven model cannot be reformed—it must be replaced with new visions of society grounded in justice, care, and collective well-being.

Today, that crisis has only deepened. Global fascism is on the rise, fueled by white nationalism and bankrolled by billionaires. Endless wars persist, economic inequality has reached staggering levels, and the climate crisis accelerates—marked by fiercer storms, prolonged droughts, and rising seas. These overlapping catastrophes are displacing millions, intensifying global migration, and ravaging our planet.

At the same time, racial, gender, and sexual violence remain rampant, sustained by entrenched systems of oppression. State-sanctioned brutality continues to target the most vulnerable. The global threat posed by these intersecting crises is urgent and undeniable, as centuries-old systems of exploitation grow more violent.

Any meaningful transformation of societies must confront the intersecting oppressions of class, race, gender, colonialism, and environmental destruction. Human rights lawyer and feminist Erika Guevara Rosas underscores this imperative:

> Solutions can be found only through collective and connected efforts at community, national and global levels. ... It is not about system recovery after COVID-19, it must be system redesign and transformation, eliminating all forms of gender-based violence and discrimination, while addressing their root causes.[15]

The leadership, strategies, and visions of historically excluded communities—especially low-income Black, Indigenous, and other marginalized women of color—must be central to this process. Across the globe, feminist movements continue to offer imagination, hope, and radical pathways toward a future grounded in collective action, care, and solidarity.

Final Reflections

Revisiting Herstories: The Young Lords Party centers the ideas, strategies, and actions of U.S. feminists of color in the late 1960s and early 1970s. As Puerto Rican women activists, we were part of a global movement for societal transformation, where working-class and marginalized women of color played leading roles. Facing internal tensions and external pressures, we contributed to reshaping the revolutionary movement—pushing its boundaries, challenging its assumptions, and making it more inclusive of the struggles women faced. These lessons of resistance and collective organizing remind us that people committed to revolutionary principles and actions have the power to create change that benefits all of humanity.

This defining moment calls to all who believe in justice, liberation, and the dignity of life. Our response—our actions—will shape what comes next. Our goals remain unwavering: the liberation of all oppressed peoples, the dismantling of racism and gender-based exploitation, and the creation of a world rooted in human needs and social justice.

Fig 25. Former members of the Young Lords Party. 2015.
L to R: Wilma, Denise, Minerva, Olguie, Gloria Rodríguez, Iris,
Cookie, and Martha

Fig 26. 50th Anniversary of the Young Lords Party. July 2019.
(Photos courtesy: José Angel Figueroa)

ACKNOWLEDGMENTS

I am thankful for the opportunity to publish this revised edition of *Revisiting Herstories: The Young Lords Party*. It allowed me to return to the original work with a more critical and reflective lens—to address gaps, clarify key concepts, and incorporate my evolving perspectives. This edition represents a deepening of purpose: to more fully honor the voices, complexities, and legacies that shape this herstory.

I am especially grateful to Dr. Jacqueline Lazú, whose thoughtful and multilayered introduction brings depth to the narrative and places its relevance within both scholarly and activist communities. Her insightful review of the original edition inspired me to invite her to contribute to this volume. Collaborating with her has been a true joy and a reminder of the strength found in solidarity. Through our work together, we have connected histories that have too often been treated in isolation, reaffirming their shared visions for justice and liberation.

My deepest respect to all the Young Lords who took part in the struggle for social justice, Puerto Rican rights, and the national liberation of Puerto Rico—and who remained true to revolutionary principles and practices despite the many obstacles placed in our path, both within and beyond the organization.

I am honored to have been active in struggle alongside remarkable, caring, and dedicated African American, Latina, Indigenous, and Asian feminists—women who carried out the day-to-day work of revolutionary change. Women were the heart of the Young Lords Party, and I want to acknowledge the women in New York with whom I worked most closely: Mecca Adai, Micky Agrait, Marta Arguello, Bernadette Baken, Iris Benítez, Diana Caballero, Lulu Carreras, Gloria Colón, Carmen Copeland, Aida Cruset, Yolanda DeJesus, Yvonne Dominguez, Jenny Figueroa, Elena González, Mirta González, Beverly Kruset, Elsie López, Lulu Limardo, Letty Lozano, Doleza Miah, Myrna Martínez, Nydia Mercado, Carmen Mercado, Connie Morales, Elsie Morales, Denise Oliver, Isa Ríos, Olguie Robles, Gloria Rodríguez, Miriam Rodríguez, Elba Saavedra, Marlin Segarra, Lydia Silva, Cleo Silvers, and Becky Serrano.

This book is the result of many hearts and histories coming together. I want to acknowledge those whose support, labor, and commitment made its completion possible.

First, I thank my mother Almida Roldan for her guiding spirit and perseverance in the face of adversity.

I thank my compañero, José Angel Figueroa, for his steadfast support. His belief in this book and consistent reassurance encouraged me to write—and to keep writing. His comments, insights, and poetic reflections on many drafts inspired me to dig deeper to recover forgotten stories.

My heartfelt thanks to my dear friend, Dr. Deborah Paredez, whose early reading of the manuscript gave me the confidence to move forward with the project.

I owe a debt of gratitude to Dr. Edna Acosta-Belén for graciously reading an early draft of the manuscript. Her thoughtful comments and notes prompted further research that significantly enriched the content. I thank her for her guidance, patience, and scholarship.

I offer special thanks to Dr. Barbara Ransby—historian, scholar, and activist—whose work on social justice movements and Black women freedom fighters I have long admired. I am deeply honored to have her support for this book.

Several scholars, colleagues, and friends read drafts of sections or chapters and offered invaluable feedback that shaped the historical framing and narrative. My sincere thanks to Dr. Ujju Aggawal, Dr. Nicole Burrows, Dr. Claudia Sofía Garriga-López, Dr. Rebeca Hey-Colón, Dr. Vanessa Valdes, Dr. Wilson Valentin Escobar, and Karina Hurtado-Ocampo for their probing questions, suggested readings, and technical comments. I also thank Dr. Ariana Mangual for her wise counsel on an initial proposal, and Dr. Jillian Baez and Dr. Claudine Taffee for their early encouragement. Thank you to Felicitas N. Nunez, Carmen Rivera, and Carmen Vivian Rivera for reading sections of the manuscript, and to Wendy Barrales and Maya García for conducting preliminary research.

I thank my friend Michael Abramson for allowing me to include his iconic photographs in this book. It has been a pleasure to collaborate with him on multiple projects over many years.

Craig Wilse provided a meticulous editorial review of the manuscript. His analysis and observations pushed me to see the bigger picture in the details. I also thank Norman Ware for his careful and thorough final editing.

Writing during the isolation of the pandemic made staying connected with family and friends vital to my spirit and well-being. They sustained me during the most difficult moments and reminded me that I was not alone in the work. My son Adrien was a thoughtful and steady presence. My grandson Lorenzo made me laugh—often and loudly. My sister, Yolanda, shared beautiful reminiscences. I'm thankful to my friends Vernon Douglas, Patricia Leonard, Anna Gyorgy, Francia Castro, Lori Salmon, who sent texts, photos, and caring messages. Thank you to Ángel Antonio Ruiz, DK Dyson, Magdalena Gomez, Lisa Jones, and Betsy Salas for your kind check-ins.

I extend special thanks to Dr. Darrel Enck-Wanzer for *The Young Lords: A Reader*, which was a key resource for many of the Young Lords' documents referenced in this book.

JT Tagaki and Roselly Torres deserve recognition for their excellent work promoting and distributing the documentary, *¡Palante Siempre Palante! The Young Lords*. My thanks to Dr. Yarimar Bonilla, then Director of the Center for Puerto Rican Studies, and Dr. Frances Negrón-Muntaner for hosting a commemoration of the film's 25th anniversary and to Edgardo Miranda Rodríguez, Vanessa Roman, and Patria Rodríguez for their participation.

Finally, I wish to recognize Newsreel and Third World Newsreel for the production and distribution of *¡El Pueblo Se Levanta! The People Rise Up!* Since 1971, this cinema verité documentary has helped keep alive a visual history of the Young Lords Party and the social justice and anti-colonial struggles of the Puerto Rican people.

APPENDIX

- 13-Point Program & Platform (Written October 1969)
- 13-Point Program & Platform, (Revised, December 1970)
- Young Lords Party Position Paper on Women (September 1970)
- Why a Women's Union? (June 1971)
- Women's Union 12-Point Program (June 1971)

13 POINT PROGRAM
AND PLATFORM
YOUNG LORDS ORGANIZATION
OCTOBER 1969

THE YOUNG LORDS ORGANIZATION IS A REVOLUTIONARY
POLITICAL PARTY FIGHTING FOR THE LIBERATION OF ALL
OPPRESSED PEOPLE

1. WE WANT SELF-DETERMINATION FOR PUERTO RICANS-- LIBERATION ON THE ISLAND AND INSIDE THE UNITED STATES

For 500 years, first spain and then the united states have colonized our country. Billions of dollars in profits leave our country for the united states every year. In every way we are slaves of the gringo. We want liberation and the Power in the hands of the People, not Puerto Rican exploiters.
QUE VIVA PUERTO RICO LIBRE!

2. WE WANT SELF-DETERMINATION FOR ALL LATINOS

Our Latin Brothers and Sisters, inside and outside the united states, are oppressed by amerikkkan business. The Chicano people built the Southwest, and we support their right to control their lives and their land. The people of Santo Domingo continue to fight against gringo domination and its puppet generals. The armed liberation stuggles in Latin America are part of the same war of Latinos against imperialism.
QUE VIVA LA RAZA!

3. WE WANT LIBERATION OF ALL THIRD WORLD PEOPLE

Just as Latins first slaved under spain and then the yanquis, Black people, Indians and Asians slaved to build the wealth of this country. For 400 years they have fought for freedom and dignity against racist Babylon (decadent empire). Third World people have led the fight for freedom. All the colored and oppressed peoples of the world are one nation under oppression.
NO PUERTO RICAN IS FREE UNTIL ALL PEOPLE ARE FREE!

4. WE ARE REVOLUTIONARY NATIONALISTS AND OPPOSE RACISM

The Latin, Black, Indian and Asian people inside the u.s. are colonies fighting for liberation. We know that washington, wall street, and city hall will try to make our nationalism into racism; but Puerto Ricans are of all colors and we resist racism. Millions of poor white people are rising up to demand freedom and we support them. These are the ones in the u.s. that are stepped on by the rulers and the government. We each organize our people, but our fights are the same against oppression and we will defeat it together.
POWER TO ALL OPPRESSED PEOPLE!

5. WE WANT COMMUNITY CONTROL OF OUR INSTITUTIONS AND LAND

We want control of our communities by our people and programs to guarantee that all institutions serve the needs of our people. People's control of police, health services, churches, schools, housing, transportation and welfare are needed. We want an end to attacks on our land by urban removal, highway destruction, universities and corporations.
LAND BELONGS TO ALL THE PEOPLE!

6. WE WANT A TRUE EDUCATION OF OUR CREOLE CULTURE AND SPANISH LANGUAGE

We must learn our history of fighting against cultural, as well as economic genocide by the yanqui. Revolutionary culture, culture of our people, is the only true teaching.
LONG LIVE BORICUA!   LONG LIVE EL JIBARO!

7. WE OPPOSE CAPITALISTS AND ALLIANCES WITH TRAITORS

Puerto Rican rulers, or puppets of the oppressor, do not help our people. They are paid by the system to lead our people down blind alleys, just like the thousands of poverty pimps who keep our communities peaceful for business, or the street workers who keep gangs divided and blowing each other away. We want a society where the people socialistically control their labor.
VENCEREMOS!

8. WE OPPOSE THE AMERIKKKAN MILITARY

We demand immediate withdrawal of us military forces and bases from Puerto Rico, Vietnam, and all oppressed communities inside and outside the us. No Puerto Rican should serve in the u.s. army against his Brothers and Sisters, for the only true army of oppressed people is the people's army to fight all rulers.
U.S. OUT OF VIETNAM, FREE PUERTO RICO!

9. WE WANT FREEDOM FOR ALL POLITICAL PRISONERS

We want all Puerto Ricans freed because they have been tried by the racist courts of the colonizers, and not by their own people and peers. We want all freedom fighters released from jail.
FREE ALL POLITICAL PRISONERS!

10. WE WANT EQUALITY FOR WOMEN. MACHISMO MUST BE REVOLUTIONARY...NOT OPPRESSIVE

Under capitalism, our people have been oppressed by both the society and our own men. The doctrine of machismo has been used by our men to take out their frustrations against their wives, sisters, mothers, and children. Our men must support their women in their fight for economic and social equality, and must recognize that our women are equals in every way within the revolutionary ranks.
FORWARD, SISTERS, IN THE STRUGGLE!

11. WE FIGHT ANTI-COMMUNISM WITH INTERNATIONAL UNITY.

Anyone who resists injustice is called a communist by "the man" and condemned. Our people are brainwashed by television, radio, newspapers, schools, and books to oppose people in other countries fighting for their freedom. No longer will our people believe attacks and slanders, because they have learned who the real enemy is and who their real friends are. We will defend our Brothers and Sisters around the world who fight for justice against the rich rulers of this country.
VIVA CHE!

12. WE BELIEVE ARMED SELF-DEFENSE AND ARMED STRUGGLE ARE THE ONLY MEANS TO LIBERATION

We are opposed to violence--the violence of hungry children, illiterate adults, diseased old people, and the violence of poverty and profit. We have asked, petitioned, gone to courts, demonstrated peacefully, and voted for politicians full of empty promises. But we still ain't free. The time has come to defend the lives of our people against repression and for revolutionary war against the businessman, politician, and police. When a government oppresses our people, we have the right to abolish it and create a new one.
BORICUA IS AWAKE!   ALL PIGS BEWARE!

13. WE WANT A SOCIALIST SOCIETY

We want liberation, clothing, free food, education, health care, transportation, utilities, and employment for all. We want a society where the needs of our people come first, and where we give solidarity and aid to the peoples of the world, not oppression and racism.
HASTA LA VICTORIA SIEMPRE!

Fig. 27. 13-Point Program. October 1969.

YOUNG LORDS PARTY

13 POINT PROGRAM

AND PLATFORM

TENGO PUERTO RICO EN MI CORAZON

YLP

THE YOUNG LORDS PARTY IS A REVOLUTIONARY POLITICAL PARTY FIGHTING FOR THE LIBERATION OF ALL OPPRESSED PEOPLE

1. WE WANT SELF-DETERMINATION FOR PUERTO RICANS, LIBERATION ON THE ISLAND AND INSIDE THE UNITED STATES.

For 500 years, first spain and then the united states have colonized our country. Billions of dollars in profits leave our country for the united states every year. In every way we are slaves of the gringo. We want liberation and the Power in the hands of the People, not Puerto Rican exploiters. QUE VIVA PUERTO RICO LIBRE!

2. WE WANT SELF-DETERMINATION FOR ALL LATINOS.

Our Latin Brothers and Sisters, inside and outside the united states, are oppressed by amerikkkan business. The Chicano people built the Southwest, and we support their right to control their lives and their land. The people of Santo Domingo continue to fight against gringo domination and its puppet generals. The armed liberation struggles in Latin America are part of the war of Latinos against imperialism. QUE VIVA LA RAZA!

3. WE WANT LIBERATION OF ALL THIRD WORLD PEOPLE.

Just as Latins first slaved under spain and the yanquis, Black people, Indians, and Asians slaved to build the wealth of this country. For 400 years they have fought for freedom and dignity against racist Babylon. Third World people have led the fight for freedom. All the colored and oppressed peoples of the world are one nation under oppression. NO PUERTO RICAN IS FREE UNTIL ALL PEOPLE ARE FREE!

4. WE ARE REVOLUTIONARY NATIONALISTS' AND OPPOSE RACISM

The Latin, Black, Indian and Asian people inside the u.s. are colonies fighting for liberation. We know that washington, wall street, and city hall will try to make our nationalism into racism; but Puerto Ricans are of all colors and we resist racism. Millions of poor white people are rising up to demand freedom and we support them. These are the ones in the u.s. that are, stepped on by the rulers and the government. We each organize our people, but our fights are the same against oppression and we will defeat it together. POWER TO ALL OPPRESSED PEOPLE!

5. WE WANT EQUALITY FOR WOMEN. DOWN WITH MACHISMO AND MALE CHAUVANISM.

Under capitalism, women have been oppressed by both society and our men. The doctrine of machismo has been used by men to take out their frustrations on wives, sisters, mothers, and children. Men must fight along with sisters in the struggle for economic and social equality and must recognize that sisters make up over half of the revolutionary army; sisters and brothers are equals fighting for our people. FORWARD SISTERS IN THE STRUGGLE!

6. WE WANT COMMUNITY CONTROL OF OUR INSTITUTIONS AND LAND.

We want control of our communities by our people and programs to guarantee that all institutions serve the needs of our people. People's control of police, health services, churches, schools, housing, transportation and welfare are needed. We want an end to attacks on our land by urban renewal, highway destruction, and university corporations. LAND BELONGS TO ALL THE PEOPLE!

7. WE WANT A TRUE EDUCATION OF OUR AFRO-INDIO CULTURE AND SPANISH LANGUAGE.

We must learn our long history of fighting against cultural, as well as economic genocide by the spaniards and now the yanquis. Revolutionary culture, culture of our people, is the only true teaching. JIBARO SI, YANQUI NO!

8. WE OPPOSE CAPITALISTS AND ALLIANCES WITH TRAITORS.

Puerto Rican rulers, or puppets of the oppressor, do not help our people. They are paid by the system to lead our people down blind alleys, just like the thousands of poverty pimps who keep our communities peaceful for business, or the street workers who keep gangs divided and blowing each other away. We want a society where the people socialistically control their labor. VENCEREMOS!

9. WE OPPOSE THE AMERIKKKAN MILITARY.

We demand immediate withdrawal of all u.s. military forces and bases from Puerto Rico, VietNam, and all oppressed communities inside and outside the u.s. No Puerto Rican should serve in the u.s. army against his Brothers and Sisters, for the only true army of oppressed people is the People's Liberation Army to fight all rulers. U.S. OUT OF VIETNAM, FREE PUERTO RICO NOW!

10. WE WANT FREEDOM FOR ALL POLITICAL PRISONERS AND PRISONERS OF WAR.

No Puerto Rican should be in jail or prison, first because we are a nation, and amerikkka has no claims on us; second, because we have not been tried by our own people (peers). We also want all freedom fighters out of jail, since they are prisoners of the war for liberation. FREE ALL POLITICAL PRISONERS AND PRISONERS OF WAR!

11. WE ARE INTERNATIONALISTS.

Our people are brainwashed by television, radio, newspapers, schools and books to oppose people in other countries fighting for their freedom. No longer will we believe these lies, because we have learned who the real enemy is and who our real friends are. We will defend our sisters and brothers around the world who fight for justice and are against the rulers of this country. QUE VIVA CHE GUEVARA!

12. WE BELIEVE ARMED SELF-DEFENSE AND ARMED STRUGGLE ARE THE ONLY MEANS TO LIBERATION

We are oppose to violence - the violence of hungry children, illiterate adults, diseased old people, and the violence of poverty and profit. We have asked, petitioned, gone to courts, demonstrated peacefully, and voted for politicians full of empty promises. But we still ain't free. The time has come to defend the lives of our people against repression and for revolutionary war against the businessmen, politicians, and police. When a government oppresses the people, we have the right to abolish it and create a new one. ARM OURSELVES TO DEFEND OURSELVES!

13. WE WANT A SOCIALIST SOCIETY.

We want liberation, clothing, free food, education, health care, transportation, full employment and peace. We want a society where the needs of the people come first, and where we give solidarity and aid to the people of the world, not oppression and racism. HASTA LA VICTORIA SIEMPRE!

Fig. 28. 13-Point Program. Revised, December 1970.

YLP POSITION PAPER ON WOMEN
CENTRAL COMMITTEE

Puerto Rican, Black, and other Third World (colonized) women are becoming more aware of their oppression in the past and today. They are suffering three different types of oppression under capitalism. First, they are oppressed as Puerto Ricans or Blacks. Second, they are oppressed as women. Third, they are oppressed by their own men. The Third World woman becomes the most oppressed person in the world today.

Economically, Third World women have always been used as a cheap source of labor and as sexual objects. Puerto Rican and Black women are used to fill working class positions in factories, mass assembly lines, hospitals, and all other institutions. Puerto Rican and Black women are paid lower wages than whites and kept in the lowest positions within society. At the same time, giving Puerto Rican and Black women jobs means that the Puerto Rican and Black man is kept from gaining economic independence, and the family unit is broken down. Capitalism defines manhood according to money and status; the Puerto Rican and Black man's manhood is taken away by making the Puerto Rican and Black woman the breadwinner. This situation keeps the Third World man divided from his woman. The Puerto Rican and Black man either leaves the household, or he stays and becomes economically dependent on the woman, undergoing psychological damage. He takes out all of his frustrations on his woman, beating her, repressing, and limiting her freedom. Because this society produces these conditions, our major enemy is capitalism rather than our oppressed men.

Third World Women have an integral role to play in the liberation of oppressed people as well as in the struggle for the liberation of women. Puerto Rican and Black women make up over half of the revolutionary army, and in the struggle for national liberation they must press for the equality of women. The woman's struggle is the revolution within the revolution. Puerto Rican women will be neither behind nor in front of their brothers but always alongside them in mutual respect and love.

Historical

In the past women were oppressed by several institutions, one of which was marriage. When a woman married a man, she became his property and lost her last name. A man could have several wives in order to show other men what wealth he had and enhance his position in society. In Eastern societies men always had several wives and a number of women who were almost prostitutes, called concubines, purely sexual objects. Women had no right to own anything, not even their children; they were owned by her husband. This was true in places all over the world. In many societies, women had no right to be divorced, and in India it was the custom of most of the people that when the husband died, all his wives became the property of his brother.

In Latin America and Puerto Rico, the man had a wife, and another woman called la corteja. This condition still exists today. The wife was there to be a homemaker, to have children and to maintain the family name and honor. She had to be sure to be a virgin and remain pure for the rest of her life, meaning she could never experience sexual pleasure. The wife had to have children in order to enhance the man's concept of virility and his position within the Puerto Rican society. La corteja became his sexual instrument. The man could have set her up in another household, paid her rent, bought her food, and paid her bills. He could have children with this woman, but they are looked upon as by-products of a sexual relationship. Both women had to be loyal to the man. Both sets of children grew up very confused and insecure and developed negative attitudes about the role.

Women have always been expected to be wives and mothers only. The community respects them for being good cooks, good housewives, and good mothers but never for being intelligent, strong, educated, or militant. In the past, women were not educated, only the sons got an education, and mothers were respected for the number of sons they had, not daughters. Daughters were worthless, and the only thing they could do was marry early to get away from home. At home, the role of the daughter was to be a nursemaid for the other children and kitchen help for her mother.

The daughter was guarded like a hawk by her father, brothers, and uncles to keep her a virgin. In Latin America, the people used dueñas or old lady watchdogs to guard the purity of the daughters. The husband must be sure that his new wife never has been touched by another man because that would ruin the "merchandise." When he marries her, her purpose is to have sons and keep his home but not to be a sexual partner.

Sex was a subject that was never discussed, and women were brainwashed into believing that the sex act was dirty and immoral, and its only function was for the making of children. In Africa, many tribes performed an operation on young girls to remove the clitoris so they would not get any pleasure out of sex and would become better workers.

The Double Standard, Machismo, and Sexual Fascism

Capitalism sets up standards applied differently to Puerto Rican and Black men from the way they are applied to Puerto Rican and Black women. These standards are also applied differently to Third World people than they are applied to whites. These standards must be understood since they are created to divide oppressed people in order to maintain an economic system that is racist and oppressive.

Puerto Rican and Black men are looked upon as rough, athletic, and sexual, but not as intellectuals. Puerto Rican women are not expected to know anything except about the home, kitchen, and bedroom. All that they are expected to do is look pretty and add a little humor. The Puerto Rican man sees himself as superior to his woman, and his superiority, he feels, gives him license to do many things—curse, drink, use drugs, beat women, and run around with many women. As a matter of fact these things are considered natural for a man to do, and he must do them to be considered a man. A woman who curses, drinks, and runs around with a lot of men is considered dirty scum, crazy, and a whore.

Today Puerto Rican men are involved in a political movement. Yet the majority of their women are home taking care of the children. The Puerto Rican sister that involves herself is considered aggressive, castrating, hard, and unwomanly. She is viewed by the brothers as sexually accessible because what else is she doing outside of the home. The Puerto Rican man tries to limit the woman's role because he feels the double standard is threatened; he feels insecure without it as a crutch.

Machismo has always been a very basic part of Latin American and Puerto Rican culture. Machismo is male chauvinism and more. Machismo means "mucho macho" or a man who puts himself selfishly at the head of everything without considering the woman. He can do whatever he wants because his woman is an object with certain already defined roles: wife, mother, and good woman.

Machismo means physical abuse, punishment, and torture. A Puerto Rican man will beat his woman to keep her in place and show her who's boss. Most Puerto Rican men do not beat women publicly because in the eyes of other men that is a weak thing to do. So, they usually wait until they're home. All the anger and violence of centuries of oppression that should be directed against the oppressor is directed at the woman. The aggression is also directed at daughters. The daughters hear their fathers saying, "the only way a woman is going to do anything, or listen is by hitting her." The father applies this to the daughter, beating her so that she can learn *respeto*. The daughters grow up with messed-up attitudes about their role as women and about manhood. They grow to expect that men will always beat them.

Sexual fascists are very sick people. Their illness is caused in part by this system, which mouths puritanical attitudes and laws and yet exploits the human body for profit.

Sexual Fascism is tied closely to the double standard and machismo. It means that a man or woman thinks of the opposite sex solely as sexual objects to be used for gratification and then discarded. Sexual fascists do not consider people's feelings; all they see everywhere is a pussy or a dick. They will use any rap, especially political, to get sex.

Prostitution

Under capitalism, Third World women are forced to compromise themselves because of their economic situation. The facts that her man cannot get a job and that the family is dependent on her for support means she hustles money by any means necessary. Black and Puerto Rican sisters are put into a situation where jobs are scarce or nonexistent and are forced to compromise body, mind, and soul; they are then called whores or prostitutes. Puerto Rican and Black sisters are made to prostitute themselves in many other ways. The majority of these sisters on the street are also hard-core drug addicts, taking drugs as an escape from oppression. These sisters are subjected to sexual abuse from dirty old men who are mainly white racists who view them as the ultimate sexual objects. Also, he has the attitude that he cannot really prove his manhood until he has slept with a Black or Puerto Rican woman. The sisters also suffer abuse from the pimps, really small-time capitalists, who see the woman as private property that must produce the largest possible profit.

Because this society controls and determines the economic situation of Puerto Rican and Black women, sisters are forced to take jobs at the lowest wages, and at the same time take insults and other indignities in order to keep the job. In factories, our men are worked like animals and cannot complain because they will lose their jobs—their labor is considered abundant and cheap. In hospitals, our women comprise the majority of the nurses' aides, kitchen workers, and clerks. These jobs are unskilled; the pay is low, and there is no chance for advancement. In offices, our positions are usually as clerks, typists, and no-promotion jobs. In all of these jobs, our sisters are subjected to racial slurs, jokes, and other indignities such as being leered at, manhandled, propositioned, and assaulted. Our sisters are expected to prostitute themselves and take abuse of any kind or lose these subsistence jobs.

Everywhere our sisters are turned into prostitutes. The most obvious example is the sisters hustling their bodies on the streets, but the other forms of prostitution are also types of further exploitation of the Third World woman. The only way to eliminate prostitution is to eliminate this society, which creates the need. Then we can establish a socialist society that meets the economic needs of all the people.

Birth Control, Abortion, Sterilization-Genocide

We have no control over our bodies, because capitalism finds it necessary to control the woman's body to control population size. The choice of motherhood is being taken out of the mother's hands. She is sterilized to prevent her from having children, or she has to have a child because she cannot get an abortion.

Third World sisters are caught up in a complex situation. On one hand, we feel that genocide is being committed against our people. We know that Puerto Ricans will not be around very long if Puerto Rican women are sterilized at the rate, they are being sterilized now. . . .. Part of this genocide is also the use of birth control pills, which were tested for 15 years on Puerto Rican sisters (guinea pigs) before being sold in the U.S. market. Even now many doctors feel that these pills cause cancer and death from blood clotting.

Abortions in hospitals that are butcher shops are little better than the illegal abortions our women used to get. The first abortion death in NYC under the new abortion law was Carmen Rodríguez, a Puerto Rican sister who died in Lincoln Hospital. Her abortion was legal, but the conditions in the hospital were deadly. On the other hand, we believe that abortions should be legal if they are community controlled, if they are safe, if our people are educated about the risks, and if doctors do not sterilize our sisters while performing abortions. We realize that under capitalism our sisters and brothers cannot support large families and the more children we have, the harder it is to support them. We say, change the system so that women can freely be allowed to have as many children as they want without suffering any consequences.

Day Care Centers

One of the main reasons why many sisters are tied to the home and cannot work or become revolutionaries is the shortage of day care centers for children. The centers that already exist are overcrowded, expensive, and are only super-baby-sitting centers. Day care centers should be free, should be open 24 hours a day, and should be centers where children are taught their revolutionary history and culture. Many sisters leave their children with a neighbor, or the oldest child is left to take care of the younger ones. Sometimes they are left alone, and all of us have read the tragic results in the newspapers of what happens to children left alone—they are burned to death in fires, or they swallow poison, or fall out of windows to their death.

Revolutionary Women

Throughout history, women have participated and been involved in liberation struggles. But the writers of history have never given full acknowledgment to the role of revolutionary women.

MARIANA BRACETTI was a Puerto Rican woman who together with her husband fought in the struggle for independence in Lares. She was called "El Brazo de Oro" because of her unlimited energy. For her role in the struggle, she was imprisoned. She sewed the first flag of El Grito de Lares.

Another nationalist woman was LOLA RODRÍGUEZ DE TIÓ, a poet who expressed the spirit of liberty and freedom in "La Borinqueña" in 1867. Besides being a nationalist, she was a fighter for women's rights. She refused to conform to the traditional customs concerning Puerto Rican women and at one point cut her hair very short.

BLANCA CANALES was a leader of the revolution in Jayuya in 1950.

LOLITA LEBRÓN, together with three other patriots, opened fire on the House of Representatives [in Washington, DC] in an armed attack in 1954 bringing the attention of the world to Puerto Rico's colonial status. She emptied a .45 automatic from the balcony of the Congress onto the colonial legislators. She then draped herself in the Puerto Rican flag and cried, "Viva Puerto Rico Libre." The result was five legislators [were] shot, and one critically wounded. She was imprisoned in a federal penitentiary and sentenced to 50 years and is still in prison for this heroic act.

Only recently, a 19-year-old coed, ANTONIA MARTÍNEZ, was killed in Puerto Rico in a demonstration against the presence of amerikkkan military recruiting centers. She was murdered when she yelled, "Viva Puerto Rico Libre!"

SOJOURNER TRUTH was born a slave in New York around 1800. She traveled in the north speaking out against slavery and for women's rights. She was one of the most famous Black orators in history.

KATHLEEN CLEAVER is a member of the Central Committee of the Black Panther Party. The Black Panthers are the vanguard of the Black liberation struggle in the United States. Another Panther sister, ERICKA HUGGINS, is imprisoned in Connecticut for supposedly being a member of a conspiracy. She was forced to have her child in prison and was given no medical attention while she was pregnant. Her child was later taken away from her because of her political beliefs.

ANGELA DAVIS is a Black revolutionary sister who is being hunted by the f.b.i. and is on their 10 most wanted list because she has always defended her people's right to armed self-defense and because of her Marxist-Leninist philosophy.

In other parts of the world, women are fighting against imperialism and foreign invasion. Our sisters in Vietnam have struggled alongside their brothers for 26 years; first against the french colonizer, then against the japanese invaders, and now against the amerikkkan aggressors. Their military capability and efficiency have been demonstrated in so many instances that a women's brigade was formed in the National Liberation Front of the North Vietnamese Army.

LA THI THAM was born in a province constantly bombarded by U.S. planes. After her fiancé was killed in action, she sought and got a job with a time bomb detecting team. She scanned the sky with field glasses and when the enemy dropped bombs along the countryside, she would locate those that had not yet exploded, and her teammates would open them and clear the road for traffic.

KAN LICH, another Vietnamese sister, fought under very harsh and dangerous conditions. She became a brilliant commander, decorated many times for her military ability. Her practice to "hit at close quarters, hit hard, withdraw quickly" proved to be valid.

The Central Committee of the Young Lords Party has issued this position paper to explain and to educate about the role of sisters in the past and how we see sisters in the struggle now and in the future. We criticize those brothers who are "machos" and who continue to treat our sisters as less than equals. We criticize sisters who remain passive, who do not join in the struggle against our oppression. We are fighting every day within our party against male chauvinism because we want to make a revolution of brothers and sisters, together, in love and respect for each other.

Palante, vol. 2, no. 12, September 25, 1970

WHY A WOMEN'S UNION?

June 1971

The Third World Woman is exploited in many ways.

First, we are used as a source of cheap labor. As workingwomen, we get the dirtiest jobs at the lowest wages. We get paid less than men and less than white women for the same amount of work. Because we work out of necessity, we have to put up with abuse and manhandling from the bosses to keep our jobs. We are worked like animals in factories, especially in the garment industry where we spend most of our lives making clothes for other people while we can barely clothe ourselves. Our labor is considered abundant and cheap. If we speak up against the mistreatment, the boss fires us and gets himself another "girl." In the hospitals, we make up the majority of the workers as nurses' aides, kitchen workers, and clerks. In offices, we work as clerks and typists. They squeeze out our sweat and blood and still we don't make enough for a decent life.

Second, we are the women that are forced to prostitute ourselves in order to survive within a system that excludes us because there are no jobs. We sell our bodies like merchandise in order to stay alive. We are forced into a situation where we depend on the streets for our survival. Most of us are the street hustlers selling our bodies and barely making a living at it. A lot of us are prostituting because we depend on drugs that the rich pushers bring into our communities, and the government doesn't do anything because it benefits them. Or we're on welfare taking government handouts that are not enough to support ourselves and our children.

Third, as women our bodies are used for experimentation. Puerto Rican women have been sterilized to stop us from having "too many babies." This kind of murder leaves ⅓ of Puerto Rican women sterile today. The birth control pill was tested on Puerto Rican women for 15 years before it was sold in the u.s. Puerto Rican women have the highest death rate from butcher performed abortions, like the case of Carmen Rodríguez who was killed at Lincoln Hospital in New York City when she went for an abortion.

This government also uses us as sexual objects. We have always been portrayed as very exotic and sexual, but with no brains. We are used as objects with which to sell different things, which we then are brainwashed into buying. Women buy the most products. We are taught from the time we are born to look at ourselves negatively. Puerto Ricans refer to a baby girl as a *chancleta*—a slipper. Consciously and non-consciously, we believe we are inferior. So, then businessmen make products promising us that we will look better and be happier. Things like padded bras, girdles, false eyelashes, wigs, make-up, vaginal sprays, and crash diets are just a few examples. We are taught to look pretty, get married, have children, take care of them, do the housekeeping, and serve the husband as his slave. Depending on how well we do these things, determines how good a woman we are. A good woman does all the housework alone, even if she works [outside the home as well]. A good woman obeys her husband and never talks back to him. We're not supposed to have the brains to think, and we're supposed to remain passive and conform to the role of being shy, timid. Women aren't supposed to be fighters.

Yet our history has always had women fighters. . ...

Why a Women's Union?

Because as women we can best organize other women for the liberation of Puerto Rico and for the self-determination of all oppressed people. Because as women, we best understand our own oppression and can organize ourselves for our liberation, always remembering that we will not be free until all our people are free.

We don't want to be cheap labor horses anymore. We don't want to be used as guinea pigs anymore. We want to be respected and treated as human beings by our men. We want all our people to be treated like human beings, and if not, we will fight till we are.

La Luchadora, vol. 1, no. 1, June 1971

WOMEN'S UNION
12-POINT PROGRAM

1) We believe in the liberation of all Puerto Ricans—liberation on the island and inside the U.S.

2) We believe in the self-determination of all third world people.

3) We want equality for women—down with machismo and sexism.

4) We want full employment and equal pay for all women with day care facilities provided by the work institution.

5) We want an end to the present welfare system; community-worker boards must be established in all welfare centers to [e]nsure the protection of women and their needs.

6) We want an end to the particular oppression of prostitutes and drug-addict sisters.

7) We want the withdrawal of the American military force from our communities and an end to their sexual abuse of women.

8) We want freedom for all political prisoners and prisoners of war and an end to the sexual brutalization and torture enforced on sisters by prison officials.

9) We want an end to the experimentation and genocide committed on sisters through sterilization, forced abortions, contraceptives, and unnecessary gynecological exams.

10) We want a true education of our story as women.

11) We believe in the right to defend ourselves against rapes, beatings, muggings, and general abuse.

12) We want a socialist society.

ENDNOTES

PREFACE

[1] Nicole Acevedo, Gabe Gutierrez, and Annie Rose Ramos, "Puerto Ricans Flood Streets, Demand Resignation of Governor in Huge Protest," NBC News, last modified July 23, 2019, https://www.nbcnews.com/news/latino/march-people-puerto-rico-mobilizes-largest-protest-gov-rossell-s-n1032286.

[2] Sandra Guzmán, "Meet the Women Leading Puerto Rico's Feminist Revolution," Shondaland, August 9, 2019, https://www.shondaland.com/change-makers/a28653844/puerto-rico-protests-feminist-revolution.

[3] "Boricua" means Puerto Rican.

[4] Thirteen-Point Program and Platform, in Darrel Enck-Wanzer, ed., *The Young Lords: A Reader* (New York: New York University Press, 2010), 9.

[5] Patricia Hill Collins, *Black Feminist Thought: Knowledge, Consciousness, and the Politics of Empowerment* (New York: Routledge, 2000), ix.

[6] Jacqueline Lazú "Sí, pero... Truth and Reckonings: Revisiting Herstories: The Young Lords Party," Centro Journal 35, no. 1 (2025): 45–62.

[7] Andrés Torres, "Introduction: Political Radicalism in the Diaspora—The Puerto Rican Experience," in *The Puerto Rican Movement: Voices from the Diaspora*, ed. Andrés Torres and José E. Velázquez (Philadelphia: Temple University Press, 1998), 4.

[8] Audre Lorde, *Sister Outsider: Essays and Speeches* (1984; Berkeley, CA: Crossing Press, 2007), 138.

[9] Edna Acosta-Belén, "Introduction: Unveiling and Preserving a Puerto Rican Historical Memory," in *Through the Eyes of Rebel Women: The Young Lords, 1969–1976*, by Iris Morales (New York: Red Sugarcane Press, 2016), 1.

[10] Elizabeth Fee and Michael Wallace, "The History and Politics of Birth Control," *Feminist Studies* 5, no. 1 (Spring 1979): 202.

[11] Michel-Rolph Trouillot, *Silencing the Past: Power and the Production of History* (Boston: Beacon Press, 1995), 22.

[12] Maylei Blackwell, *¡Chicana Power! Contested Histories of Feminism in the Chicano Movement* (Austin: University of Texas Press, 2011), 102.

[13] Trouillot, *Silencing the Past,* 22.

[14] Lucille Clifton, "Why Some People Be Mad at Me Sometimes," The Dewdrop, June 10, 2020, https://thedewdrop.org/2020/06/10/lucille-clifton-why-some-people-be-mad-at-me-sometimes/.

PART I. ANOTHER CYCLE OF GRASSROOTS MILITANCY

[1] Zuleica Romay Guerra, "New World Coming: Race in Socialist Cuba," YouTube, November 19, 2021, https://www.youtube.com/watch?v=5jJQBtPTPks.

Chapter 1. Human Rights, Not Just Civil Rights

[1] Kym Klass, "Gwen Patton, Lifelong Civil Rights Activist, Dies," *Washington Times*, May 21, 2017, https://www.washington-times.com/news/2017/may/21/gwen-patton-lifelong-civil-rights-activist-dies/.

[2] Raquel M. Ortiz and Iris Morales, *Vicki and a Summer of Change! ¡Vicki Y Un Verano de Cambio!* (New York: Red Sugarcane Press, Inc. 2021). The first children's book about the Young Lords.

[3] Judy Klemesrud, "Young Women Find a Place in High Command of Young Lords," *New York Times*, November 11, 1970, 78.

[4] Edna Acosta-Belén and Carlos E. Santiago, *Puerto Ricans in the United States: A Contemporary Portrait* (Boulder, CO: Lynne Rienner, 2006), 81.

[5] Acosta-Belén and Santiago, *Puerto Ricans in the United States*, 75-80.

[6] Pedro Caban, "Puerto Rico, Colonialism in," Scholars Archive, University at Albany, State University of New York, 2005, https://scholarsarchive.li-brary.albany.edu/cgi/viewcontent.cgi?article=1018&context=lacs_fac_scholar: 517.

[7] Maura Toro-Morn and Ivis García Zambrano, "Gendered Fault Lines: A Demographic Profile of Puerto Rican Women in the United States," *Centro Journal* 29, no. 3 (Fall 2017): 17.

[8] "35% of Puerto Rican Women Sterilized," Chicago Women's Liberation Union, Herstory Project, September 19, 2016, https://www.cwluher-story.org/health/35-of-puerto-rican-women-sterilized.

[9] Puerto Rico is an archipelago comprising various islands—Puerto Rico proper, Vieques, Mona, Desecheo, and Culebra.

[10] Acosta-Belén and Santiago, *Puerto Ricans in the United States*, 81.

[11] Matthew Gandy, "Between Borinquen and the *Barrio*: Environmental Justice and New York City's Puerto Rican Community, 1969–1972," *Antipode* 34, no. 4 (September 2002): 732.

[12] Lorrin Thomas, *Puerto Rican Citizen: History and Political Identity in Twentieth-Century New York City* (Chicago: University of Chicago Press, 2010), 56–59.

[13] Komozi Woodward, "Rethinking the Black Power Movement," *Africana Age*, Schomburg Center for Research in Black Culture, New York Public Library, http://exhibitions.nypl.org/africanaage/essay-black-power.html.

[14] NewsOne Staff, "Malcolm X's Most Iconic Speeches," NewsOne, last modified May 19, 2022, https://newsone.com/3903093/malcolm-x-most-iconic-speeches/.

[15] Barbara Ransby, *Ella Baker and the Black Freedom Movement: A Radical Democratic Vision* (Chapel Hill: University of North Carolina Press, 2003), 344.

[16] Ransby, *Ella Baker*, 344.

[17] "Achieving the Dream: Death of a Panther," WTTW Digital Archives, http://www.wttw.com/main.taf?p=76,4,6,1.

[18] Erin Blakemore, "Why People Rioted after Martin Luther King Jr.'s Assassination," History, April 2, 2018; last modified, December 13, 2021, https://www.history.com/news/mlk-assassination-riots-occupation.

[19] Karen A. Secrist, "Occupy Lincoln Park: The Militant Drama of the Young Lords Organization," *Journal of African American Studies* 23, no. 4 (December 2019): 393, doi:10.1007/s12111-019-09449-3.

[20] Secrist, "Occupy Lincoln Park," 394.

[21] Frank Browning, "From Rumble to Revolution: The Young Lords," *Ramparts*, October 1970, 20.

[22] "Cosmoe Speaks," *Y.L.O.* (newspaper of the Chicago Young Lords Organization) 1, no. 4 (1969).

[23] Ella Turney, "Human Rights vs Civil Rights," US Institute of Diplomacy and Human Rights, March 17, 2021, https://usidhr.org/human-rights-vs-civil-rights.

[24] Terence McArdle, "The 'Law and Order' Campaign That Won Richard Nixon the White House 50 Years Ago," *Washington Post*, November 5, 2018, https://www.washingtonpost.com/history/2018/11/05/law-order-campaign-that-won-richard-nixon-white-house-years-ago/.

[25] "Nixon Adviser Admits War on Drugs Was Designed to Criminalize Black People," Equal Justice Initiative, last modified March 25, 2016, https://eji.org/news/nixon-war-on-drugs-designed-to-criminalize-black-people/.

[26] "People in Jail and Prison in 2020," Vera Institute of Justice, January 25, 2021, https://www.vera.org/publications/people-in-jail-and-prison-in-2020.

[27] Vincent Browne, "Richard Nixon Committed Far Greater Crimes Than the Watergate Break-In," *Irish Times*, June 19, 2013, https://www.irishtimes.com/news/politics/richard-nixon-committed-far-greater-crimes-than-the-watergate-break-in-1.1433510.

[28] Taylor Owen and Ben Kiernan, "Making More Enemies Than We Kill? Calculating U.S. Bomb Tonnages Dropped on Laos and Cambodia, and Weighing Their Implications," *Asia-Pacific Journal*, April 27, 2015, https://apjjf.org/Ben-Kiernan/4313.html.

[29] "Richard Nixon," Encyclopedia Britannica, https://www.britannica.com/biography/Richard-Nixon.

[30] "Nixon Insists That He Is 'Not a Crook,'" History, November 16, 2009; last modified, November 14, 2019, https://www.history.com/this-day-in-history/nixon-insists-that-he-is-not-a-crook.

[31] According to 1970 census data, 817,712 Puerto Ricans lived in New York, or roughly 10 percent of the city's population. "On Arrival: Puerto Ricans in Post-World War II New York," Teachers College - Columbia University, n.d. https://www.tc.columbia.edu/che/projects/past-projects/blog-posts/on-arrival-puerto-ricans-in-post-world-war-ii-new-york/.

[32] Mark Schmitt, "Liberalism's Mayor," *American Prospect*, May 21, 2010, https://prospect.org/article/liberalism-s-mayor/.

[33] Seymour P. Lachman and Robert Polner, *The Man Who Saved New York: Hugh Carey and the Great Fiscal Crisis of 1975* (Albany: State University of New York Press, 2010), 58.

[34] Stephen Brier, "Why the History of CUNY Matters: Using the CUNY Digital History Archive to Teach CUNY's Past," *Radical Teacher* 108, no. 1 (Spring 2017): 30.

[35] Puerto Rican Forum, *A Study of Poverty Conditions in the New York Puerto Rican Community* (New York: Puerto Rican Forum, 1970).

[36] Acosta-Belén and Santiago, *Puerto Ricans in the United States*, 73.

[37] "The Fight for Survival During the 50s," *Palante* 5, no. 9 (October 30–November 20, 1973): 5.

[38] Alice Colón-Warren, "The Feminization of Poverty among Women in Puerto Rico and Puerto Rican Women in the Middle Atlantic Region of the United States," *Brown Journal of World Affairs* 5, no. 2 (Summer–Fall 1998): 272, https://www.jstor.org/stable/24590326?read-now=1&seq=15.

[38] Colón-Warren, "The Feminization of Poverty," 272.

[39] Colón-Warren, "The Feminization of Poverty," 264.

[40] "New York School Boycott," Civil Rights Digital Library, December 17, 2020, https://crdl.usg.edu/events/ny_school_boycott/?Welcome.

[41] Felipe Hinojosa, *Apostles of Change: Latino Radical Politics, Church Occupations, and the Fight to Save the Barrio* (Austin: University of Texas Press, 2021), 98.

[42] Brier, "Why the History of CUNY Matters," 31–32. Brier describes rallies and confrontations in the spring of 1969, culminating in student strikes and building occupations at the City College of New York, Brooklyn College, Queens College, Bronx Community College, and the Borough of Manhattan Community College. Administrators called police on several campuses to retake the occupied buildings. Students of color led class boycotts and were supported by many white students and faculty.

[43] Tia Tenopia, "Latinopia Event 1969 Denver Youth Conference," Latinopia, March 4, 2012, https://latinopia.com/latino-history/latinopia-event-1969-denver-youth-conference/.

[44] Luis Aponte-Parés, "The East Harlem Real Great Society, a Puerto Rican Chapter in the Fight for Self-Determination," Planners Network, March 12, 1999, https://www.plannersnetwork.org/1999/03/the-east-harlem-real-great-society-a-puerto-rican-chapter-in-the-fight-for-self-determination/.

[45] Roxanne Dunbar-Ortiz, *An Indigenous Peoples' History of the United States* (Boston: Beacon Press, 2014), 2.

[46] Anne Garland Mahler, *From the Tricontinental to the Global South: Race, Radicalism, and Transnational Solidarity* (Durham, NC: Duke University Press, 2018), 121.

[47] Alan Maass, *The Case for Socialism*, 3rd ed. (Chicago: Haymarket Books, 2010), 5.

[48] Van Gosse, *Rethinking the New Left: An Interpretative History* (New York: Palgrave Macmillan, 2005), 2.

[49] Rose Muzio, *Radical Imagination, Radical Humanity: Puerto Rican Political Activism in New York* (Albany: State University of New York Press, 2017), 3.

Chapter 2. Serving The People. We are Revolutionary Nationalists

[1] Mao Tse-tung, *Quotations from Chairman Mao Tse-tung*, Marxists Internet Archive, https://www.marxists.org/ebooks/mao/Quotations_from_Chairman_Mao_Tse-tung.pdf. *The Little Red Book* explains the meaning of "Serving the People:" "Our point of departure is to serve the people whole-heartedly and never for a moment divorce ourselves from the masses, to proceed in all cases from the interests of the people and not from one's self-interest or from the interests of a small group."

[2] Subcommander Marcos, *The Zapatistas' Dignified Rage: Final Public Speeches of Subcommander Marcos*, ed. Nick Henck, trans. Henry Gales (Chico, CA: AK Press, 2018), 52.

[3] Gary Eidsvold, Anthony Mustalish, and Lloyd F. Novick, "The New York City Department of Health: Lessons in a Lead Poisoning Control Program," *American Journal of Public Health* 64, no. 10 (October 1974): 956–62, https://ajph.aphapublications.org/doi/pdf/10.2105/AJPH.64.10.956.

[4] Theresa Horvath, "The Health Initiatives of the Young Lords Party: How a Group of 1960s Radicals Made Health a Revolutionary Concern," Hofstra University, 5, https://www.hofstra.edu/pdf/community/culctr/culctr_events_healthcare0310_%20horvath_paper.pdf.

[5] Eidsvold, Mustalish, and Novick, "The New York City Department of Health," 957.

[6] Horvath, "The Health Initiatives of the Young Lords Party," 6.

[7] Eidsvold, Mustalish, and Novick, "The New York City Department of Health," 957.

[8] Browning, "From Rumble to Revolution," 23.

[9] Iris Benítez, *Y.L.O*, January 1970, 20.

[10] "Young Lords Defy Take-Over Order," *New York Times*, January 3, 1970.

[11] "*¡Palante Radio!* Latin Liberation News and the Young Lords Organization of New York," Down and to the Left, December 2, 2013, https://downandtotheleft.wordpress.com/2013/12/02/palante-radio-liberation-news-and-the-new-york-young-lords-organization/.

[12] Mahler, *From the Tricontinental to the Global South*, 121–22. The phrase "within the belly of the beast" is from a writing by Cuban poet and political exile José Martí about his time living in New York City.

[13] Mahler, *From the Tricontinental to the Global South*, 96.

[14] Jorge Duany, "Nation on the Move: The Construction of Cultural Identities in Puerto Rico and the Diaspora," *American Ethnologist* 27, no. 1 (February 2000): 7, doi:10.1525/ae.2000.27.1.5.

[15] Edna Acosta-Belén, email correspondence, September 8, 2021.

[16] Edna Acosta-Belén, email correspondence, September 8, 2021.

[17] Felipe Luciano, "On Revolutionary Nationalism," in Enck-Wanzer, *The Young Lords: A Reader*, 133.

[18] MerriCatherine, "Huey P. Newton's Interview with The Movement (1968)," Medium, January 13, 2018, https://medium.com/@merricatherine/huey-p-newtons-interview-with-the-movement-magazine-1968-a328e6b78c32.

[19] MerriCatherine, "Huey P. Newton's Interview."

[20] Loretta Ross, "Fighting White Supremacy and White Privilege to Build a Human Rights Movement," *Understanding and Dismantling Privilege* 6, no. 1 (April 2016): 3.

[21] Elizabeth "Betita" Martínez, "What Is White Supremacy?" Catalyst Project, 2013, https://collectiveliberation.org/wp-content/uploads/2013/01/What_Is_White_Supremacy_Martinez.pdf.

[22] Young Lords Party, Michael Abramson, and Iris Morales, *Palante: Voices and Photographs of the Young Lords, 1969–1971* (Chicago: Haymarket Books, 2011), 67.

[23] Report of Central Committee Evaluation and Retreat, December 21–23, 1970, 20. Recap of activities from July to December 1970 and goals for 1971. Iris Morales files.

[24] Mahler, *From the Tricontinental to the Global South*, 124–25.

[25] Iris Morales, "Puerto Rican Racism" ("Racismo borincaño"), in Enck-Wanzer, *The Young Lords: A Reader*, 136.

[26] Marta I. Cruz-Janzen, "Out of the Closet: Racial Amnesia, Avoidance, and Denial; Racism among Puerto Ricans." *Race, Gender and Class* 10, no. 3 (2003): 71.

[27] Marilisa Jiménez García, *Side by Side: U.S. Empire, Puerto Rico, and the Roots of American Youth Literature and Culture* (Jackson: University Press of Mississippi, 2021), 17.

[28] Vanessa K. Valdés, *Diasporic Blackness: The Life and Times of Arturo Alfonso Schomburg* (Albany: State University of New York Press, 2017), 8.

[29] Young Lords Party Central Committee, *The Ideology of the Young Lords Party* (pamphlet), 1971, 4. Afro-Boricuas are defined as a "mixture of mostly Spanish and African who developed in the sugarcane plantations and coasts of Puerto Rico, … and whose ancestors were slaves. … [T]he culture and customs [of Puerto Ricans] are mostly African, and the racist societies of Spain and Amerikkka treat them as though they are inferior."

[30] Carlos Aponte, "Loiza Aldea," *Palante* 2, no. 9 (1970): 6.

[31] Jorge Duany, "Neither White nor Black: The Politics of Race and Ethnicity among Puerto Ricans on the Island and in the U.S. Mainland," paper presented at the Conference on the Meaning of Race and Blackness in the Americas: Contemporary Perspectives, Providence, Rhode Island, February 10–12, 2000, 4, http://maxweber.hunter.cuny.edu/eres/docs/eres/SOC217_PIMENTEL/duany.pdf.

[32] Margaret Power, "Seeing the U.S. Empire through the Eyes of Puerto Rican Nationalists Who Opposed It," *Modern American History* 2, no. 2 (July 2019): 190, doi:10.1017/mah.2019.18.

[33] Jorell Meléndez-Badillo, *Puerto Rico: A National History* (Princeton, NJ: Princeton University Press, 2024), 97.

[34] Edgardo Pratts, "A 85 años de la masacre de Río Piedras," 80 Grados, November 13, 2020, https://www-80grados-net.translate.goog/a-85-anos-de-la-masacre-de-rio-piedras/?_x_tr_sl=es&_x_tr_tl=en&_x_tr_hl=en&_x_tr_pto=sc.

[35] Pratts, "A 85 años de la masacre de Río Piedras."

[36] Charles R. Venator Santiago, "The Other Nationalists: Marcus Garvey and Pedro Albizu Campos" (master's thesis, University of Massachusetts Amherst, 1996), 33, https://scholarworks.umass.edu/cgi/viewcontent.cgi?article=3676&context=theses.

[37] Yenica Cortes, "Remembering Puerto Rico's Ponce Massacre," *Liberation*, March 1, 2007, https://www.liberationnews.org/07-03-01-remembering-puerto-ricos-ponce-html/.

[38] Jose Colon, "Estado Libre Asociado: The Constitutionality of Puerto Rico's Legal Status," Chicana/o Latina/o Law Review 7, no. 0 (1984): 105, doi:10.5070/c770020957.

[39] Venator Santiago, "The Other Nationalists," 33.

[40] Jorell Meléndez-Badillo, *Puerto Rico: A National History*, 115.

[41] Margaret Pour, "Puerto Rican Women Nationalist vs. U.S. Colonialism: An Exploration of Their Conditions and Struggles in Jail and Court," *Chicago-*

Kent Law Review 87, no. 2 (April 2012): 465, https://scholarship.kent-law.iit.edu/cklawreview/vol87/iss2/9.

[42] "Utuado Uprising," Military Wiki, https://military-history.fan-dom.com/wiki/Utuado_Uprising.

[43] Pedro Caban, "Puerto Rican Nationalist Uprising," Latin American, Caribbean, and U.S. Latino Studies Faculty Scholarship 22 (2005), Scholars Archive, University at Albany, State University of New York, https://scholarsar-chive.library.albany.edu/lacs_fac_scholar/22.

[44] Pedro A. Malavet, *America's Colony: The Political and Cultural Conflict between the United State and Puerto Rico* (New York: New York University Press, 2004) 92.

[45] Antonia Darder, "Pedro Albizu Campos," Encyclopedia Britannica, n.d.https://www.britannica.com/biography/Pedro-Albizu-Campos.

[46] Malavet, *America's Colony*, 92.

[47] Venator Santiago, "The Other Nationalists," 36.

[48] Antonia Darder, "Pedro Albizu Campos," Encyclopedia Britannica, n.d.https://www.britannica.com/biography/Pedro-Albizu-Campos.

[49] Manuel Maldonado-Denis, "Prospects for Latin American Nationalism: The Case of Puerto Rico," *Latin American Perspectives* 3, no. 3 (Summer 1976): 39.

[50] Maldonado-Denis, "Prospects for Latin American Nationalism," 41.

[51] Felipe Luciano, "On Revolutionary Nationalism," in Enck-Wanzer, *The Young Lords: A Reader*, 134.

[52] Anne McClintock, "Family Feuds: Gender, Nationalism and the Family," *Feminist Review*, no. 44 (Summer 1993), 77 doi:10.2307/1395196:

Chapter 3. The Rise of the Women's Caucus

[1] Ana Lydia Vega, "Cloud Cover Caribbean," in *Short Stories by Latin American Women: The Magic and the Real*, ed. Celia Correas de Zapata (New York: Modern Library, 2003), 223.

[2] Browning, "From Rumble to Revolution," 23.

[3] Young Lords Party, Abramson, and Morales, *Palante*, 40.

[4] McClintock, "Family Feuds," 77.

[5] Santa Cruz Feminist of Color Collective, "Building on 'the Edge of Each Other's Battles': A Feminist of Color Multidimensional Lens." *Hypatia* 29, no. 1 (Winter 2014): 28-29.

[6] Santa Cruz Feminist of Color Collective, "Building on 'the Edge of Each Other's Battles,'" 24.

[7] María Lugones, "Indigenous Movements and Decolonial Feminism," Department of Women's, Gender, and Sexuality Studies, Ohio State University, 2, https://wgss.osu.edu/sites/wgss.osu.edu/files/LugonesSeminarReadings.pdf.

[8] Santa Cruz Feminist of Color Collective, "Building on 'the Edge of Each Other's Battles,'" 27.

[9] Carole Boyce Davies, *Left of Karl Marx: The Political Life of Black Communist Claudia Jones* (Durham, NC: Duke University Press, 2008), 23.

[10] Kathryn Blackmer Reyes and Julia E. Curry Rodríguez, "*Testimonio*: Origins, Terms, and Resources," *Equity and Excellence in Education* 45, no. 3 (2012): 525, doi:10.1080/10665684.2012.698571. The authors link the use of *testimonio* to liberation efforts and anti-imperialist movements in Third World nations.

[11] Kristie Soares, "Joy, Rage, and Activism: The Gendered Politics of Affect in the Young Lords Party," *Signs: Journal of Women in Culture and Society* 46, no. 4 (Summer 2021): 940, doi:10.1086/713295.

[12] Lisa Gail Collins, "Activists Who Yearn for Art That Transforms: Parallels in the Black Arts and Feminist Art Movements in the United States," *Signs: Journal of Women in Culture and Society* 31, no. 3 (Spring 2006): 727, doi:10.1086/498991.

[13] Isabel Allende, *The Soul of a Woman* (New York: Ballantine Books, 2021), 13.

[14] Thirteen-Point Program and Platform, in Enck-Wanzer, *The Young Lords: A Reader*, 9–10.

[15] Young Lords Organization, "13-Point Program and Platform," *Palante* 2, no. 2 (1970): 19.

[16] Anne McClintock, "Family Feuds: Gender, Nationalism and the Family," *Feminist Review*, no. 44 (Summer 1993), 63, doi:10.2307/1395196.

[17] BlackPast, "(1981) Audre Lorde, 'The Uses of Anger: Women Responding to Racism,'" August 12, 2012, https://www.blackpast.org/african-american-history/speeches-african-american-history/1981-audre-lorde-uses-anger-women-responding-racism/.

[18] *Women in the Colonies*, episode 2 of 3, Pacifica Radio Archives, March 1970, https://www.pacificaradioarchives.org/recording/bb383502.

[19] Young Lords Party, Abramson, and Morales, *Palante*, 13.

[20] Ernesto Che Guevara, *Man and Socialism in Cuba* (Havana: Guairas Book Institute, 1967).

[21] Young Lords Party, Abramson, and Morales, *Palante*, 48.

[22] BlackPast, "(1970) Huey P. Newton, 'The Women's Liberation and Gay Liberation Movements,'" April 17, 2018, https://www.blackpast.org/african-american-history/speeches-african-american-history/huey-p-newton-women-s-liberation-and-gay-liberation-movements/.

[23] BlackPast, "(1970) Huey P. Newton."

[24] Enck-Wanzer, *The Young Lords: A Reader*, 23.

[25] Firuzeh Shokooh Valle, "Getting into the Mainstream: The Virtual Strategies of the Feminist Movement in Puerto Rico" (master's thesis, Northeastern University, 2010), 58.

[26] María I. Bryant, "Puerto Rican Women's Roles in Independence Nationalism: Unwavering Women" (PhD diss., American University, 2011), 216.

[27] Becky Serrano, "Ana Roqué," *Palante* 3, no. 1 (1971): 11.

[28] Sojourner Truth, "Ain't I a Woman?," December 1851, Modern History Sourcebook, Fordham University, https://sourcebooks.fordham.edu/mod/sojtruth-woman.asp.

PART II. FEMINISTS OF COLOR AND GENDER JUSTICE MOVEMENTS

[1] "Women Who Disagree," in *Mujer en pie de lucha*, ed. Dorinda Moreno (Mexico City: Espina del Norte, 1973), 29.

Chapter 4. Sterilization Politics and Struggles for Reproductive Justice

[1] Diane Feeley, "Antoinette Konikow: Marxist and Feminist," in *Revolutionary Traditions of American Trotskyism*, ed. Paul Le Blanc (New York: Fourth Internationalist Tendency, 1988), 5. Reprinted from *International Socialist Review* 33 (January 1972): 19–23.

[2] Natasha Lennard, "The Long, Disgraceful History of American Attacks on Brown and Black Women's Reproductive Systems," The Intercept, September 17, 2020, xx, https://theintercept.com/2020/09/17/forced-sterilization-ice-us-history/.

[3] Enck-Wanzer, *The Young Lords: A Reader*, 165. See also Iris Morales, "Sterilized Puerto Ricans," *Palante* 2, no. 2 (1970): 8. Reprinted in *Palante* 2, no. 10 (1970): 5.

[4] Jennifer A. Nelson, "'Abortions under Community Control': Feminism, Nationalism, and the Politics of Reproduction among New York City's Young Lords," *Journal of Women's History* 13, no. 1 (Spring 2001): 157, doi:10.1353/jowh.2001.0031.

[5] Ranjani Chakraborty, "The U.S. Medical System Is Still Haunted by Slavery," *Vox*, December 7, 2017, https://www.vox.com/health-care/2017/12/7/16746790/health-care-black-history-inequality.

[6] Sylviane A. Diouf, "Remembering the Women of Slavery," Schomburg Center for Research in Black Culture, New York Public Library, March 27, 2015, https://www.nypl.org/blog/2015/03/27/remembering-women-slavery.

[7] Liz Barnes, review of *When Rape Was Legal: The Untold History of Sexual Violence during Slavery*, by Rachel A. Feinstein, Reviews in History, October 2019, https://reviews.history.ac.uk/review/2344.

[8] Stephanie E. Jones-Rogers, *They Were Her Property: White Women as Slave Owners in the American South* (New Haven: Yale University Press, 2019).

[9] Isabel Wilkerson, *Caste: The Origins of Our Discontents* (New York: Random House, 2020), 79.

[10] Laura Briggs, *Reproducing Empire: Race, Sex, Science, and U.S. Imperialism in Puerto Rico* (Berkeley: University of California Press, 2003), 83.

[11] Briggs, *Reproducing Empire*, 87.

[12] Elizabeth Fee and Michael Wallace, "The History and Politics of Birth Control," *Feminist Studies* 5, no. 1 (Spring 1979): 202.

[13] Blanca Noelle Martínez, "Puertorriqueña Power and *Testimonio*: Puerto Rican Women's Fight for Reproductive Freedom in the 1930s through the 1970s" (master's thesis, University of California, San Diego, 2018), 8.

[14] This reference is to the Puerto Rican Socialist Party founded in 1899 by Santiago Iglesias Pantín.

[15] Carlos Sanabria, *Puerto Rican Labor History, 1898–1934: Revolutionary Ideals and Reformist Politics* (Lanham, MD: Lexington Books, 2018), 92

[16] Martínez, "Puertorriqueña Power and *Testimonio*," 8.

[17] Briggs, *Reproducing Empire*, 90.

[18] Annette B. Ramírez de Arellano and Conrad Seipp, *Colonialism, Catholicism, and Contraception: A History of Birth Control in Puerto Rico* (Chapel Hill: University of North Carolina Press, 2017), 28–29.

[19] Briggs, *Reproducing Empire*, 76.

[20] César J. Ayala and Rafael Bernabe, *Puerto Rico in the American Century: A History since 1898* (Chapel Hill: University of North Carolina Press, 2017), 207.

[21] Briggs, *Reproducing Empire*, 77.

[22] Ruth Arroyo, Rafael Bernabe, and Nancy Herzig, "Confronting Anti-Choice Forces in Puerto Rico," Marxists Internet Archive, https://www.marxists.org/history/etol/newspape/atc/4725.html.

[23] "35% of Puerto Rican Women Sterilized," Chicago Women's Liberation Union, Herstory Project.

[24] Iris Ofelia López, *Matters of Choice: Puerto Rican Women's Struggle for Reproductive Freedom* (New Brunswick, NJ: Rutgers University Press, 2008), 13.

[25] Briggs, *Reproducing Empire*, 80.

[26] Nick Thimmesch, "Puerto Rico and Birth Control," *Journal of Marriage and Family* 30, no. 2 (May 1968): 257.

[27] "Puerto Rico," Eugenics Archives, https://eugenicsarchive.ca/discover/tree/530ba18176f0db569b00001b.

[28] Erin Blakemore, "The First Birth Control Pill Used Puerto Rican Women as Guinea Pigs," History, May 9, 2018; last modified, March 11, 2019, https://www.history.com/news/birth-control-pill-history-puerto-rico-enovid.

[29] Martínez, "Puertorriqueña Power and *Testimonio*," 24.

[30] Olivia Kinnear, "Sterilization: The Untold Story of Puerto Rico," Pasquines, September 1, 2015, https://pasquines.us/2015/09/01/sterilization-the-untold-story-of-puerto-rico/.

[31] López, *Matters of Choice*, 15.

[32] Briggs, *Reproducing Empire*, 102.

[33] Briggs, *Reproducing Empire*, 104.

[34] "Puerto Rico," Eugenics Archives.

[35] Briggs, *Reproducing Empire*, 108.

[36] Bianca González, "Eugenics and Contraceptives in Puerto Rico: A History of Manipulation and Unethical Experimentation," *Liberal Currents*, May 22, 2020, https://www.liberalcurrents.com/eugenics-and-contraceptives-in-puerto-rico-a-history-of-manipulation-and-unethical-experimentation/.

[37] Katherine Andrews, "The Dark History of Forced Sterilization of Latina Women," Panoramas, October 30, 2017, https://www.panoramas.pitt.edu/health-and-society/dark-history-forced-sterilization-latina-women.

[38] Ella Jordan-Smith, "A Historical Analysis of U.S. Imperialism on Women in Puerto Rico" (honors thesis, State University of New York at New Paltz, 2019), 10, https://soar.suny.edu/bitstream/handle/20.500.12648/1329/Jordan-Smith_Honors.pdf?sequence=1&isAllowed=y.

[39] Kathryn Krase, "The History of Forced Sterilization in the United States," *Our Bodies Ourselves,* last modified September 21, 2020, https://www.our-bodiesourselves.org/book-excerpts/health-article/forced-sterilization.

[40] Ana María García, dir., *La operación*, Cinema Guild, 1982. The film documents the 1950s and 1960s sterilization campaign in Puerto Rico.

[41] Rodríguez Trías advocated for health services for poor and working-class women and children and served as director of the Lincoln Hospital Pediatrics Department in the Bronx. She was the first Latina president of the American Public Health Association, a founding member of its women's caucus, and a recipient of the Presidential Citizens Medal.

[42] Alexandra Minna Stern, "Forced Sterilization Policies in the U.S. Targeted Minorities and Those with Disabilities—and Lasted into the 21st Century," Institute for Healthcare Policy and Innovation, September 23, 2020, https://ihpi.umich.edu/news/forced-sterilization-policies-us-targeted-minorities-and-those-disabilities-and-lasted-21st.

[43] Alexandra Minna Stern, "That Time the United States Sterilized 60,000 of Its Citizens," *Huffington Post*, January 7, 2016, https://www.huffpost.com/entry/sterilization-united-states_n_568f35f2e4b0c8beacf68713.

⁴⁴ Nicole L. Novak and Natalie Lira, "California Once Targeted Latinas for Forced Sterilization," *Smithsonian Magazine*, March 22, 2018, https://smithsonianmag.com/history/california-targeted-latinas-forced-sterilization-180968567/.

⁴⁵ The Student Nonviolent Coordinating Committee, "Genocide in Mississippi," Tulane University Digital Library, last modified 1964, https://digitallibrary.tulane.edu/islandora/object/tulane%3A21196.

⁴⁶ Paola Alonso, "Autonomy Revoked: The Forced Sterilization of Women of Color in 20th Century America," Texas Woman's University, n.d., https://twu.edu/media/documents/history-government/Autonomy-Revoked-The-Forced-Sterilization-of-Women-of-Color-in-20th-Century-America.pdf.

⁴⁷ Alonso, "Autonomy Revoked."

⁴⁸ Blake T. Hilton, "Frantz Fanon and Colonialism: A Psychology of Oppression," *Journal of Scientific Psychology*, December 2011, 54, https://www.psyencelab.com/uploads/5/4/6/5/54658091/frantz_fanon_and_colonialism.pdf.

⁴⁹ Sandra Knispel, "Coerced Sterilization of Native Women Occurred in the 70s," *Futurity*, October 24, 2019, https://www.futurity.org/sterilizations-native-american-women-2192722-2/. See also Beth Adams, "'Reproduction on the Reservation': The History of Forced Sterilization of Native American Women," WXXI News, Rochester, New York, October 28, 2019, https://www.wxxinews.org/post/reproduction-reservation-history-forced-sterilization-native-american-women.

⁵⁰ J. Nelson, "Abortions under Community Control," 167.

⁵¹ José E. Velázquez, Carmen V. Rivera, and Andres Torres, eds., *Revolution Around the Corner: Voices from the Puerto Rican Socialist Party in the United States* (Philadelphia: Temple University Press, 2021), 148.

⁵² Sue Davis, "A Doctor Who Fought Sterilization Abuse," *Workers World*, April 20, 2005, http://www.workers.org/2005/us/rakow-0428.

⁵³ Renee Tajima-Peña, dir., *No más bebés*, PBS, 2015. Mothers involved in the *Madrigal v. Quilligan* trial recount the day they were sterilized.

⁵⁴ Juliana Jiménez J., "California Compensates Victims of Forced Sterilizations, Many of Them Latinas," NBC News, July 23, 2021, https://www.nbcnews.com/news/latino/california-compensates-victims-forced-sterilizations-many-latinas-rcna1471.

⁵⁵ Briggs *Reproducing Empire*, 124.

⁵⁶ Sharon Smith, "Women's Liberation: The Marxist Tradition," *International Socialist Review*, no. 93 (Summer 2014), https://isreview.org/issue/93/womens-liberation-marxist-tradition/index.html.

⁵⁷ Drew C. Pendergrass and Michelle Y. Raji, "The Bitter Pill: Harvard and the Dark History of Birth Control," *Harvard Crimson*, September 28, 2017, https://www.thecrimson.com/article/2017/9/28/the-bitter-pill/.

⁵⁸ Pendergrass and Raji, "The Bitter Pill."

[59] "The Puerto Rico Pill Trials," PBS, January 4, 2018, https://www.pbs.org/wgbh/americanexperience/features/pill-puerto-rico-pill-trials/.

[60] Blakemore, "The First Birth Control Pill."

[61] Chana Gazit, "The Pill," PBS, 2007, https://www.pbs.org/wgbh/amex/pill/index.html.

[62] Theresa Vargas, "Guinea Pigs or Pioneers? How Puerto Rican Women Were Used to Test the Birth Control Pill," *Washington Post*, May 9, 2017, https://www.washingtonpost.com/news/retropolis/wp/2017/05/09/guinea-pigs-or-pioneers-how-puerto-rican-women-were-used-to-test-the-birth-control-pill/.

[63] Amanda Brownlee, "A Virtue Ethics Analysis of the Puerto Rico Birth Control Trials," April 24, 2020, STS Research Paper, 13.

[64] Brownlee, "A Virtue Ethics Analysis," 14.

[65] Vargas, "Guinea Pigs or Pioneers?"

[66] Pendergrass and Raji, "The Bitter Pill."

Chapter 5. Solidarities with African American and Chicana Feminists

[1] Angela Davis, quoted in Max Peterson, "The Revolutionary Practice of Black Feminisms," National Museum of African American History and Culture, Smithsonian Institution, March 4, 2019, https://nmaahc.si.edu/explore/stories/revolutionary-practice-black-feminisms.

[2] Yuderkys Espinosa Miñoso, "Why We Need Decolonial Feminism: Differentiation and Co-Constitutional Domination in Western Modernity," Afterall, July 1, 2020, https://www.afterall.org/article/why-we-need-decolonial-feminism-differentiation-and-co-constitutional-domination-of-western-modernit.

[3] Karen Vieira Powers, *Women in the Crucible of Conquest: The Gendered Genesis of Spanish American Society, 1500–1600* (Albuquerque: University of New Mexico Press, 2005), 178.

[4] Angela Y. Davis, *Women, Race and Class* (New York: Vintage Books, 1983), 21.

[5] "Overview Essay: Women in Resistance," Slave Resistance: A Caribbean Study, n.d., http://scholar.library.miami.edu/slaves/womens_resistance/womens.html.

[6] Powers, *Women in the Crucible of Conquest*, 178.

[7] Sharon Smith, *Women and Socialism: Class, Race, and Capital* (Chicago: Haymarket Books, 2015), xii.

[8] Davies, *Left of Karl Marx*, 39.

[9] Claudia Jones, "An End to the Neglect of the Problems of the Negro Woman!," University of Central Florida Digital Library, June 1949, 4, http://purl.flvc.org/FCLA/DT/1927554.

[10] Erik S. McDuffie, *Sojourning for Freedom: Black Women, American Communism, and the Making of Black Left Feminism* (Durham, NC: Duke University Press, 2011), 3.

[11] Jones, "An End to the Neglect," 15–17.

[12] "Kimberlé Crenshaw on Intersectionality, More Than Two Decades Later," Columbia Law School, June 8, 2017, https://www.law.columbia.edu/news/archive/kimberle-crenshaw-intersectionality-more-two-decades-later.

[13] Ashley Bohrer, "Intersectionality and Marxism: A Critical Historiography," *Historical Materialism* 26, no. 2 (June 2018): 49, doi:10.1163/1569206x-00001617.

[14] Benita Roth, *Separate Roads to Feminism: Black, Chicana, and White Feminist Movements in America's Second Wave* (Cambridge: Cambridge University Press, 2004), 12.

[15] Kimberly Springer, *Living for the Revolution: Black Feminist Organizations, 1968–1980* (Durham, NC: Duke University Press, 2006), 3.

[16] Kathleen A. Laughlin, Julie Gallagher, Dorothy Sue Cobble, Eileen Boris, Premilla Nadasen, Stephanie Gilmore, and Leandra Zarnow, "Is It Time to Jump Ship? Historians Rethink the Waves Metaphor," *Feminist Formations* 22, no. 1 (Spring 2010): 76–78, doi:10.1353/nwsa.0.0118.

[17] Laughlin et al., "Is It Time to Jump Ship?," 77–81.

[18] Jasmin A. Young, "Strapped: A Historical Analysis of Black Women and Armed Resistance, 1959–1979" (PhD diss., Rutgers University, 2018), 209.

[19] Young, "Strapped," 209.

[20] Linda Burnham, "The Wellspring of Black Feminist Theory," Women of Color Resource Center, Working Paper Series, no. 1, 2001, 5, https://solidarity-us.org/pdfs/cadreschool/fws.burnham.pdf.

[21] Ransby, *Ella Baker*, 352.

[22] Ransby, *Ella Baker*, 352.

[23] "Dr. Gwen Patton: A Long Time Movement Activist," Civil Rights Movement Archive, 2017, https://www.crmvet.org/vet/patton.htm.

[24] Ashley D. Farmer, "Remembering Gwen Patton, Activist and Theorist," June 14, 2017, https://www.ashleydfarmer.com/blog/2017/6/14/remembering-gwen-patton-activist-and-theorist.

[25] Patricia Romney, *We Were There: The Third World Women's Alliance and the Second Wave* (New York: Feminist Press, 2021), 47.

[26] Frances M. Beal, "Double Jeopardy: To Be Black and Female," *Meridians* 8, no. 2 (2008): 166, https://www.jstor.org/stable/40338758.

[27] Beal, "Double Jeopardy," 166.

[28] Young, "Strapped," 210–11.

[29] Beal, "Double Jeopardy," 174–75.

[30] BlackPast, "The Black Panthers' Ten Point Program," https://www.black-past.org/african-american-history/primary-documents-african-american-history/black-panther-party-ten-point-program-1966/.

[31] Kathleen Neal Cleaver, "Women, Power, and Revolution (1998)," History Is a Weapon, https://www.historyisaweapon.com/defcon1/cleaverwomen-powerrev.html.

[32] Mary Phillips, "The Feminist Leadership of Ericka Huggins in the Black Panther Party," *Black Diaspora Review* 4, no. 1 (Winter 2014): 200.

[33] Salamishah Tillet, "The Panthers' Revolutionary Feminism," *New York Times*, October 2, 2015, 12, https://www.nytimes.com/2015/10/04/movies/the-panthers-revolutionary-feminism.html.

[34] Phillips, "The Feminist Leadership of Ericka Huggins," 200.

[35] Phillips, "The Feminist Leadership of Ericka Huggins," 190–93.

[36] Meera White, "Seeing Black Women in Power," National Museum of African American History and Culture, Smithsonian Institution, July 28, 2017, https://nmaahc.si.edu/explore/stories/collection/seeing-black-women-power.

[37] Nicole Martin, "Women Were Key in the Black Panther Party," Clayman Institute for Gender Research, Stanford University, January 6, 2014, https://gender.stanford.edu/news-publications/gender-news/women-were-key-black-panther-party.

[38] Tracye A. Matthews, "'No One Ever Asks What a Man's Role in the Revolution Is': Gender Politics and Leadership in the Black Panther Party, 1966–71," in *Sisters in the Struggle: African American Women in the Civil Rights–Black Power Movement*, ed. Bettye Collier-Thomas and V. P. Franklin (New York: New York University Press, 2001), 246, https://libcom.org/files/No%20one%20ever%20asks%20what%20a%20man's%20role%20in%20the%20revolution%20is.pdf.

[39] Springer, *Living for the Revolution*, 27.

[40] Young, "Strapped," 213. It is unclear if the Puerto Rican activists who requested membership in the BWA were members of other nationalist, socialist, or feminist organizations.

[41] Springer, *Living for the Revolution*, 48.

[42] Frances Beal, interviewed by Loretta J. Ross, Oakland, March 18, 2005, Voices of Feminism Oral History Project, Sophia Smith Collection, Smith College, 5, https://www.smith.edu/libraries/libs/ssc/vof/transcripts/Beal.pdf.

[43] Patricia Romney, *We Were There: The Third World Women's Alliance and the Second Wave* (New York: Feminist Press, 2021).

[44] Springer, *Living for the Revolution*, 78.

[45] Lee Bebout, *Mythohistorical Interventions: The Chicano Movement and Its Legacies* (Minneapolis: University of Minnesota Press, 2011); Maylei Blackwell, ¡*Chicana Power!:Contested Histories of Feminism in the Chicano*

Movement (Austin: University of Texas Press, 2011); and Maria E. Cotera, review of *Mythohistorical Interventions* by Lee Bebout and *¡Chicana Power!* by Maylei Blackwell, *Signs: Journal of Women in Culture and Society* 38, no. 3 (Spring 2013), https://www.journals.uchicago.edu/doi/10.1086/668556.

[46] Rodolfo Gonzales and Alurista, "El Plan Espiritual de Aztlán," *El Grito del Norte* 2, no. 9 (July 6, 1969): 5, https://icaa.mfah.org/s/en/item/803398#?c=&m=&s=&cv=1&xywh=793%2C2029%2C1029%2C576.

[47] Amy D. Rublin, "'Though All Women Are Women, No Woman Is Only a Woman': Black, White, and Chicana Feminist Consciousness Development from 1955 to 1985" (honors thesis, University of Pennsylvania, 2007), 52.

[48] Rublin, "Though All Women Are Women," 42.

[49] Alma M. García, ed., *Chicana Feminist Thought*: *The Basic Historical Writings* (New York: Routledge, 1997), 29.

[50] Tia Tenopia, "Latinopia Event 1969 Denver Women's Caucus," Latinopia, March 3, 2013, https://latinopia.com/latino-history/latinopia-event-1969-denver-womens-caucus/.

[51] García, *Chicana Feminist Thought*, 1.

[52] Clarissa Dominguez, "Emergence of the Chicana Movement," Feminist Poetry Movement, December 10, 2018, https://sites.williams.edu/engl113-f18/dominguez/emergence-of-the-chicana-movement/.

[53] García, *Chicana Feminist Thought*, 6.

[54] Alma M. García, "The Development of Chicana Feminist Discourse, 1970–1980," *Gender and Society* 3, no. 2 (June 1989): 223, http://www.jstor.org/stable/189983.

[55] Miroslava Chávez-García, "A Genealogy of Chicana History, the Chicana Movement, and Chicana Studies," in *Routledge Handbook of Chicana/o Studies*, ed. Francisco A. Lomelí, Denise A. Segura, and Elyette Benjamin-Labarthe (Abingdon, Oxon., England: Routledge, 2019), Academia.edu - Share Research, https://www.academia.edu/410638736.

[56] García, "The Development of Chicana Feminist Discourse," 220.

[57] Mirta Vidal, "Chicanas Speak Out—Women: New Voice of La Raza," Duke University Libraries, Repository Collections and Archives, October 1971, 3, https://repository.duke.edu/dc/wlmpc/wlmms01005.

[58] García, *Chicana Feminist Thought*, 3.

[59] Dionne Espinoza "'Revolutionary Sisters': Women's Solidarity and Collective Identification among Chicana Brown Berets in East Los Angeles, 1967–1970," *Aztlán* 26, no. 1 (Spring 2001): 18.

[60] Elvira Rodríguez, "Covering the Chicano Movement: Examining Chicano Activism through Chicano, American, African American, and Spanish-Language Periodicals, 1965–1973" (PhD diss., University of California, Riverside, 2013), 30.

[61] Espinoza, "Revolutionary Sisters," 19.

[62] Sonia A. López, "The Role of the Chicana within the Student Movement," in *Chicana Feminist Thought: The Basic Historical Writings*, ed. Alma M. García (New York: Routledge, 2007), 103.

[63] Blackwell, *¡Chicana Power!*, 68.

[64] Espinoza "Revolutionary Sisters," 17.

[65] Espinoza "Revolutionary Sisters," 17.

[66] Blackwell, *¡Chicana Power!*, 8.

[67] Blackwell, *¡Chicana Power!*, 68.

[68] Blackwell, *¡Chicana Power!*, 30.

[69] Blackwell, *¡Chicana Power!*, 31.

[70] García, "The Development of Chicana Feminist Discourse," 226.

[71] García, "The Development of Chicana Feminist Discourse," 227.

[72] Vidal, "Chicanas Speak Out," 21.

[73] Vicki L. Ruíz, *From Out of the Shadows: Mexican Women in Twentieth-Century America* (New York: Oxford University Press, 2008), 107.

Chapter 6. Demands of The Women's Caucus

[1] Audre Lorde, *A Burst of Light and Other Essays* (Ithaca, NY: Firebrand Books, 1988).

[2] McClintock, "Family Feuds," 77.

[3] "The Long Feminist History of Fighting for Universal Childcare," Bitch Media, September 4, 2020, https://www.bitchmedia.org/article/universal-childcare-feminist-history.

[4] "Young Lords Council Removes Luciano as National Chairman," *New York Times*, September 5, 1970. See also "Press Release on Felipe," *Palante 2*, no.11 (1970): 2.

[5] Enck-Wanzer, *The Young Lords: A Reader*, 175. See also Jenny Figueroa, "World of Fantasy," *Palante* 3, no. 2 (1971): 4.

[6] Lulu Rovira, "Makeup and Beauty," *Palante* 3, no. 12 (1971): 9.

[7] "YLP Editorial," *Palante* 2, no. 4 (1970): 11.

[8] "Contract for the Murder of Chairman Felipe," *Palante* 2, no. 8 (1970): 2.

[9] "Young Lords Council Removes Luciano," *New York Times*, 21.

[10] Young Lords Party Central Committee, "On Felipe Luciano," *Palante* 2, no. 11 (1970): 2.

[11] "Young Lords Council Removes Luciano," *New York Times*, 21.

[12] Nydia Mercado, "Revolutionary Wedding," *Palante* 2, no. 9 (1970): 9.

[13] Erica González, "Mujeres of the Young Lords," Colorlines, August 19, 2009, https://www.colorlines.com/articles/mujeres-young-lords.

[14] Young Lords Party, Abramson, and Morales, *Palante*, 48.

[15] Young Lords Party, Abramson, and Morales, *Palante*, 50.

[16] Enck-Wanzer, *The Young Lords: A Reader*, 169. See also Young Lords Party Central Committee, "Young Lords Party Position on Women," *Palante* 2, no. 12 (1970): 12.

[17] "La posición del Partido de los Young Lords cuanto a las Mujeres." Spanish-language version of "Young Lords Party Position on Women," *Palante* 2, no. 13 (1970): 11.

[18] "Women in Cuba: The Revolution within the Revolution," in *Anthropology for the Nineties: Introductory Readings*, ed. Johnnetta B. Cole (New York: Free Press, 1988), 533.

[19] Debra Evenson, "Women's Equality in Cuba: What Difference Does a Revolution Make?," *Minnesota Journal of Law and Inequality* 4, no. 2 (June 1986): 309, https://scholarship.law.umn.edu/cgi/viewcontent.cgi?article=1328&context=lawineq.

[20] Klemesrud, "Young Women Find a Place," 78.

Chapter 7. Queer Liberation and the Young Lords Party

[1] Princess Harmony, "Queer People and the U.S. Communist Movement, 1969–1979," *Workers World*, January 14, 2022, https://www.workers.org/2022/01/61137/?utm_source=rss&utm_medium=rss&utm_campaign=queer-people-and-the-u-s-communist-movement-1969-1979.

[2] Emily K. Hobson, *Lavender and Red: Liberation and Solidarity in the Gay and Lesbian Left* (Oakland: University of California Press, 2016), 25–26.

[3] "Gay Liberation in New York City," Out History, Page One, n.d., https://outhistory.org/exhibits/show/gay-liberation-in-new-york-cit/3rd-world/pg-1.

[4] "Third World Gay Liberation Statement, 1970," in *Dear Sisters: Dispatches from the Women's Liberation Movement*, ed. Rosalyn Baxandall and Linda Gordon (New York: Basic Books, 2000), 64.

[5] "Gay Liberation in New York City," Out History.

[6] BlackPast, "(1970) Huey P. Newton."

[7] Ronald K. Porter, "A Rainbow in Black: The Gay Politics of the Black Panther Party," in *Sexualities in Education: A Reader*, ed. Erica R. Meiners and Therese Quinn, special issue, *Counterpoints* 367 (2012): 364–75.

[8] Hobson, *Lavender and Red*, 32.

[9] BlackPast, "(1970) Huey P. Newton."

[10] BlackPast, "(1970) Huey P. Newton."

[11] BlackPast, "(1970) Huey P. Newton."

[12] BlackPast, "(1970) Huey P. Newton."

[13] Joshua Bloom and Waldo E. Martin Jr., *Black against Empire: The History and Politics of the Black Panther Party* (Oakland: University of California Press, 2013), 306.

[14] Black Panther Party, "*Black Panther* Newspaper Insert on People's Revolutionary Constitutional Convention, June 11, 1970," Roz Payne Sixties Archive, https://rozsixties.unl.edu/items/show/667.

[15] George Katsiaficas, "Organization and Movement: The Case of the Black Panther Party and the Revolutionary People's Constitutional Convention of 1970," in *1963–2013: A Civil Rights Retrospective*, ed. Richard Cambridge, special issue, *About Place Journal* 2, no. 4 (February 2014), https://aboutplacejournal.org/issues/civil-rights/future-perfect/george-katsiaficas/#notes.

[16] Porter, "A Rainbow in Black," 364–75.

[17] Jared E. Leighton, "Freedom Indivisible: Gays and Lesbians in the African American Civil Rights Movement" (PhD diss., University of Nebraska–Lincoln, 2013), 372.

[18] Leighton, "Freedom Indivisible," 364.

[19] Leighton, "Freedom Indivisible," 366.

[20] Third World Gay Revolution, "Sixteen Point Platform and Program," Pinko, last modified October 15, 2019, https://pinko.online/pinko-1/third-world-gay-revolution-archive.

[21] Greta Olson and Mirjam Horn-Schott, "Introduction: Beyond Gender—Toward a Decolonized Queer Feminist Future," in *Beyond Gender: An Advanced Introduction to Futures of Feminist and Sexuality Studies*, ed. Greta Olson, Daniel Hartley, Mirjam Horn-Schott, and Leonie Schmidt (Abingdon, Oxon., England: Routledge, 2018), 14.

[22] Gillian Brockell, "The Transgender Women at Stonewall Were Pushed Out of the Gay Rights Movement. Now They Are Getting a Statue in New York," *Washington Post*, June 12, 2019, https://www.washingtonpost.com/history/2019/06/12/transgender-women-heart-stonewall-riots-are-getting-statue-new-york/.

[23.] Sylvia Rivera, "I'm Glad I Was in the Stonewall Riot," interview by Leslie Feinberg, *Workers World*, July 2, 1998, https://www.solidarity-us.org/files/SylviaRiveraInterview.pdf.

[24] Samuel Galen Ng, "Trans Power! Sylvia Lee Rivera's STAR and the Black Panther Party," *Left History* 17, no. 1 (Spring–Summer 2013): 22, doi:10.25071/1913-9632.39213.

[25] Rivera, "I'm Glad I Was in the Stonewall Riot."

[26] Young Lords Party, Abramson, and Morales, *Palante*, 40.

[27] Young Lords Party, Abramson, and Morales, *Palante*, 40.

[28] Ross, "Fighting White Supremacy."

[29] Young Lords Party Central Committee, July 1971 Retreat Paper, 6. Summarizes activities from January 1 to June 3, 1971. It announces the national liberation of Puerto Rico as the organization's political priority and gender and racial justice struggles as secondary. Iris Morales Files.

[30] Young Lords Party Central Committee, "Communiqué of Central Committee, Meeting of December 7–28, 1971," 1. Reviews activities from September to December 1971, including the rectification movement, the demotions of leading members, the Women's Union, and the YLP Party Congress. Iris Morales files.

PART III. "WE DO NOT LIVE SINGLE-ISSUE LIVES"

[1]Audre Lorde, *Sister Outsider: Essays and Speeches* (New York: Ten Speed Press, 2007), 138.

Chapter 8. Poverty Is a Health Issue

[1] Enck-Wanzer, *The Young Lords: A Reader*, 188.

[2] Lloyd Ultan and Barbara Unger, *Bronx Accent: A Literary and Pictorial History of the Borough* (New Brunswick, NJ: Rutgers University Press, 2000), 192.

[3] "Empire Roundup: Caught in the Squeeze," *Health/PAC Bulletin*, Health Policy Advisory Center, October 1970, https://www.healthpacbulletin.org/wp-content/uploads/1970/10/1970-October_Corrected.pdf.

[4] Michael T. Kaufman, "Lincoln Hospital: Case History of Dissension That Split Staff," *New York Times*, December 21, 1970, 1.

[5] "Lincoln History: A Bronx Legacy," NYC Health + Hospitals, n.d., https://www.nychealthandhospitals.org/lincoln/about-lincoln-hospital/history/.

[6] Kaufman, "Lincoln Hospital: Case History of Dissension," 1.

[7] Merlin Chowkwanyun, "The New Left and Public Health, the Health Policy Advisory Center, Community Organizing, and the Big Business of Health, 1967–1975," *American Journal of Public Health* 101, no. 2 (February 2011): 242, doi:10.2105/ajph.2009.189985.

[8] Chowkwanyun, "The New Left and Public Health."

[9] Interview with Cleo Silvers, March 12, 2007, Bronx African American History Project, BAAHP Digital Archive, Fordham University.

[10] "Editorial: Institutional Organizing," *Health/PAC Bulletin*, no. 37, Health Policy Advisory Center, January 1972, https://www.healthpacbulletin.org/healthpac-bulletin-january-1972/.

[11] Interview with Cleo Silvers, March 12, 2007.

[12] Fitzhugh Mullan, *White Coat, Clenched Fist: The Political Education of an American Physician* (Ann Arbor: University of Michigan Press, 2006), 139.

[13] Richard Fleming, "Could It Ever Happen Here? Lincoln Hospital Making Unprecedented Changes in Health Care," UCSF Synapse Archive, University of California, San Francisco, November 15, 1973, https://synapse.library.ucsf.edu/?a=d&d=ucsf19731115-01.2.13&e=-------en--20--1--txt------txIN--.

[14] Mullan, *White Coat, Clenched Fist*, 141.

[15] Mullan, *White Coat, Clenched Fist*, 142.

[16] Carl Pastor, "Socialism at Lincoln," *Palante* 2, no. 8 (1970): 5.

[17] Stephen Torgoff, "HRUM Sums Up Hospital Organizing," Marxists Internet Archive, December 27, 1972, https://www.marxists.org/history/erol/ncm-1/hrum.htm.

[18] "Your Asian Wasn't Quiet," Tumblr, n.d., https://asianamericanactivism.tumblr.com/post/68946140266/i-wor-kuen-12-point-party-platform-i-wor-kuen.

[19] "Empire Roundup: Caught in the Squeeze," *Health/PAC Bulletin*.

[20] Bella August, "El Barrio: A People's Health Movement," *Health/PAC Bulletin*, Health Policy Advisory Center, February 1970, http://www.healthpacbulletin.org/healthpac-bulletin-february-1970-2/.

[21] Health Revolutionary Unity Movement, *"Ideology,"* 4.

[22] Health Revolutionary Unity Movement, "Ideology, History, Patients' and Workers' Rights," 10.

[23] "Editorial: Institutional Organizing," *Health/PAC Bulletin*.

[24] Health Revolutionary Unity Movement, *"Ideology,"* 8.

[25] Health Revolutionary Unity Movement, *"Ideology,"* 9.

[26] Health Revolutionary Unity Movement, *"Ideology,"* 11–12.

[27] Ritch Whyman, "How Do We Fight Racism and Capitalism?," Socialist.ca, International Socialists, February 1, 2012, https://www.socialist.ca/node/745.

[28] Health Revolutionary Unity Movement, *"Ideology,"* 8.

[29] Health Revolutionary Unity Movement, *"Ideology,"* 6–7.

[30] Merlin Chowkwanyun, "Have You Heard of the Lincoln Collective?," History of Medicine and Public Health, New York Academy of Medicine Library Blog, May 17, 2016, https://nyamcenterforhistory.org/2016/05/17/have-you-heard-of-the-lincoln-collective/.

[31] Pastor, "Socialism at Lincoln," 5.

[32] Alfonso A. Narvaez, "Young Lords Seize Lincoln Hospital Building," *New York Times*, July 15, 1970, 34, https://www.nytimes.com/1970/07/15/archives/young-lords-seize-lincoln-hospital-building-offices-are-held-for-12.html.

[33] Mullan, *White Coat, Clenched Fist*, 146.

[34] Mullan, *White Coat, Clenched Fist*, 146.

[35] Pastor, "Socialism at Lincoln," 5.

[36] "Editorial: Institutional Organizing," *Health/PAC Bulletin*.

[37] Willard Cates Jr., David A. Grimes, and Kenneth F. Schulz, "The Public Health Impact of Legal Abortion: 30 Years Later," *Perspectives on Sexual and Reproductive Health* 35, no. 1 (January–February 2003): 25, doi:10.1363/3502503.

[38] Julia Jacobs, "Remembering an Era before Roe, When New York Had the 'Most Liberal' Abortion Law," *New York Times*, July 19, 2018, https://www.nytimes.com/2018/07/19/us/politics/new-york-abortion-roe-wade-nyt.html.

[39] Martin Gansberg, "Abortion Death Reported by City," *New York Times*, July 21, 1970, 32.

[40] Charlayne Hunter, "Community Dispute Cuts Service at City Hospital," *New York Times*, August 26, 1970, 1.

[41] Mullan, *White Coat, Clenched Fist*, 148–49.

[42] Kaufman, "Lincoln Hospital: Case History of Dissension," 1.

[43] Edward Hudson, "Doctors Stay Out at Hospital Here," *New York Times*, August 28, 1970, 24, https://www.nytimes.com/1970/08/28/archives/doctors-stay-out-at-hospital-here-injunction-fails-to-influence-27.html.

[44] Hudson, "Doctors Stay Out."

[45] Jennifer Nelson, *Women of Color and the Reproductive Rights Movement* (New York: New York University Press, 2003), 102.

[46] Nelson, *Women of Color and the Reproductive Rights Movement*, 108.

[47] Le Pioufle, "Feminism and the Puerto Rican Independence Movement."

[48] Enck-Wanzer, *The Young Lords: A Reader*, 178. See also Gloria Colón, "Abortions," *Palante* 3, no. 5 (1971): 12.

[49] See generally J. Nelson, "Abortions under Community Control," 157–80.

[50] Enck-Wanzer, *The Young Lords: A Reader*, 178.

[51] J. Nelson, "Abortions under Community Control," 170, and Nelson's interview with Olguie Robles, New York City, April 18, 2000, in the same article.

[52] Enck-Wanzer, *The Young Lords: A Reader*, 169.

[53] Sean Gardiner, "Heroin: From the Civil War to the 70s, and Beyond," *City Limits*, July 5, 2009, https://citylimits.org/2009/07/05/heroin-from-the-civil-war-to-the-70s-and-beyond/.

[54] Joseph Lelyveld, "Obituary of a Heroin User Who Died at 12," New York Times, January 12, 1970, 1.

[55] Viola H. Huang, "Between Protest, Compromise, and Education for Radical Change: Black Power Schools in Harlem in the Late 1960s," (PhD diss., Columbia University, 2019).

[56] Thomas F. Brady, "St. Luke's Yields on Drug Facility," *New York Times*, January 18, 1970, 56.

[57] Alondra Nelson, "'Genuine Struggle and Care': An Interview with Cleo Silvers," *American Journal of Public Health* 106, no. 10 (October 2016), doi:10.2105/AJPH.2016.303407.

[58] Merlin Chowkwanyun, "On Fitzhugh Mullan's *White Coat, Clenched Fist*," *Social Medicine* 2, no. 2 (April 2007): 103, https://www.socialmedicine.info/index.php/socialmedicine/article/download/124/238.

[59] "Editorial: Institutional Organizing," *Health/PAC Bulletin*.

[60] "N.Y.C. Human Rights Commission Releases Report on Einhorn Case; Blames All Parties," Jewish Telegraphic Agency, July 16, 1971, https://www.jta.org/1971/07/16/archive/n-y-c-human-rights-commission-releases-report-on-einhorn-case-blames-all-parties.

[61] A. Nelson, "Genuine Struggle and Care."

[62] Chowkwanyun, "The New Left and Public Health," 242.

[63] "Editorial: The Medical Industrial Complex," *Health/PAC Bulletin*, Health Policy Advisory Center, November 1969, https://www.healthpacbulletin.org/healthpac-bulletin-november-1969/.

Chapter 9. Uprisings against New York City Criminal Justice System

[1] Assata Shakur, *Assata: An Autobiography* (Chicago: Lawrence Hill, 2001), 1.

[2] Sarah Childress, "Michelle Alexander: 'A System of Racial and Social Control,'" Frontline, April 29, 2014, https://www.pbs.org/wgbh/frontline/article/michelle-alexander-a-system-of-racial-and-social-control/.

[3] Wendy Sawyer and Peter Wagner, "Mass Incarceration: The Whole Pie, 2020," Prison Policy Initiative, March 24, 2020, https://www.prisonpolicy.org/reports/pie2020.html?c=pie&gclid=CjwKCAiA1uKMBhAGEiwAxzvX96qz7gcnuY4urRqElLQlx7DegMV2ZO7NnC1nkgwVjmF.

[4] Willie Mack, "'Traitors in Our Midst': Race, Corrections, and the 1970 Tombs Uprising," Gotham Center for New York City History, October 1, 2020, https://www.gothamcenter.org/blog/traitors-in-our-midst-race-corrections-and-the-1970-tombs-uprising.

[5] Orisanmi Burton, "Organized Disorder: The New York City Jail Rebellion of 1970," *Black Scholar* 48, no. 4 (October 2018): 30, https://doi:10.1080/00064246.2018.1514925.

[6] Heather Ann Thompson, "How a Series of Jail Rebellions Rocked New York—and Woke a city," *The Nation*, March 21, 2019, https://www.thenation.com/article/archive/new-york-jail-rebellion-1970-tombs-mdc/.

[7] William J. vanden Heuvel, interviewed by Jeffrey A. Kroessler, February 2, 2011, Justice in New York: An Oral History no. 12, Lloyd Sealy Library Digital Collections, http://dc.lib.jjay.cuny.edu/index.php/Detail/Object/Show/object_id/657.

[8] Emily L. Thuma, *All Our Trials: Prisons, Policing, and the Feminist Fight to End Violence* (Urbana: University of Illinois Press, 2019), 24.

[9] Thompson, "How a Series of Jail Rebellions Rocked New York."

[10] "The House of D: A Panel on the Women's House of Detention," Village Preservation, August 27, 2020, https://www.villagepreservation.org/event/the-house-of-d/.

[11] Olga Jiménez de Wagenheim, *Nationalist Heroines, Puerto Rican Women History Forgot, 1930s to 1950s* (Princeton: Markus Wiener Publishers, 2016), 228.

[12] Wagenheim, *Nationalist Heroines*, 230.

[13] "Smith Act," Wikipedia, last modified September 13, 2022, https://en.wikipedia.org/wiki/Smith_Act.

[14] Wagenheim, *Nationalist Heroines*, 232-233.

[15] Hobson, *Lavender and Red*, 25–26.

[16] Hugh Ryan, "The Queer History of the Women's House of Detention," *Activist History Review*, May 31, 2019, https://activisthistory.com/2019/05/31/the-queer-history-of-the-womens-house-of-detention/. Daughters of Bilitis, founded in San Francisco in 1955, took its name from a poetry collection called *Songs of Bilitis.* Bilitis was the female character romantically associated with Sappho, the female Greek lyric poet. https://www.britannica.com/topic/Daughters-of-Bilitis

[17] Ryan, "The Queer History of the Women's House of Detention."

[18] For a discussion of the history of International Women's Day, see Temma Kaplan, "On the Socialist Origins of International Women's Day," *Feminist Studies* 11, no. 1 (Spring 1985): 163–71, doi:10.2307/3180144.

[19] Minnie Bruce Pratt, "1970: Reviving the Fighting Spirit of Int'l Women's Day," *Workers World*, February 23, 2005, https://www.workers.org/2005/us/womens-day-0303/.

[20] Pratt, "1970: Reviving the Fighting Spirit."

[21] Pratt, "1970: Reviving the Fighting Spirit."

[22] Hobson, *Lavender and Red*, 46.

[23] Hobson, *Lavender and Red*, 6.

[24] "Prison Struggle 1970–71," *Critical Resistance*, last modified March 9, 2012, https://criticalresistance.org/resources/prison-struggle-1970-1-5/.

[25] Thompson, "How a Series of Jail Rebellions Rocked New York."

[26] Burton, "Organized Disorder," 34.

[27] Thompson, "How a Series of Jail Rebellions Rocked New York."

[28] Thompson, "How a Series of Jail Rebellions Rocked New York."

[29] Burton, "Organized Disorder," 32.

[30] Burton, "Organized Disorder," 32.

[31] Thompson, "How a Series of Jail Rebellions Rocked New York."

[32] Burton, "Organized Disorder," 34.

[33] Thompson, "How a Series of Jail Rebellions Rocked New York."

[34] Burton, "Organized Disorder," 36.

[35] Burton, "Organized Disorder," 37.

[36] Burton, "Organized Disorder," 39.

[37] Bruce Jackson, *Law and Disorder: Criminal Justice in America* (Urbana: University of Illinois Press, 1984), 85.

[38] Philip Quarles, "An Unexplained Death and an Unacceptable System," WNYC, New York Public Radio, September 21, 2017, https://www.wnyc.org/story/unexplained-death-and-unacceptable-system/.

[39] I Wor Kuen translates as "Fist of Harmony"; the phrase originates from the Chinese fight to overthrow imperialism and colonialism during the Boxer Rebellion of 1900.

[40] Los Siete de la Raza were seven young Latinos from San Francisco's Mission District accused of murdering a policeman in 1969. The men were acquitted in 1970.

[41] Michael T. Kaufman, "200 Armed Young Lords Seize Church after Taking Body There," *New York Times*, October 19, 1970, 26.

[42] Kaufman, "200 Armed Young Lords Seize Church," 26.

[43] Mecca Adai, "Free Our Sisters," *Palante* 2, no. 17 (December 1970): 19.

[44] Adai, "Free Our Sisters," 19.

[45] Adai, "Free Our Sisters," 19.

[46] Afeni Shakur, "Women's House of Detention," *Palante* 2, no. 17 (1970): 3.

[47] Shakur, "Women's House of Detention," 3.

[48] Shakur, "Women's House of Detention," 3.

[49] Angela Y. Davis, *Are Prisons Obsolete?* (New York: Seven Stories Press, 2003), 60–83.

[50] Davis, *Are Prisons Obsolete?* 83.

[51] Ellen Pierce, "Demonstration at the House of D," Wisconsin Historical Society, GT Press Collection, 1964–1977, https://content.wisconsinhistory.org/digital/collection/p15932coll8/id/62636.

[52] Adai, "Free Our Sisters," 19.

[53] Adai, "Free Our Sisters," 19.

[54] Pierce, "Demonstration at the House of D."

[55] Adai, "Free Our Sisters," 19.

[56] Tony Platt, quoted in "Organizing the Prisons in the 1960s and 1970s: Part One, Building Movements," Process: A Blog for American History, September 20, 2016, https://www.processhistory.org/prisoners-rights-1/.

[57] "Words from Prison—Did You Know …?" American Civil Liberties Union, https://www.aclu.org/other/words-prison-did-you-know.

[58] Thuma, *All Our Trials*, 4.

[59] Michele Goodwin, "The New Jane Crow: Women's Mass Incarceration," Just Security, July 20, 2020, https://www.justsecurity.org/71509/the-new-jane-crow-womens-mass-incarceration/.

Chapter 10. Free Puerto Rico Now! Organizing with Students

[1] Puerto Rican Student Union, "Somos Puertorriqueños y estamos despertando," pamphlet, New York, 1970, 1. Iris Morales files.

[2] Brier, "Why the History of CUNY Matters," 30.

[3] Sean Molloy, "SEEK's Fight for Racial and Social Justice at CUNY (1965–1969)," CUNY Digital History Archive, June 23, 2017, https://cdha.cuny.edu/secondary-sources/seek.

[4] Zita Dixon, "Creating, Passing, and Protecting a Racially Equitable Higher Education Social Policy Program: A Critical Historical Case Study of a State's Policymaking Process and Its Participants" (PhD diss., Brandeis University, 2021), 10.

[5] Danny Shaw, "NYC Ruling Class Targets Black, Latino City University Students," *Liberation*, November 1, 2006, https://www.liberationnews.org/06-11-01-nyc-ruling-class-targets-black-html/#.XzcFPPJ7kSI.

[6] "Minutes from 4/8/1965 CCNY Faculty Council Meeting · CUNY Digital History Archive," Home · CUNY Digital History Archive, last modified April 8, 1965, https://cdha.cuny.edu/items/show/6982.

[7] Frederick Douglass Opie, *Upsetting the Apple Cart: Black-Latino Coalitions in New York City from Protest to Public Office* (New York: Columbia University Press, 2014), 74.

[8] Christopher Gunderson, "The Struggle for CUNY: A History of the CUNY Student Movement, 1969–1999," 7, https://eportfolios.macaulay.cuny.edu/hainline2014/files/2014/02/Gunderson_The-Struggle-for-CUNY.pdf.

[9] Gunderson, "The Struggle for CUNY," 8.

[10] In 1971, the MPI became the Puerto Rican Socialist Party (Partido Socialista Puertorriqueño).

[11] Ashley Leane Black, "From San Juan to Saigon: Shifting Conceptions of Puerto Rican Identity during the Vietnam War" (master's thesis, University of British Columbia, 2012), 40–42, https://central.bac-lac.gc.ca/.item?id=TC-BVAU-42499&op=pdf&app=Library&oclc_number=1032917918.

[12] Mirta González, "Free Puerto Rico," *Y.L.O.*, January 1970, 8.

[13] L.U.C.H.A. (Latinos Unidos Con Honor y Amistad), student organization formed at New York University in 1969.

[14] Frederick D. Opie, *Upsetting the Apple Cart: Black-Latino Coalitions in New York City from Protest to Public Office* (New York: Columbia University Press, 2014), 74-75.

[15] "La historia de la Unión Estudiantil Boricua, movimiento estudiantil revolucionario," pamphlet. Iris Morales files.

[16] Richie Pérez, "Puerto Rican Student Union," *Palante* 3, no. 3 (1971): 7.

[17] "Proposal for Unifying the Puerto Rican Student Movement," document from the student section of the Puerto Rican Revolutionary Workers Organization. Iris Morales files.

[18] Ben Lieber, "Latins Demand 'Free Puerto Rico,'" Marxists Internet Archive, September 24, 1970, https://www.marxists.org/history/erol/ncm-8/pl-latins.htm. First published in the *Columbia Daily Spectator* 115, no. 2 (September 24, 1970).

[19] Lieber, "Latins Demand 'Free Puerto Rico.'"

[20] Olga Jiménez de Wagenheim, "Remembering March 1, 1954," 80 Grados, March 9, 2019, https://www.80grados.net/remembering-march-1-1954/

[21] Marisol LeBrón, "Puerto Rico and the Colonial Circuits of Policing," North American Congress on Latin America, September 27, 2017, https://nacla.org/news/2017/09/27/puerto-rico-and-colonial-circuits-policing.

[22] "Jayuya Uprising," Military Wiki, https://military-history.fandom.com/wiki/Jayuya_uprising.

[23] "La Revolución Nacionalista," YouTube, October 6, 2007, https://www.youtube.com/watch?v=RfOJj0nmGEU.

[24] The Associated Press, "Revolt Flares in Puerto Rico; Soon Quelled With 23 Dead," The New York Times, October 31, 1950, 1.

[25] Olivia Kinnear, "Women in Puerto Rican History: Blanca Canales," Pasquines, June 15, 2015, https://pasquines.us/2015/06/15/women-in-the-history-of-puerto-rico-blanca-canales/.

[26] Davies, *Left of Karl Marx*, 141.

[27] Davies, *Left of Karl Marx*, xxiv-xxvii.

[28] Davies, *Left of Karl Marx*, 110–11.

[29] Davies, *Left of Karl Marx*, 110–13.

[30] Olivia Kinnear, "Women in Puerto Rican History: Blanca Canales," Pasquines, June 15, 2015, https://pasquines.us/2015/06/15/women-in-the-history-of-puerto-rico-blanca-canales/.

PART IV. NATIONALISMS AND FEMINISMS

[1] Skyler Gomez, "On Love and Identity: 6 Poems by Julia de Burgos," Literary Ladies Guide, June 14, 2019, https://www.literaryladiesguide.com/classic-women-authors-poetry/poems-julia-de-burgos-puerto-rican-poet/.

Chapter 11. Rebellion Rushin' Down the Wrong Road

[1] This line from "Five Nights of Bleeding," published by poet-musician Linton Kwesi Johnson in 1973, resonates as a metaphor for the Young Lords' move to Puerto Rico. At eleven years old, Johnson emigrated from Jamaica to

South London to join his mother. In his final year of secondary school, he joined the Black Panther Party of England. See Johnson's work at: Robert J. Stewart, "Linton Kwesi Johnson: Poetry Down a Reggae Wire," New West Indian Guide/Nieuwe West-Indische *Gids* 67, nos. 1–2 (1993): 69–89.

[2] Young Lords Party, Abramson, and Morales, *Palante*, 72.

[3] Pablo "Yoruba" Guzmán, "Why the Young Lords Party," *Palante* 2, no. 17 (1970).

[4] Report of Central Committee Evaluation and Retreat, December 21–23, 1970, 15.

[5] Gloria González, "Rompe Cadenas," *Palante* 3, no. 2 (1971): 12–13.

[6] Report of Central Committee Evaluation and Retreat, 13.

[7] Juan González and Juan "Fi" Ortiz, "Letter from Puerto Rico," *Palante* 2, no. 11 (1970): 4.

[8] Report of Central Committee Evaluation and Retreat, 14.

[9] The Young Lords defined "lumpen" or lumpenproletariat as the unemployable—people on drugs or in jail, sex workers, and welfare mothers. A jibaro was defined as an agricultural worker.

[10] Report of Central Committee Evaluation and Retreat, 12–15.

[11] Roberto P. Rodríguez-Morazzani, "Political Cultures of the Puerto Rican Left in the United States," in *The Puerto Rican Movement: Voices from the Diaspora*, ed. Andrés Torres and José E. Velázquez (Philadelphia: Temple University Press, 1998), 42.

[12] Report of Central Committee Evaluation and Retreat, 5.

[13] Report of Central Committee Evaluation and Retreat, 5.

[14] Report of Central Committee Evaluation and Retreat, 3.

[15] Carlos Aponte, letter to Young Lords Party's Central Committee, circa February 1971, UCLA, Asian American Studies Center.

[16] YLP Ministry of Defense, "Beware of What You Say (Bugging)," *Palante* 3, no. 3 (1971): 14.

[17] Young Lords Party Central Committee, July 1971 Retreat Paper, 2.

[18] Young Lords Party, "Police Agents," *Palante*, 3, no. 3 (1971): Defense Supplement, 14.

[19] Carlos Aponte, letter to Young Lords Party Central Committee, ca. February 1971, UCLA Asian American Studies Center, Los Angeles.

[20] Carlos Aponte, letter to Young Lords Party Central Committee.

[21] Juan González Papers, Box 29, Folders 10 and 11, Center for Puerto Rican Studies Library and Archives at Hunter College, New York City.

[22] Young Lords Party, Abramson, and Morales, *Palante*, 72.

[23] Report of Central Committee Evaluation and Retreat, 20.

[24] "Pig of the Year," *Palante* 3, no. 1 (1971): 14.

[25] Marisabel Brás, "The Changing of the Guard: Puerto Rico in 1898," World of 1898: The Spanish-American War, Hispanic Division, Library of Congress, https://www.loc.gov/rr/hispanic/1898/bras.html.

[26] Acosta-Belén and Santiago, *Puerto Ricans in the United States*, 57.

[27] Young Lords Party Central Committee, "Two Years of Struggle," *Palante* 3, no. 13 (1971): 10.

[28] Andrés Torres, "A Brief History of the Puerto Rican Socialist Party in the United States," in *Revolution around the Corner: Voices from the Puerto Rican Socialist Party in the United States*, ed. José E. Velázquez, Carmen V. Rivera, and Andrés Torres (Philadelphia: Temple University Press, 2021), 29.

[29] Torres, "Introduction: Political Radicalism in the Diaspora," 7.

[30] Torres, "A Brief History of the Puerto Rican Socialist Party," 28.

Chapter 12. The Women's Union and The 12-Point Program

[1] The Women's Union, *La Luchadora* 1, no.1. (June 1971)

[2] Report of Central Committee "Evaluation and Retreat," 17.

[3] Report of Central Committee Evaluation and Retreat, 19.

[4] Report of Central Committee Evaluation and Retreat, 18. In the lumpen group, Pérez identified "prostitutes, drug addicts, welfare mothers, hustlers, the street people, unemployed, and prisoners in jail and all political prisoners."

[5] Young Lords Party Central Committee, *The Ideology of the Young Lords Party* (pamphlet), 1971.

[6] BlackPast, "(1965) The Moynihan Report: The Negro Family, the Case for National Action," January 21, 2007, https://www.blackpast.org/african-american-history/moynihan-report-1965/.

[7] Susan Greenbaum, "Opinion: Where's the Obituary for the Moynihan Report?" Al Jazeera America, October 10, 2015, http://america.aljazeera.com/opinions/2015/10/wheres-the-obituary-for-the-moynihan-report.html.

[8] Chong Chon-Smith, *East Meets Black: Asian and Black Masculinities in the Post–Civil Rights Era* (Jackson: University Press of Mississippi, 2015), 17.

[9] Kay S. Hymowitz, "The Black Family: 40 Years of Lies," *City Journal*, Summer 2005, https://www.city-journal.org/html/black-family-40-years-lies-12872.html.

[10] Chon-Smith, *East Meets Black*, 16–18.

[11] Daniel Geary, "Moynihan's Anti-Feminism," *Jacobin*, July 1, 2015, https://www.jacobinmag.com/2015/07/moynihans-report-fiftieth-anniversary-black-family/.

[12] Geary, "Moynihan's Anti-Feminism."

[13] Greenbaum, "Opinion: Where's the Obituary?"

[14] Springer, *Living for the Revolution*, 17.

[15] Young Lords Party Central Committee, July 1971 Retreat Paper, 20.

[16] Women's Union 12-Point Program and Platform. See appendix in this volume.

17 bell hooks, *Feminism Is for Everybody: Passionate Politics* (Cambridge, MA: South End Press, 2000), 42.

[18] Matthew Yarrow, "Colonial Legacy and Military Strategy: The U.S. Military in Puerto Rico," Latin America/Caribbean Program, American Friends Service Committee Peacebuilding Unit, n.d., https://www.afsc.org/sites/default/files/documents/2000%20Colonial%20Legacy%20and%20Military%20Strategy%20The%20US%20Military%20in%20Puerto%20Rico.pdf.

[19] Women's Union, *La Luchadora*, centerfold, 1971.

[20] Women's Union, "Esclava de casa," *La Luchadora* 1, no. 1 (July 1971): 2.

[21] Women's Union, "Machismo," *La Luchadora* 1, no. 2 (August 1971): 4.

[22] Friedrich Engels, *Origins of the Family, Private Property, and the State*, II. The Family, 4. The Monogamous Family, Marxists Internet Archive, https://www.marxists.org/archive/marx/works/1884/origin-family/ch02d.htm.

[23] Women's Union, "Esclava de casa," 2.

[24] Muzio, *Radical Imagination, Radical Humanity*, 1.

[25] Torres, "A Brief History of the Puerto Rican Socialist Party," 71.

[26] Carmen Vivian Rivera, "Our Movement: One Woman's Story," in *The Puerto Rican Movement: Voices from the Diaspora*, ed. Andrés Torres and José E. Velázquez (Philadelphia: Temple University Press, 1998), 204.

[27] Muzio, *Radical Imagination, Radical Humanity*, 38.

[28] Torres, "A Brief History of the Puerto Rican Socialist Party," 69.

[29] Zoilo Torres, "What the Puerto Rican Socialist Party Nurtured in Me," in *Revolution around the Corner: Voices from the Puerto Rican Socialist Party in the United States*, ed. José E. Velázquez, Carmen V. Rivera, and Andrés Torres (Philadelphia: Temple University Press, 2021), 282.

[30] Ruth Robinett, "Report on Canadian Conference with Indochinese Women," May 3, 1971, Marxists Internet Archive, https://www.marxists.org/history/etol/document/youth/ysa/ysa-docs-min-1971/04-AWWP-women-con-NEC-mins-07.pdf.

[31] Robinett, "Report on Canadian Conference," 2.

[32] Position on Women's Liberation in Darrel Enck-Wanzer, ed., *The Young Lords: A Reader* (New York: New York University Press, 2010), 180.

[33] Enck-Wanzer, *The Young Lords: A Reader,* 181.

[34] Enck-Wanzer, *The Young Lords: A Reader,* 181.

[35] Enck-Wanzer, *The Young Lords: A Reader*, 180.

[36] Enck-Wanzer, *The Young Lords: A Reader*, 182

[37] Denise Comanne, "How Patriarchy and Capitalism Combine to Aggravate the Oppression of Women," Committee for the Abolition of Illegitimate Debt,

May 28, 2020, https://www.cadtm.org/How-Patriarchy-and-Capitalism-Com-bine-to-Aggravate-the-Oppression-of-Women.

Chapter 13. From Revolutionary to narrow nationalism

[1] Aja Monet, *My Mother Was a Freedom Fighter* (Chicago: Haymarket Books, 2017), 3.

[2] Stephen Zunes and Jesse Laird, "The U.S. Anti-Vietnam War Movement (1964–1973)," International Center on Nonviolent Conflict, January 2010, https://www.nonviolent-conflict.org/us-anti-vietnam-war-movement-1964-1973/.

[3] "Pentagon Papers," History, August 2, 2011; last modified June 9, 2021, https://www.history.com/topics/vietnam-war/pentagon-papers.

[4] Katherine T. McCaffrey, Military Power and Popular Protest: The U.S. Navy in Vieques, Puerto Rico (Chicago: Rutgers University Press, 2002), 68.

[5] Michael Staudenmaier, "Puerto Rican Independence Movement, 1898–Present," Marxists Internet Archive, 2798, https://www.marxists.org/his-tory/erol/ncm-8/history-independence-movement.pdf.

[6] Young Lords Party Central Committee, July 1971 Retreat Paper, 6.

[7] Central Committee, July 1971 Retreat Paper, 3.

[8] Central Committee, July 1971 Retreat Paper, 5.

[9] Central Committee, July 1971 Retreat Paper," 5.

[10] Iris Morales, *Through the Eyes of Rebel Women: The Young Lords, 1969–1976* (New York: Red Sugarcane Press, 2016), 183; see also Palante 2, no. 12 (1970): 11.

[11] Central Committee, July 1971 Retreat Paper, 5.

[12] Central Committee, July 1971 Retreat Paper, 14.

[13] Central Committee, July 1971 Retreat Paper, 15.

[14] Central Committee, July 1971 Retreat Paper, 6.

[15] Central Committee, July 1971 Retreat Paper, 4.

[16] Central Committee, July 1971 Retreat Paper, 6.

[17] Young Lords Party Central Committee, *The Ideology of the Young Lords Party*, 31.

[18] Central Committee, July 1971 Retreat Paper, 6.

[19] Central Committee, July 1971 Retreat Paper, 6.

[20] Central Committee, July 1971 Retreat Paper, 6.

[21] Central Committee, July 1971 Retreat Paper, 3.

[22] Young Lords Party Central Committee, "Communiqué," 1.

[23] Third World Students' League, "United We Stand, Divided We Walk," *Palante* 3, no. 19 (1971): 5.

[24] Puerto Rican Student Union, "The Puerto Rican Studies Conference," *Palante* 3, no. 20 (1971): 9.

[25] Bryant, "Puerto Rican Women's Roles," 130.

[26] Rivera, "Our Movement: One Woman's Story," 205.

[27] Bryant, "Puerto Rican Women's Roles," 64.

[28] Bryant, "Puerto Rican Women's Roles," 67.

[29] Bryant, "Puerto Rican Women's Roles," 69.

[30] Bryant, "Puerto Rican Women's Roles," 77.

[31] Lina Sunseri, "Moving Beyond the Feminism Versus National Dichotomy: An Anti-Colonial Feminist Perspective on Aboriginal Liberation Struggles," *Canadian Woman Studies/Le Cahiers de la Femme* 20, no. 2 (2000), https://cws.journals.yorku.ca/index.php/cws/article/view/7621.

[32] Radwa Saad and Sara Soumaya Abed, "A Revolution Deferred: Sexual and Gender-Based Violence in Egypt," in *Gender, Protests and Political Change in Africa*, ed. Awino Okech (Cham, Switzerland: Palgrave Macmillan, 2020), 81–106.

[33] Ranjoo Seodu Herr, "The Possibility of Nationalist Feminism," *Hypatia* 18, no. 3 (August 2003): 137, doi:10.1111/j.1527-2001.2003.tb00825.

[34] Herr, "The Possibility of Nationalist Feminism," 142.

[35] Camille Le Pioufle, "Feminism and the Puerto Rican Independence movement since the 1950s: From Unrequited Love to a Matching pair?" Dumas - Dépôt Universitaire De Mémoires Après Soutenance, last modified 2019, https://dumas.ccsd.cnrs.fr/dumas-02172215/ file/2018_MM2_Le_Pioufle C. pdf. 92.

[36] Pablo "Yoruba" Guzmán, "Report to Central Committee, December 7, 1971," 13. In this forty-five-page report, Guzmán discusses his trip to China and presents ideas for the future of the Young Lords Party. Iris Morales files.

[37] Pablo "Yoruba" Guzmán, "Our Present Situation: Statement, Analysis, Suggestions, Draft Paper for Discussion," November 10, 1971, 1. Iris Morales files.

[38] Pablo "Yoruba" Guzmán, "Report #1 to Juan González and Gloria Fontanez, November 14, 1971," 1–2. This two-page report describes the YLP's deteriorating conditions and Guzmán's meetings with national staff members regarding this situation. Iris Morales files.

[39] Guzmán, "Report to the Central Committee, December 7, 1971," 17–18.

[40] Central Committee, "Communiqué," 1.

[41] Central Committee, "Communiqué," 5.

[42] Central Committee, "Communiqué," 23–24.

[43] Yellow Seeds broadside, Balch Institute for Ethnic Studies, Historical Society of Pennsylvania, http://www2.hsp.org/exhibits/Balch%20exhibits/chinatown/yellowseeds.html.

[44] Jean Tepperman, "The Material Basis of Women's Oppression in Capitalist Society," Marxists Internet Archive, last modified July 1981, https://www.marxists.org/history/erol/ncm-8/19812302.htm.

[45] Central Committee, "Communiqué," 17.

[46] Lulu Rovira, "Children's Center Opens," *Palante* 4, no. 11 (1972): 6.

[47] Women's Union, "FBI and City Threaten to Close Down Day Care Center," *Palante* 4, no. 19 (1972): 6.

[48] Lydia Silva, "Why a Women's Union," *Palante* 4, no. 8 (1972): 6.

[49] Juan González, "On Our Errors," *Palante* 4, no. 4 (1972): 12.

[50] González, "On Our Errors," 12.

[51] Central Committee, "Communiqué," 21.

[52] Young Lords Party Central Committee, "Faction Leaves Young Lords Party," *Palante* 4, no. 12 (1972), special edition.

[53] PRRWO, "Resolutions and Speeches," 14.

[54] Juan González Papers, Box 29, Folders 10 and 11, Center for Puerto Rican Studies Library and Archives at Hunter College, New York City.

[55] Juan González Papers, Box 29, Folders 10 and 11, Center for Puerto Rican Studies Library and Archives at Hunter College, New York City.

[56] PRRWO, "Resolutions and Speeches," 2.

[57] Puerto Rican Revolutionary Workers Organization (PRRWO), "Resolutions and Speeches," First Party Congress, 1972, 31.

[58] PRRWO, "Resolutions and Speeches," 32.

[59] Morales, *Through the Eyes of Rebel Women*, 118–23.

PART V. RECKONING WITH THE PAST

[1] Eduardo Galeano, *Open Veins of Latin America: Five Centuries of the Pillage of a Continent* (New York: Monthly Review Press, 1973), 267.

Chapter 14. State Surveillance, Police Violence, and Enemy Within

[1] Brian Glick, preface to *The COINTELPRO Papers: Documents from the FBI's Secret Wars against Dissent in the United States*, by Ward Churchill and Jim Vander Wall (Boston: South End Press, 1990), xv.

[2] Carmin Maffea, "The Fight to Abolish the Police Is the Fight to Abolish Capitalism," Left Voice, June 10, 2020, https://www.leftvoice.org/the-fight-to-abolish-the-police-is-the-fight-to-abolish-capitalism/.

[3] Aryeh Neier, "Surveillance by the FBI," *Index on Censorship* 10, no. 2 (April 1981): 44, https://journals.sagepub.com/toc/ioca/10/2.

[4] Alex Zambito, "The FBI's War on the Left: A Short History of COINTELPRO," Midwestern Marx, October 4, 2020, https://www.midwesternmarx.com/articles/the-fbis-war-on-the-left-a-short-history-of-cointelpro-by-alex-zambito.

[5] Ward Churchill and Jim Vander Wall, *The COINTELPRO Papers: Documents from the FBI's Secret Wars against Dissent in the United States* (Boston: South End Press, 1990), 209.

[6] "Black Panther Greatest Threat to U.S. Security," *Desert Sun* (Palm Springs, CA), July 16, 1969, at the California Digital Newspaper Collection, https://cdnc.ucr.edu/?a=d&d=DS19690716.2.89&e=-------en--20--1--txt-txIN--------1.

[7] Nina Renata Aron, "When the Black Justice Movement Got Too Powerful, the FBI Got Scared and Got Ugly," Medium, February 9, 2017, https://timeline.com/black-justice-fbi-scared-ebcf2986515c.

[8] Aron, "When the Black Justice Movement Got Too Powerful."

[9] Zambito, "The FBI's War on the Left."

[10] "Police Kill Two Members of the Black Panther Party," History, November 13, 2009; last modified December 1, 2021, https://www.history.com/this-day-in-history/police-kill-two-members-of-the-black-panther-party.

[11] Staudenmaier, "Puerto Rican Independence Movement," 2769.

[12] César Ayala, "Political Persecution in Puerto Rico: Uncovering Secret Files," *Against the Current*, no. 85 (March–April 20000), https://againstthecurrent.org/atc085/p1685/.

[13] Churchill and Vander Wall, *The COINTELPRO Papers*, 69.

[14] "The Basics on COINTELPRO and How to Counter It," Real People's Media, March 10, 2020, https://realpeoples.media/the-basics-on-cointelpro-and-how-to-counter-it/.

[15] Glick, preface to *The COINTELPRO Papers*, x.

[16] Ryan Wong, "The Long 1960s, Seen through NYPD Surveillance Photographs," Hyperallergic, December 8, 2017, https://hyperallergic.com/403347/the-long-1960s-seen-through-nypd-surveillance-photographs/.

[17] Kristian Williams, *Our Enemies in Blue: Police and Power in America* (Cambridge, MA: South End Press, 2007), 155.

[18] Marilynn S. Johnson, "Challenging Police Repression: Federal Activism and Local Reform in New York City," in *Uniform Behavior: Police Localism and National Politics*, ed. Stacy K. McGoldrick and Andrea McArdle (New York: Palgrave Macmillan, 2006), 86.

[19] Sherry Wolf, "Spies, Lies, and War: Lessons of COINTELPRO," *International Socialist Review*, September–October 2006, at Third World Traveler, https://thirdworldtraveler.com/FBI/Lessons_COINTELPRO.html.

[20] Chisun Lee, "Why the NYPD Is Fighting for the Right to Spy on You," *Village Voice*, December 18, 2002, 33.

[21] Churchill and Vander Wall, *The COINTELPRO Papers*, 69.

[22] Kevin Zeese and Margaret Flowers, "Police Violence and Racism Have Always Been Tools of Capitalism," Countercurrents, June 22, 2020, https://countercurrents.org/2020/06/police-violence-and-racism-have-always-been-tools-of-capitalism/.

[23] Neier, "Surveillance by the FBI," 45.

[24] YLP Defense Ministry, "Beware of What You Say (Bugging)," *Palante* 3, no. 3 (1971): 10.

[25] This information was obtained from various Freedom of Information Act files dated from December 1968 to December 20, 1972.

[26] Hernan Flores, "Repression against the Young Lords," *Palante* 3, no. 3 (1971): 9.

[27] "Handschu V. Special Services Division (Challenging NYPD Surveillance Practices Targeting Political Groups)," New York Civil Liberties Union, https://www.nyclu.org/en/cases/handschu-v-special-services-division-challenging-nypd-surveillance-practices-targeting.

[28] Josmar Trujillo, "No Backspace: NY's Rules for Policing Political Activity Still Need Tightening," *City Limits*, March 17, 2017, https://citylimits.org/2017/03/17/no-backspace-nys-rules-for-policing-political-activity-still-need-tightening/.

[29] Joseph Goldstein, "Old New York Police Surveillance Is Found, Forcing Big Brother Out of Hiding," *New York Times*, June 16, 2016, https://www.nytimes.com/2016/06/17/nyregion/old-new-york-police-surveillance-is-found-forcing-big-brother-out-of-hiding.html?searchResultPosition=3.

Chapter 15. "The Past Does Not Exist Independently From The Present"

[1] Romay Guerra, "New World Coming: Race in Socialist Cuba." YouTube video, https://www.youtube.com/watch?v=5jJQBtPTPks

[2] Sylvia Walby, "Theorising Patriarchy," *Sociology* 23, no. 2 (May 1989): 214, https://www.jstor.org/stable/42853921.

[3] Soares, "Joy, Rage, and Activism," 947.

[4] Rose M. Brewer, "Black Radical Theory and Practice: Gender, Race, and Class," *Socialism and Democracy* 17, no. 2 (Winter–Spring 2003), ttps://sdonline.org/issue/33/black-radical-theory-and-practice-gender-race-and-class.

[5] "Women at the Core of the Fight against COVID-19 Crisis," Organisation for Economic Co-operation and Development, April 1, 2020, https://www.oecd.org/coronavirus/policy-responses/women-at-the-core-of-the-fight-against-covid-19-crisis-553a8269/.

[6] Kate Power, "The COVID-19 Pandemic Has Increased the Care Burden of Women and Families," *Sustainability: Science, Practice and Policy* 16, no. 1 (2020), https://www.tandfonline.com/doi/full/10.1080/15487733.2020.1776561.

[7] Justin Fox and Elaine He, "The Pandemic Was Historically Bad for Working-Class Women," *Bloomberg*, March 30, 2021, https://www.bloomberg.com/opinion/articles/2021-03-30/covid-19-job-losses-were-historic-for-black-and-hispanic-women.

[8] Rick W. A. Smith, "How Imperialism Gave Us 2020," *Sapiens*, February 16, 2021, https://www.sapiens.org/culture/imperialism-2020/.

[9] Edna Acosta-Belén and Christine E. Bose, "From Structural Subordination to Empowerment: Women and Development in Third World Contexts," Gender and Society 4, no. 3 (1990): 300, doi:10.1177/089124390004003003.

[10] Natália M. De Souza and Lara M. Rodrigues Selis, "Gender violence and feminist resistance in Latin America," International Feminist Journal of Politics 24, no. 1 (2022): 7, doi:10.1080/14616742.2021.2019483.

[11] Marisol LeBrón, "Where Were You When We Were Being Killed? How Puerto Rican Feminists Help Us Understand Policing and State Violence," Society and Space, October 1, 2020, https://www.societyandspace.org/articles/where-were-you-when-we-were-being-killed-how-puerto-rican-feminists-help-us-understand-policing-and-state-violence.

[12] Juan C. Dávila and Osvaldo Budet, "Organizing to End Gender-Based Violence in PR," When We Fight, We Win, podcast audio, https://www.whenwefightwewin.com/listen/season-2-episode-2-estadodeemergencia-organizing-to-end-gender-based-violence-in-pr/.

[13] Geoff Gilliard, "New Research Reveals Power of Women's Movements over the Past 50 Years - SFU News - Simon Fraser University," Simon Fraser University, last modified March 6, 2020, https://www.sfu.ca/sfunews/stories/2020/03/new-research-reveals-power-of-women-s-movements-over-the-past-50.html.

[14] Carin Zissis et al., "Explainer: Abortion Rights in Latin America," Americas Society/Council of the Americas, last modified June 28, 2022, https://www.as-coa.org/articles/explainer-abortion-rights-latin-america.

[15] Erika Guevara Rosas, "From Mobilization to Solidarity: The Power of Feminist Struggles in Latin America," openDemocracy, December 2, 2021, https://www.opendemocracy.net/en/north-africa-west-asia/from-mobilization-to-solidarity-the-power-of-feminist-struggles-in-latin-america/.

INDEX

ABOUT THE AUTHOR

Iris Morales is an activist, educator, attorney, media producer, and author whose work is grounded in social justice and the fight for Puerto Rico's decolonization. Her activism spans several decades of organizing with movements alongside tenants, students, workers, feminists, community advocates, and media makers—uplifting the voices and struggles of those impacted by inequality and oppression.

Morales's commitment to justice and liberation bridges diverse fields—including community organizing, education, law, media, and philanthropy. Within media, she has led independent organizations, launched literacy initiatives for children and youth, and designed innovative television production training programs. She is the founder of Red Sugarcane Press, a publishing project dedicated to documenting the histories and legacies of Black, Indigenous, and other peoples of color in the Americas, with a focus on the Puerto Rican experience.

Morales is the editor and author of several books, including the anthologies: *Voices from Puerto Rico: Post-Hurricane María*; *Latinas: Struggles & Protests in 21st Century USA*; and *Latinas: Gender, Race and Class*. She coauthored the children's picture book *Vicki: A Summer of Change*, and wrote *A Flag's Journey*, her first chapter book for young readers.

Morales is also the author of the only published works documenting women's contributions to the Young Lords Party and its important role in the Puerto Rican diaspora. Her book *Through the Eyes of Rebel Women: The Young Lords 1969–1976*, and her award-winning documentary *¡Palante, Siempre Palante!*, which aired nationally on public television, preserve and share these histories. She was a leading member of the Young Lords for more than five years and cofounder of both its Women's Caucus and Women's Union.

Based in New York City, Morales holds a J.D. from New York University School of Law and an M.F.A. in Integrated Media Arts from Hunter College.

About Red Sugarcane Press

R ed Sugarcane Press, Inc. is dedicated to preserving and promoting the histories and cultures of Black, Indigenous, and other peoples of color in the Americas, with a focus on the Puerto Rican experience. It aims to amplify the voices of Indigenous and African-descended communities who, from the era of enslavement to the present, have survived and thrived through the courage and tenacity of many generations.

Red Sugarcane Press publishes both established and emerging writers, artists, and activists whose work break new ground. Books and related projects are collaborative endeavors, offering diverse perspectives and artistic styles. These works reflect radical imaginations and distinct voices that spark dialogue and inspire action toward a more just and equitable world.

Current publications span a variety of genres, including poetry collections, plays, political histories, children's stories, and anthologies. Several titles are bilingual in English and Spanish. Books are available in both print and e-book formats and can be purchased through a range of online platforms accessible to individuals, bookstores, and libraries.

For more information, visit:

www.RedSugarcanePress.com
facebook.com/redsugarcanepress
instagram@redsugarcane
info@redsugarcanepress.com

www.ingramcontent.com/pod-product-compliance
Lightning Source LLC
Chambersburg PA
CBHW070548130626
46556CB00001B/62